A
SPECIAL
ASSIGNMENT

Varindra Tarzie Vittachi

A
SPECIAL
ASSIGNMENT
a trilogy comprising
A REPORTER IN SUBUD
ASSIGNMENT SUBUD
A MEMOIR OF SUBUD

BY
VARINDRA TARZIE VITTACHI

SUBUD PUBLICATIONS INTERNATIONAL

SUBUD is a spiritual process, not a theory or teaching.
Statements about Subud should be considered as reflecting
the author's own personal experience and understanding.
They are not to be regarded as authoritative pronouncements
nor are they intended to be a Subud doctrine.

This edition first published 1996 by
Subud Publications International Ltd,
Loudwater Farm, Loudwater Lane,
Rickmansworth, Herts WD3 4HG, England.

ISBN 1 869822 69 2

Typesetting by Leonard Hurd
Cover design by Marcus Bolt
Printed in Great Britain by Watkiss Studios Ltd, Biggleswade Bedfordshire.

Publishing history:

Assignment Subud
published 1965 by Dharma Publications, New York
A Reporter in Subud
published 1963 by Dharma Publications, New York

A Reporter's Assignment in Subud
A double volume, comprising:
A Reporter in Subud and *Assignment Subud*
published 1971 by Subud Publications International Ltd

A Memoir of Subud
published 1988 by Subud Publications International Ltd

ONE morning in London in 1959 Reynold
Osborne of New York, Richard Lacey of
Johannesburg and I were discussing books
about Subud. We agreed that no-one should
write about Subud as our understanding of
experience changed with time. I said that
although writing was my trade I would never
write about Subud. They laughed.
Richard said: "Will you give that to us in
writing?" Here it is – in writing.

CONTENTS

PUBLISHER'S NOTE

The books in this trilogy were written specifically for members of Subud, present and future. They arise out of a certain spiritual experience, which is reflected by the language. This does not mean that others will not be interested, even fascinated. The sheer quality of the story telling and character studies, as well as the author's fresh reflections about our age and the meaning of life, ensure that something real and rare may well come across to anyone with an open mind and open feelings.

The name 'Bapak' refers to Muhammad Subuh Sumohadiwidjojo (1901-1987), the Indonesian founder of Subud.

INTRODUCTION

VARINDRA TARZIE VITTACHI'S three books on Subud and his close relationship with Bapak are some of the most valuable writings we have, apart from those of Bapak himself. He entered Subud together with the first westerners at Coombe Springs at Kingston-on-Thames in 1957. As he mentions near the end of this volume Bapak told him many things because he knew that he was by nature a communicator and would share them with others. He was more than just that. He was a compelling talker and an inimitable raconteur who always laced his words with humour. And he knew that this was the finest story he would ever tell.

He was born, the eldest of thirteen children, on September 21st 1921 in Pillikiathuwa near the town Gampaha, north of Colombo. His father, who was the village schoolmaster, gave him the name Aleya (fearless) Gamini. Soon however his agility among the trees in the garden and the adjoining forest earned him the nickname Tarzan, which was quickly abbreviated to Tarzie. He was never known as anything else until he also became Varindra in 1964 [see page 108].

He grew up in a small country famous for its age-old toleration, which along with the climate and rich landscape, earned the name 'paradise island'. He was brought up as a Buddhist but was a natural sceptic. This from an early age took the form of challenging what others around him said they believed in – Buddhism, Christianity, nationalism, patriotism or any other explanations of existence or tenets of right conduct.

His deep curiosity, and his love of words and writing, led him into journalism at an early age. Most unusually he was drawn not only to examine the roots of the injustice and violence, the lies and cruelty he saw around him. He was equally interested in the processes of his own mind and emotions. Already at twelve he was asking the big questions – the why and wherefore of existence – and searching for true values.

His exuberant participation in life as a brilliant Fleet Street trained journalist led to his becoming at the age of thirty-two the editor of the *Ceylon Observer*, the oldest newspaper in Asia. He had connections everywhere and moved easily in the highest places, as he campaigned for toleration of minorities and for linguistic equality. He loved lampooning pomposity. Under the pseudonym Flybynight, he set the English speaking middle classes of Ceylon laughing with a series of Jungle Stories, in which a large cast of animal politicians played out their power games with recognisable style and gusto.

It is hard to imagine from the account here of the year 1958 when Subud came to Ceylon that he was the witness and chronicler of racial violence that changed the whole history of the island. In between the second visit of Icksan Ahmed which ended in April and the arrival of Bapak and his party in October came a defining moment in his life. In May a state of emergency had been declared along with a curfew and censorship of the press. He heard a scuffle, a cry and a lot of laughter in the street below his office window. Looking out he saw a roundly pregnant woman, a Tamil of the sweeper class, grotesquely trotting down the street as urchins took flying kicks at her swollen belly. A truckload of armed Sinhalese police, parked across the street, roared with laughter as each kick landed on its mark.

Tarzie (as he then was) was filled with rage – outrage. He refused to be silent, temporarily left his job and in five weeks wrote a strictly factual but vehement book about the forces and policies which were finally destroying the age old toleration and harmony of his homeland. He took the typescript to London himself and found a publisher, Andre Deutsch, who brought the book out within three weeks. *Emergency 58* was at once banned in Ceylon, and became an immediate best-seller in Asia. Bapak is reported to have said it was his best book, because of the sincerity of its passion. It won him the prestigious Asian award for journalism and literature, the Ramon Magsaysay Prize.

Tarzie made a great many friends, but he never minded making enemies. He began to receive regular telephone threats to his life. Bapak, who knew at once the quality and capacity of everyone he encountered, also foresaw the part he would play in Subud. When this part was about to be terminated by his assassination Bapak called him out of danger to Bombay.

Thrown into exile with his wife Sunetra (Harianti) and four children, he could now have two roles. As Tarzie he became a peripatetic teacher of journalism all over Asia, a 'newspaper doctor' as he liked to call himself. He was the inspirational animator of numerous international seminars and conferences. With his strong sense of what ordinary people want he co-pioneered the concept of development journalism. A colleague said of him: 'In whichever country he was he seemed to be part of the people'. He wrote frequently in the international press, and, for a while, based in Hong Kong, edited his own newspaper, *The Asian*.

Being a constant traveller – he used to say he wrote well at 33,000 feet – he could as Varindra at the same time fit in continual service for Subud.

He became – as he was variously called – Bapak's courier, messenger-boy, leg-man, ambassador, reporting regularly back to Jakarta. He was the ideal link-man between sprouting Subud groups in numerous countries – and never needed to ask for expenses. His visiting presence brought lightness and laughter, and he was expert at finding a practical way between quarrelling helpers and committee members. He would observe, though, that dealing with Subud members, who themselves were going through an individualised spiritual process, could be more troubled and delicate than the relationships he faced later in the United Nations.

Already in 1963 at the Second Subud World Congress in Briarcliff, New York, Bapak made him international chairman of Subud, a position he retained for thirty years – almost until his death. He wished to resign more than once and be an ordinary member, doing his latihan (the Subud spiritual exercise) two or three times a week. But Bapak had reasons to keep him there. One was that he would never, as Bapak knew, exercise responsibility as power but only as service, and the other that he would never allow a strong central organisation to take over Subud.

By the 1970s Varindra had become a global person, moving to New York. When he wrote an article questioning the current policies of the United Nations on population, he was invited to join that branch of the UN. He was then able to influence the way in which this crucial issue was handled – not through prescriptive birth control measures by governments, but by both addressing the conditions of life of poor people and empowering women so that they could choose the size of their families.

By now with his second wife Lestari he was living in New York. In 1980 he joined the brilliant team at the head of UNICEF, working for the health and protection of the world's children. The late Jim Grant, Executive Director of UNICEF, called him 'a unique pioneer in the most important revolution in our time – the advancement of the human being everywhere'. The London *Times* said of him that 'his global vision and unaffected love of humanity made him at all levels a brilliant mobiliser for action on questions of poverty and the environment and especially for children'.

Varindra had a horror of everything sanctimonious. 'Don't you go spiritual on me,' he would say to close friends. Bureaucracy was an incubus that had to be watched out for, exposed and laughed at. At the end of his life he was warning us that some of the same forces which were crippling the UN, the universities and the churches could undermine Subud too.

He was a realist about human nature, especially his own. He never hid his own weaknesses. Rukman Hundeide, the Norwegian founder of the biggest Subud social enterprise, International Child Development Programme, says that it was his all too human imperfections that made him so attractive. 'In some way he became a spokesman for us sinners who are still in Subud and doing our best.'

He had periods of spiritual dryness which he knew others also went through. He tells how for a whole year he lost the ability to feel or move in the latihan. (He once helped me a lot when he said 'the latihan may be ninety-eight percent lead but then comes two percent gold – worth travelling a long way for).'

When Bapak died in 1987 – the same year as Varindra's second wife, Lestari – the material for the third book of the trilogy, long meditated, was waiting to be set down: a testimony of love and gratitude, full of the pointers that Bapak kept giving us towards a different quality of life in the here and now. In the UNICEF building in New York Varindra was famous for hanging his motto, or watchword, outside his door: EVERYTHING IS ABOUT SOMETHING DIFFERENT. I was told recently that it is still remembered and quoted – especially when an impasse is reached in a discussion on policy or action.

He wrote three other books besides *Emergency 58*, all on Asian themes: *The Brown Sahib*, *The Brown Sahib Revisited* and *The Fall Of Sukarno*. There was one more book to come, though posthumously. His final concern was with the millions upon millions of the world's children who are the victims of the world situation. Why, why do they have to suffer as they do? It was part of his ultimate quarrel with God, and he never found an answer. *Between the Guns* tells a mainly UNICEF story of how over several years warring bodies ceased hostilities to save the children on both sides.

Though widely known, admired and loved, Varindra Tarzie Vittachi never became a celebrity, which means a TV star, or wished to be. Though a brilliant journalist he was finally distrustful of the newspaper world, and the vaunted freedom of the press, which is so easily manipulated by powerful interests. What was needed to bring about change, he saw, was the informed participation of people in the drama of their own lives and growth. He pointed to the non-news media for this, the NGO and religious press, local broadcasting and videos. If he had lived longer I believe he would have rejoiced to see the arrival of the Internet with its hardly realized capacity to create, without geographical boundaries, a value-based community, to set up a global debate on the struggle for truth, justice and sustainable human development.

He never swayed big conferences with his oratory. He liked to work through more intimate meetings and his wide network of friendships. He helped to create and was active in the counsels of several non-governmental organisations working for world peace and justice: The Global Forum for Spiritual and Parliamentary Leaders, The Pate Institute for Human Survival, World View International Foundation. Their gatherings had the object dear to his heart, that those who make future-forming decisions should face and if possible get to know each other personally.

He spoke to me in his last weeks of the many letters he had been receiving, and the ones that pleased him least, and most. The former were those that contained flattery, the latter those which showed he had really touched a person's feelings. He had been a mentor, but never a guru, for many people and had left 'fruitful droppings' – a typically earthy expression – in their lives. His daughter Anuradha once asked his advice when about to speak to a conference for young people. 'Teach them to say No,' he said. 'Not a miserly No, but the life-affirming No of those who hate bullies and petty rules. Never grovel because people are famous or powerful. Read tyrants as though you were a detective and learn to say No. It's not global warming that will destroy us, it's gullibility.'

He died on September 17th 1993 of inoperable liver cancer in his daughter's home at Chinnor near Oxford. A headline in *The Guardian* called him a 'Genius of Communication and Nobility'. A good part of what he tried to communicate can be found in these pages.

Matthew Barry Sullivan

PREFACE*

A TRAVELLER'S TALE

FOR ten years, between 1960 and 1970, I spent most of my time travelling from country to country, from city to city. I logged so many air-miles that some airlines tagged me as a CIP – a rather low-grade VIP, a Commercially Important Person. I learnt a great deal about the world during that time. But there were two worlds to experience wherever I went – the world of newspapers, foundations, seminars, politics and economics, and the Subud world. At first, these two worlds were distinct and even mutually exclusive. My professional life and my spiritual life were separate, even contradictory, existences. I moved from one to the other, but often with some confusion at the threshold. After a week with Bapak in Tjilandak where I had lived in a world where angels were vibrant presences to some, if not to me, and I flew away to Hong Kong or New York or London where man's work in the shape of Hilton Hotels and rocket engineering was tangibly and abundantly evident, I often wondered what was reality: the invisible world which can only be experienced in the feeling, or the visible world in which there were rotary presses and prestressed concrete buildings, overpasses and underpasses, the value of which may not be measured in terms of feeling, but in utility.

I used to ask myself when my plane landed in one of those great cities if what I saw around me – skyscrapers sprouting up where there had been only a bungalow or a two-floor store when I had passed by only a year before – was not more real than the sweet beating of butterfly wings in my feeling and on my skin that I experienced in the latihan. At such moments I even wondered whether I had imagined the ecstasy and the sadness, and the irresistible clarity of our way of receiving guidance in testing, of receiving "proof" as Bapak often put it. The Outer World was so solid that it was *evidently* real to a mind that had been taught to respect and hold to a scientific attitude towards life, that is to say, to value what was consistently logical and to remain constantly sceptical about my experience or knowledge that was not measurable on the evidence of the senses. The Inner World, as I had been taught to think, was

*This preface was originally published in the combined version of A Reporter in Subud and Assignment Subud, entitled A Reporter's Assignment in Subud.

inhabited by silly old ladies of both sexes who started life believing in Santa Claus and ended it believing in Sunday newspaper astrologers, in flying saucers and in ESP.

To my journalistic mind one of the "difficulties" of spiritual life was that its most ardent devotees were the kind of people who were ready to believe that (a) John F. Kennedy *must* have been the victim of a Texan conspiracy; (b) that when the Pope comes to his senses and publishes the Fatima document, the Second Coming will be revealed; and (c) that if Neil Armstrong had not met little moon men wearing goggles and spiral-wire antennae it is because he is one of those who hath no eyes to see nor ears to hear and not because they weren't there. Another difficulty for me was that many of us who had come to Subud because we had been repelled by the bigotry and dogma of priestcraft had ourselves become bigots and dogmatists.

But, as the years passed and Bapak's words, repeated over and over again with new weight and fresh nuances, began to reach us, we began to understand that Subud was not Sunday morning piety, not just a Monday and Thursday evening romp. It was a total experience, enveloping, interpenetrating and pervasive to the extent that we were willing to let it, and we were able to take it. Bapak had spoken of Inner and Outer. To me this was a very useful mental split which enabled one to begin to know about the nature of things and people. Everything and every being had an Inner and an Outer. Every man had an Inner self and an Outer self. Even a word had its Inner and Outer. It had a shape, a sound, a size and it had a meaning. And there were Inner meanings to words and Outer meanings. The Spiritual world was the Inner and the Material world, the Outer. My world of journalism and politics was the ambience in which my Outer self lived and the latihan was helping me to find my way about my Inner world of feeling. In my travels I recognised this distinction. I had known London for years as a city of clever, exciting people and places marvellously absorbing until I came to know Subud London which captivated me almost completely because there I met people who related to me through the feelings and not with the cleverness and the mannered outer personalities of Fleet Street and the West End.

This increasing appreciation of the essence of life made many of us retreat from the Outer world of what most people knew as "Real Life". And increasing numbers of us became lay hermits – we dressed "normally", we rode in cars and airplanes as "normal" people did, we married and raised families "normally" (perhaps not so normally) but we accepted the world in which all this activity went on only as an outer shell in which our Inner lives were to be lived. We imagined that we were different from "normal" people – and a bit superior because, even if we knew our Inners to be stinkers, we were "better" than "nice" people who lived only in their Outers. But we were behaving very much like these "normal" people who divided their world into We and They – In groups and Out groups, U and Non-U, the Beautiful and the Damned. We were rejecting the Material world – or claiming to – in our journeying through the spiritual world.

This was why so many of us found it hard to understand why Bapak watched television, why Bapak was such a natty dresser, why he preferred a Mercedes Benz to a horse and buggy, why the Subud Brotherhood needed buildings for its International Spiritual Centre when the Buddha was reported to have attained the highest state of enlightenment among men under the shade of a Bo tree. Having been city gents we were now becoming city saints – or, at any rate, sounding off as such. We were ignoring the marvellous polarity of everything in this universe. We forgot that one couldn't lift a broom by its "clean" end without also lifting its dirty, working end.

It took many years for most of us to begin to open ourselves to another insight Bapak had been giving us whenever he had spoken of Inner and Outer. He told us that Subud did not reject the material world which was also God's work, that through Subud the material world would take its due place in our lives, be under man's feet rather than on his head, that through the practice of the latihan we would be able to send material forces out to work for us. And he had told us, so often, that Inner and Outer "must come together". Our Inner and Outer lives needed to be brought together. Our Outer lives needed to be increasingly Inner-directed. He once told us that even a bank teller could worship God while doing his job and Bapak rifled through an imaginary bundle of dollar bills counting – one, two, three, four, Allah, Allah . . . I roared with laughter because my first real job was that of a junior accountant in the Bank of Ceylon and one of my duties, once a week, was to check-count the currency notes in the vault. The rupee notes were in bundles of 50 and I counted one, two, three, four . . . and always ended in 51 or 49, never 50. If I'd been an inner-directed banker I would not have been under the constant threat of dismissal as I was in that job.

Bapak is the embodiment of this principle of the essential one-ness of the Inner and Outer. Bapak the farmer, Bapak the company director,

Bapak the constitutional lawyer, Bapak the boxing fan, Bapak at the football stadium, Bapak at our latihan, Bapak testing us, Bapak explaining the nature of man and man's relationship with God – was always the same Bapak. For the first time in the spiritual history of man Subud asserts this principle clearly and without equivocation. Render unto Caesar that which is Caesar's and to God what is God's is not a plea for a schizoid existence in two worlds in which we may substitute Harvard Business School ethics for the Commandments, but an assertion that Caesar is also God's creature and would be doing His work if he would only let himself be guided from within.

Recently Bapak gave us the most poignant reminder of this principle: We can do nothing without God, he said. We need God's help to live human lives in a material environment. And God is willing to come to our help if we would only let Him. The guideposts to worship that Bapak has given us – Patience, Sincerity and Submission – stand on this single requirement: Let Him.

Ay, there's the rub.

Varindra Tarzie Vittachi

BOOK 1

A
REPORTER
IN
SUBUD

CONTENTS

PROLOGUE

BOMBAY, January 1960. The sitting-room of Bomon Behram's apartment on Nepeansea Road overlooking the ocean. Bapak, clad for the tropics in slacks and shirtsleeves, was sitting knees crossed as usual, on a long sofa reading a letter from London.

"Another book on Subud," he remarked smiling. "This letter suggests that Bapak should intercede and stop its publication on the grounds that it contains material which could be damaging to Subud. But why should Bapak interfere? Subud is not Bapak's work. It is not Man's work. How can any man damage it? If it can be endangered by Man, then it is not from God. And if it is not from God why should Bapak worry?"

"I cannot understand," I said, "how anyone in Subud can write about Subud. I am a professional writer but I feel I cannot even begin to write about Subud. My understanding of explanations and experience changes every year. How can I possibly pin them down on paper?"

"You writer, you better write," said Bapak, bypassing Anwar Zakir's services as translator.

"Write, Bapak?" I asked, "About Subud?"

"Yes, Subud," said Bapak.

"But Bapak, it will be nonsense!" I pleaded.

"Yes," agreed Bapak, "but better write."

1

Meeting in London

THE tension in my country was palpable. It was May 1957 and the two major races in Ceylon, the Sinhalese and the Tamils, were preparing for internecine brutality. As a Sinhalese and Buddhist – by far the numerically dominant community in the island – I found I was expected to go along with "my people" and condone the suppression of the minority Tamils, Hindus and Christians – by sheer force of numbers. But I was incapable of feeling racial or religious superiority – and most certainly not on numerical grounds.

When the conflict began to grow I discovered that many of my closest friends were Tamils, Hindus and Christians and that, like my parents and my wife, I had never been conscious of these distinctions in our relationship with them. The question had never arisen at all. It was quite obvious to people who thought like I did that the rift was the work of a few unscrupulous politicians who had not hesitated at the prospect of wading to power through the blood of the minority peoples.

I had been trying through my newspaper to waken the conscience of the leaders of both sides to a realization of the disaster that would surely befall our country if they continued in their efforts to fan the highly dangerous and unquenchable flames of racialism and religious fanaticism. The more conscientious of my fellow editors on the other newspapers, too, were working very hard to stop the holocaust that was coming. But we were preaching to the converted. Our newspapers never reached the kind of people who are easily moved by this sort of madness, and the power maniacs who were creating the trouble thought we were blind or "anti-national" – a new Asian phrase which connotes refusal to swim with the rising tide.

The Tamils in the North were planning a satyagraha – in the form of a "non-violent" march on Trincomalee where they were to demonstrate the unity of the Tamil people behind their cause. The All-Sinhalese Government was preparing counter-measures in the South.

∞∞∞∞

A few friends and I had been following a system of self study which had helped us very much to keep a watch on our own motivations and actions in our daily lives. These studies had enabled me to see very clearly the motivations of the politicians who were doing the damage and also many of my own weaknesses and prejudices. But I had reached an impasse. Professionally, my efforts to change people's hearts were ineffectual and, spiritually, my efforts to change myself were not much more successful.

In our small study group some of us had developed a technique of being spectators of our own actions. For instance this Spectator would sometimes break in on my conversation with someone like the managing director of my newspaper and remark, "Vittachi . . . so this is the editor who always stands up to the Boss, hm? Just listen to that ingratiating tone of your voice as you speak with him."

Or it would remark wryly, "Vittachi, did you notice how your attitude changed when you realized that the person at the other end of the telephone was a woman?"

But this Spectator, sharp as he was, always seemed to appear a fraction of a moment too late to do anything about it. It observed, but had no power to make any substantial difference to the way Vittachi thought and acted. We worked very hard at this self study: three nights a week and all our Sundays were devoted to this exercise. But we had all come to feel a sense of despair and futility. We had always been told by our teachers that help would come, but there were no signs of it for five years. We were going on like a man standing on a plank and trying to lift it. The only way in which this feat could be achieved was if a hand was offered from above. Then we could lift the plank, ourselves and all. But what hand? Who would give us this helping hand? How long, how long to wait?

One morning I was hard at it, trying to write a telling editorial appealing directly to the Tamil leaders to stop their march on Trincomalee and agree to a round-table conference at which an effort could be made to resolve their differences with the government. Suddenly, halfway through, I felt all my strength and purpose drain out of me. It was replaced by a single thought – I must get away from Ceylon for a few weeks. I felt I could not stand the tension around me any longer.

I pushed my typewriter away and walked to the managing director's room and heard myself announcing loud and rather desperately: "I'm getting the hell out of here."

By the tone of my voice he thought I was resigning my job. But when he realized that all I wanted was a temporary break, he very considerately made all the arrangements needed – leave, money, everything. As I was packing to go away to London (where do ex-colonials like myself go in such situations except London?) I had second thoughts. I told my wife that I was being theatrical – that all I needed was a few days rest in the hills, that I should cancel my trip to London and stay in Ceylon. But she, wise in my contrary ways, insisted that I go. "If you go to the hills instead and then return to work you will feel frustrated that you did not go away to England when you had the opportunity to do so," she said.

∞∞∞∞∞

I reached London on a warm summer day in June and went directly to Coombe Springs to meet John Bennett whom I had known for about seven years. As I entered the house I noticed a distinct change in the atmosphere and the people around. Everything seemed to be more relaxed than I'd ever known them. The virtuous churchfaces I had encountered there so often were not in evidence. People were laughing and talking much louder than those crumbling walls had ever heard before. Most of the women had changed their sackcloth and ashes for light summer prints and some of them had even worn a little make-up. I walked through the house and across the lawn towards the old oak tree where I had been told I would find John Bennett. Two Englishmen actually spoke to me. This fairly staggered me, but not as much as when John Bennett appeared and, seeing me, threw back his head and roared with laughter.

I was astonished. Here, indeed, was cause for wonderment. John Bennett – Mr. B. to thousands of students in many parts of the world, their model of serious, one-pointed purpose – had never laughed before in my hearing. He may have smiled and even chortled in a rather indulgent way, but laughter from the belly up was quite alien to my experience of him. I asked: "What's going on, Mr. B? There's some change at Coombe this time. People, you, everybody's behaving a bit oddly. What's the form? And what's so funny that amuses you so much?"

John Bennett replied: "Come, come upstairs to my study and I'll tell you what's different." We sat in his book-panelled room as we had on my many visits to Coombe and I told him about the impulse which had made me come to England. I told him of our study group in Ceylon and its sense of despair. I asked about the promise that help would come.

When? From where?

"Help has come," replied Bennett, in that apocalyptic tone of voice which had always enthralled and terrified me. I feared now that one of those loud and intense silences would follow. Instead, John Bennett went on: "Let me tell you a story . . ." and then followed the now familiar account of his having been told many years previously of the arrival of a man from "Dutch East India" to help and guide us with our spiritual efforts. "He is now in the next room. His name is Muhammad Subuh. You must now make up your mind whether you want to go along as you have been doing or whether you want to receive the Subud contact. For many it has been a difficult decision," he said.

"There is not the slightest difficulty for me, Mr. B," I said. "In the state in which I find myself, I am prepared to rob any temple if it will serve my purpose. But tell me why you laughed when you saw me," I insisted.

"I'll tell you why. When Pak Subuh arrived here, one of the first questions he asked me was whether there were any people in Ceylon who would be interested in these matters. I told him that there was a small group in Colombo. I suggested that it would be difficult to communicate the news to them by correspondence. But Pak Subuh only smiled and said: 'Don't worry. Something will turn up within two or three weeks.'"

"And I was the thing turned up?" I asked.

I joined in the laughter this time and it all seemed right now. I was taken to a mezzanine room which was later to be Bapak's sitting room. There were three others including Mr. Kibble of Cyprus, a South African and an American. John Bennett remarked on this – the internationalism in evidence – as some proof of the rightness of this new way we were about to enter. Then an Indonesian entered. He was dressed like an Indonesian business man. He was smoking a Dutch cheroot. I told myself, "No. It can't be. How can a Holy Man look like this?" He stubbed his cigar and smiled at us and spoke. John Bennett translated, advising us to close our eyes and relax.

Forty-five minutes later we were led into the study and Bennett asked whether we had felt anything. Kibble said he had felt a deep sense of relaxation. I said I had only felt bored, but that I'd like to continue.

For seven more days I went up to Coombe from London. I felt nothing at all. I heard and sensed other people in the exercise moving about, dancing, weeping, laughing hysterically, gibbering, spinning around like dervishes, falling like dead logs and Icksan Ahmad chanting Aw-wah,

Aw-wah, Aw-wah. One man who used to arrive at Coombe clad in bowler and striped trousers, always stood close to me stiff and proper to start with, and five minutes after the exercise started, I would hear him hiss Tchooh, Tchooh, Tchooh, slow at first, then fast, and then he stomped round the room like a train, going Tchooh, Tchooh, Tchooh ... whoo whoooooo! I laughed, suppressing the noise inside me till my sides ached.

But every night I felt terrible that the days were passing fast and I was not receiving the contact which I was now convinced that many others had definitely received, to judge by the way they sounded at the exercise and the way they spoke about their experience. I was convinced that the movements they were making were involuntary because, had it been make-believe, they would surely have preferred to adopt more graceful postures and make more spiritually appropriate noises. I asked myself how I could possibly be expected to carry this force within me to Ceylon and transmit it to others when I had not received it myself.

In acute inner agony I went one morning to meet Pak Subuh. I had a few preliminary questions and ten subsidiary philosophical questions typed out. I wanted to get the whole thing well and truly whacked. Icksan translated. I told Pak Subuh that I had now attended seven latihans and had felt nothing.

"How can I be expected to transmit this contact to the group in Ceylon when I have not received it myself yet?"

Bapak: "What made you think it was your business to take this to Ceylon?"

I said: "Mr. Bennett said that he felt that my coming here at this time had a purpose . . ."

Bapak: "That may be. But this is not your work. Or Bapak's. It is God's work. If God intends that you should be the one to open the people in Ceylon, He will see that you are equipped for the purpose. If not – then it is not your responsibility."

I felt immediate relief that this self-imposed burden had been removed from my shoulders and said so.

Bapak: "All you are required to do is to attend latihan for half an hour a day as long as you are here. Is that too much?" I agreed it was not difficult at all.

"That is another thing that troubles me," I said. "I have always been told and have believed that in spiritual matters as in worldly matters – nothing for nothing is the rule. What we receive is in proportion to what we pay in effort or devoutness."

Bapak: "All right then, what do you want to pay with?"

From the tone of Icksan's translation and the irony of his smile, I realized the absurdity of my posture in demanding that I be allowed to pay for what I received in the same counterfeit currency of spiritual effort that I had been using before.

Bapak: "Worship of God is not bargaining. You cannot buy spiritual grace. You can prepare yourself to receive it . . ."

I asked: "How? Is the layer of dirt that covers me so thick that even this force cannot penetrate it? Should I go away, try to cleanse myself and then return to receive the contact?"

Bapak: "Can you?"

I said I did not understand.

Bapak: "Can you go away and cleanse yourself?"

At this moment I felt I had my first glimpse into the meaning of the mercy of God and the concept of absolution. There was no sense in a sinner staying away from worship on the plea that he was too unclean to worship. His only hope was to worship. There was no other way.

"Any other question?" said Icksan.

I reeled off my ten-point questionnaire, filed away the answers and left*.

That evening I began the exercise, relieved of the burden of pioneering that I had been lugging around all those days. A few minutes after the exercise started I felt a peculiar sensation. My knees seemed to be buckling under me. I told myself, "Funny. Now don't you get caught, old man. You have never knelt before. Don't cut a figure. How ridiculous it would look . . ." And so, I resisted this impulse to kneel, right through the forty-five minutes. Afterwards I remarked about this to Baron Von Bissing and two others who had been at the exercise. I said I did not like the idea of cutting a figure, as everything in me revolted at the idea of

---

*A year later when I got to know Icksan better the following conversation took place in Colombo:

Icksan: "You remember you bring ten written questions about the relationship of Subud to certain teachings and so on?"

V: "Yes."

Icksan: "You remember I interpret your questions and Bapak's answers?"

V: "Yes."

Icksan: "You were satisfied with the answers?"

V: "Oh yes. Many things were made clear."

Icksan (laughing): "You think I even hear your questions? Much too heffy. But the answers were nice, h'm? Funny!"

how ridiculous it would look.

One of them said cuttingly: "Have you thought that nobody there would have cared whether you knelt or stood on your head? We were busy with our own excercise." I saw then that what was really absurd was my egoistical reluctance to let go of the picture of myself that I had been carrying about with me – the cynical, hard-boiled modern newspaperman who did not want to be caught doing something old-fashioned like reading the Bible or kneeling in worship.

At the next latihan my inner world changed for me. I found myself kneeling, and singing at the top of my voice words that had never been in my vocabulary before: "God have mercy on me". I was completely conscious of what I was saying, of the fact that I was kneeling, that I was smiling and that the tears were rolling down my face and that, for the first time in my life, I had a taste of real happiness. This wonderful sense of euphory persisted for several days. This, I knew, was what happiness was like. All my life I had known two other emotions. Unhappiness or absence of unhappiness. Now there was a taste of positive happiness.

I was now convinced that there was a force in the latihan and that I had made contact with it. My responses in the exercises changed. They turned into physical movements such as involuntary movements of the hands and head. The force was there, subtle and strong, but now my mind began its doubting again: Was this a good force or a bad force? The answer to this was only possible through experience of the way it had worked for me. Through the succeeding five years, I have had more than the meed of proof of beneficence than any man has a right to expect.

2
Waiting for Subud

AT the end of my month at Coombe, Bapak sent for me and informed me that I was not yet able to transmit the contact to others. He advised me not to speak about my experience – except what I felt I really understood – when I returned home. Since I understood nothing and could describe nothing except the exterior activity at Coombe, I realized I could say nothing at all to my friends at home, or even to my wife – only that the help we had long expected had arrived and that we would not have to wait long now. Bapak said that we should try to build up our study group to fifty in the next two or three months and he would send a competent helper to start Subud in Ceylon. I replied that this would be impossible since we had tried, vainly, for five years to increase our group but that we had not been able to grow beyond a dozen regulars. Bapak laughingly remarked that I should not be so sure about this and that the real difficulty might be how to "accommodate all who will come". I thought that this was a manner of speaking and agreed we would do our best.

I returned home armed only with a taped recording of John Bennett's account of how Pak Subud had come to England. My colleagues were waiting for me at the airport, for the first time in all my travels, brimmingly expectant through hints in my letters to my wife that I was bringing back "valuable merchandise" as one of them characteristically put it. The only merchandise I carried was the tape which I handed over with little explanation. This was run at a meeting to which the group had invited a few friends. I immediately sensed that something new was happening. People who had for years resisted our attempts to persuade them to join our study group became plainly excited by the new possibilities opened up by the news. They brought many others to listen to a replay of the tape so that by September there were fifty-four people waiting for Subud to be started in Ceylon.

One morning Aubrey Collette, a colleague in the newspaper I edited – he was a member of our study group – came in for the daily briefing session in my office and suggested that he and I do the relaxing exercises we used to practise. After three minutes of the exercise, he remarked that it had been much deeper than he had ever experienced before and that he

would practise it at home every morning before he came to work. On the
next day he came into my room, flushed and excited. "The most incredi-
ble thing happened this morning," he said. "I was doing the relaxing
exercise and suddenly my arms began to move upward and I began to cry
in prayer and I couldn't stop it even when the servant brought in my tea.
I still feel this wonderful sensation inside me."

I said to myself, "Good heavens, what have I gone and done!"

I hurriedly explained what I knew about the Subud opening and about
my own experience when the response to the contact became manifest in
me. We wrote to Bapak asking him for his advice.

Bapak's reply was: "Yes, you have opened Collette 'accidentally'. (I
understood this to mean 'Unintentionally'.) Don't open anyone deliberately yet. Do latihan with Collette in your home twice a week and say no
more about it."

It was a strange secret to keep, but we did so for several months until
the Ceylon Group was started. Collette and I, always close to each other
professionally and intellectually, came to know each other like blood
brothers. I felt nearer to him than I had ever felt towards my own brothers and sisters.

The other event was connected with my wife, Sunetra. She said to me
one day: "I want to go to London."

I replied that I could not possibly go to London again as I had just
returned from leave.

She said, "I didn't say anything about you going to London. I want to
go to London."

To appreciate the full flavour of this incident it is necessary to know
that my wife, like most middle-class women in Ceylon, had been brought
up in a very conservative family tradition, had never travelled even in a
public bus before her marriage and was not used to going about alone
even in Colombo. And now she wanted to go alone to London.

I said, "All right, but what's all this about? Why this sudden desire to
go to London?"

She replied, thoughtfully and determinedly, "Something happened to
you in England which has changed you. I also want this for myself."

I was very happy that she felt this way. I felt I was able to repay her in
some measure for having been instrumental in bringing me in contact
with the spiritual ideas and with John Bennett and Coombe Springs and
so – eventually – with Subud. I scraped together some money and sent
her on her great adventure.

Two nights after her receiving the contact from Ibu she cabled: "Thank you for giving me the opportunity of knowing what prayer is."

The study group continued, meeting three nights a week as before at Isaac Gerson's home and every Sunday, working like ununionized navvies on our farm at Kadawatta, ten miles from Colombo. There was a much more purposive and hopeful atmosphere already among us all. For Collette, Sunetra and me the talks we listened to and the self-observation tests we were given already seemed too much like techniques groping towards something much simpler and easier than we had ever imagined it would be. Sooty Banda, the bearded Socrates of our group who had helped us all enormously by his ability to simplify everything through uncannily apt and illuminating analogies,* had obviously understood our situation with his intuitive wisdom. He said: "As long as you tug at the bow nothing happens. The arrow flies only when you let go."

---

*When Subud had finally been established in Colombo an Indian who had previously practised yoga asked the helpers whether it was better to begin the latihan in the padmasan or lotus posture. Sooty's reply was: "Brother, it is raining outside. If you want to get wet all you have to do is to go out in the rain. Sit down, lie on the ground or stand on your head – it's all the same. You get wet."

3

Subud Comes to Ceylon

IN December Bapak sent Icksan Ahmad with Rachmad Pane to start the group in Ceylon. For the women he sent Bulbul (now Mariani) Arnold from Calcutta. Almost all the members of the study group were present at Colombo airport to greet the Indonesians. We were all charged with expectancy. Icksan came down the gangway, clad in a striped sports jersey with black snowboots on his feet looking like a prizefighter in training or a lumberjack on a spree. Sooty Banda's eyebrows rose quizzically. I grinned sheepishly back. Then Rachmad Pane appeared with a guitar slung on his back. The group looked at me as though I'd perpetrated a large hoax on them. I heard Sooty mutter in his beard, "I say, Tarzie, I think I want my money back!"

I could see quite well that Sooty's facetious remark had found a ready sale in the minds of the others who had the same response as I when I first saw Bapak enter the little room when I received my opening. Is this the way help comes? Are these the men who can help us to save our immortal souls? Prize fighters and guitar players?

Later, when we had sensed the Subud latihan and recognized the wonderful quality of Icksan's understanding and inner nature, we saw the difference between appearing virtuous and being virtuous. When I described my initial reaction towards Bapak – how ordinary he had looked – Sooty Banda once again explained it with memorable pithiness: "We have seen paintings of Jesus Christ – what he looked like, the clothes he wore. Long white robes and beard. So all Holy Men must look like Jesus Christ. We forget that this is the 20th century and people dress differently. Jesus Christ dressed like every other Jew in Jerusalem. In fact, my guess is that he must have been the Best Dressed Man in Palestine and regarded as a model of propriety by the Jerusalem Tailor and Cutter."

That evening there were fifty-four people waiting to receive the Subud contact. (And I had been so sure that there would not be more than a dozen). From all over the country people who had heard a whisper about Subud converged on Lesly Jayatilleke's house which was used as Icksan's headquarters. They belonged to all kinds of faiths and races – Buddhists, Mohammedans, Christians of all denominations, Hindus, Americans,

Indians, and even an Austrian and a White Russian. Their occupations
were as varied as their races and creeds – lawyers, bankers, clerks, civil
servants, taxi drivers, journalists, politicians, doctors, including three
Freudian psychiatrists, merchants, mechanics, nurses, stenographers and
teachers.

Their motives for coming were also diverse. Some came because they
were genuinely interested in trying a new way of understanding the purpose of life; some because they wanted to see Icksan perform conjuring
tricks with a couple of miracles thrown in for good measure; some
because they wanted cures for "incurable" illnesses; some came to rub
shoulders with well-known people; some came to keep watch on their
wives (or husbands); some came out of a desire to imitate; some because
something new was going on and they would not be left out. But those
who stayed on did so because something in them was touched and they
found that it was good. I know one man who came there because he
wanted to get to know Collette – the famous cartoonist on my paper. But
he stayed on because he found that through Subud his relationship with
his wife improved.

One night a small group of people stayed on for six hours hoping to
see Icksan practising hypnotism. They had heard that the smoke from
Icksan's Dunhill pipe put everyone present into a deep trance. One of
them stayed on in Subud because that night he had "felt something like a
bird moving within me" and he liked the feeling of this "bird".

Another young man walked boldly up the drive-way to where I was
seated and asked very politely: "Is there a Mr. Latihan living here?" He is
still practising latihan in Hong Kong.

Lesly's house was becoming known by a variety of names – including
Miracle House, Magic Hall, Subuddhist Mansion and Vibration Centre.

At that time the three-month-probation principle had not been introduced and people were being opened as easily as filleting fish. Latihan
went on from dusk to midnight and Icksan took the brunt of it since
Rachmad Pane was ill from an overdose of opening people in London.

Bulbul, with only three months' experience in Subud, opened streams
of women, many of whom spoke no English and therefore had no possibility of communicating verbally with her. Three hundred and forty-five
men and women were opened in three weeks.

One evening Icksan gave irrefutable proof of the faculty he had
received from Subud to judge the inner state of others. People, mostly
strangers to us, were going in and out of the latihan. Icksan, who had

been opening people and supervising the latihan for two hours, turned to Lesly and me and said: "You take over. I go dinner, come back in twenty minutes."

When he re-entered the room after dinner he interrupted my latihan and pointed to a man who was moving his hands about and gyrating his head in great abandon. Icksan whispered: "Who open him?" I said I did not know. "He not open," said Icksan, tapping the man on the shoulder and beckoning to him to follow us out. Icksan asked the man: "Who open you?" The man looked blank.

Icksan: "When you opened?"

"Open? What's open?" asked the man.

Icksan: "When you come?"

"A few minutes ago."

Icksan: "Who bring you?"

"No one. I was passing by and saw something going on. So I walked in."

Icksan told me to explain Subud to the man and open him if he wished. Later I asked Icksan how he had spotted this man from at least twenty strangers, especially since he was moving about as though the Subud force was impelling him. Icksan looked puzzled at my question.

"Why? Not difficult. All others' inner open. He like plank."

"What do you mean plank?" I persisted.

"Like plank. Like dead thing," he said, thumping the wooden table to illustrate the inner state of the man before his opening.

I observed with great wonder how these two young people, Icksan and Bulbul, sent to us by Bapak, had the inner strength, the mental stature and physical stamina to go on night after night, day after day, taking on so much and establishing a gloriously warm relationship with so many hundreds of strangers without ever assuming an attitude of superiority or resorting to verbal mysticism to capture people by confusion.

I also began to see the difference between teaching and helping people to understand. Many times Icksan said: "I don't know" when people asked him complicated questions. If a question did not fall within his own experience he would say he did not know the answer. He would say "Subud is not teaching. If Bapak were Teacher and he know ten truths he will teach only nine because if he teach all ten then he will have no more pupils."

Whenever the question asked was within the orbit of his personal experience the answer would come with a great deal of humility, but absolute certainty and clarity.

Bob Holmes (this was not his real name) was a middle-aged bachelor, an employee of the British Admiralty in Colombo. He was a lonely man, living a very quiet life in a run-down boarding house. He had come to Subud with a great personal problem. He spoke about it to Icksan:

"Icksan, I have a problem. I drink too much. Much too much. Everyday I drink half a bottle of whisky before coming to latihan. Like today. And when I go back home tonight – I shall probably finish the other half. Is this bad for my latihan?"

Icksan replied: "Bob, if I say stop, will you stop?"

Bob: "I suppose not."

Icksan: "Then why you ask me? You say you know you drink too much. As long as you like drink, you will drink. But when inner say stop, it stop."

I don't know whether Bob still drinks because he left Ceylon soon after, but he did tell me that this explanation helped him enormously by removing the sense of guilt which had accentuated the compulsiveness of the habit.

The simple clarity of Icksan's explanations was a recurrent source of joy to us. Everything he said gave proof to the most sceptical and analytical among us of the cleansing of the faculty of understanding that could come through Subud. One morning as we sat round Icksan on the verandah talking with him, two strangers walked in. They listened to our conversation for a while and one of them – the intellectual looking one – asked: "What is all this talk about God? Who knows anything about God? All this talk is just nonsense. We don't believe in God." The other man retaliated: "Speak for yourself. I believe in God."

An incomprehensible argument developed between the two. Icksan sat patiently looking at them with the indulgence of ancient wisdom. They stopped suddenly, rather embarrassedly when they realized that everyone else was listening to their wordy quarrel.

Icksan said: "Why you fight about God? You say you don't believe in God. And your friend he say he believe in God. All right. Both same. Both not from experience."

The man who did not believe in God is still in Subud and the man who believed in God stopped coming to latihan after three or four times.

4

Across the River

ICKSAN paid three visits to Ceylon within a year – twice alone and once with Bapak. He seemed to have a special place in his being for the Ceylon group, but this may be the feeling of every group which became acquainted with him. His robust attitude to life, his constant good humour and his readiness to break into laughter were highly prized by us. But these were outward attributes. None of us was able to assess his inner quality but when it was manifested in his judgements, advice or actions which had an external effect, we recognized the marvellous maturity of his soul which, although he had been in Subud for only four years, seemed as old as life itself.

When the Subud group went through the inevitable period of painful purification Icksan watched and steered it through the familiar squalls of jealousy, factionalism, cliquiness, spiritual competitiveness and office-seeking. Icksan was younger than many of the helpers in the Colombo group but he displayed one of the highest attributes of wisdom – he never once took sides in all our quarrels and never said a harsh word to anyone. But he was firm and direct in his decisions. We came to recognize that he was impartial in his attitude towards us because, *as a Subud Helper, he was incapable of partiality or favouritism.* He would often remind us:

"In Subud, in front of God, no father, no mother, no brother, no sister, no teachers, no pupils, no higher, no lower, no enemies and also no friends. Only God."

In those early days – perhaps even now – there was a great preoccupation among the more intellectually inclined members of many groups with the question of preparation for Subud. Many, with genuine concern no doubt, felt and said that in order to come to Subud and progress in the latihan it was necessary or at any rate preferable to have gone through the discipline of some spiritual training, whatever it was. This led to needless niggling jealousies in many groups where people could lay claim to the advantage of having been in this or that spiritual order or discipline or system before entering Subud. Often these loaded problems would be taken to Icksan for opinion or arbitration. It was easy to see on his face that he marvelled – in some disgust – that people who had tasted the latihan could still ask such "heffy" questions. But he never evaded an answer if the questioner seemed to find it important.

Someone who shall be nameless here remarked that he felt that his preparation for Subud through his study of a certain system of knowledge had helped him in Subud. Icksan: "Helped you to come to Subud or to progress in the latihan?"

Icksan's question gave me a clue to evaluating the function of "preparation" for Subud. Some, like me, possibly had needed some discipline, some system of preparation to make them even feel the need to worship and to keep them interested in spiritual matters. But there was no question of one kind of preparation for Subud being superior to another as long as it brought a man to ask for the contact.

Many others needed no preparation except their raw experience of life as it came to them.

The trouble arose, it seemed increasingly clear to me, when people constantly referred to the fresh experience they received through Subud in terms and language belonging to the doctrines and truths they had been taught in their pre-Subud spiritual discipline. Thus every fresh experience was reduced to an affirmation or modification of an old experience, preventing or holding back the growth of new understanding.

The members of our old study group reacted against their former teaching in two distinct ways. Some of us began to scoff at the ideas we had once valued so highly and even reviled our teachers whom we had respected so deeply before we came to Subud.

A kind of spiritual de-Stalinization process took place. Others among us found it difficult to cut loose from the old familiar ideas and described our Subud experience in the same familiar terms as we had used before. It was Icksan who helped us to see that both these attitudes were immature and unhelpful to our possibilities of growth through Subud. The picture became clearer:

One man crosses a river in a canoe and gets to the other side where there is a fine open road to walk on. Seeing this, he spits in disgust at the canoe, turns it over, curses the owner of the boat and strides off angrily down the road. Another man also crosses over and, picking the canoe up on his back, he carries it down the open road, burdened by its weight, but refusing to let go of it. A third man crosses over, gets out gratefully, moors it safely for someone else in need to use and strides off lightly down the road.

Icksan brought us to this point of understanding without lecturing or talking down to anyone. He also helped us to appreciate the fact that those who come to Subud through some previous discipline should realize that the need for it had come from their own selves and helplessness and that preparation or a practice of discipline before Subud was by no means essential for everyone. In fact, the word latihan means "training" – in this case, training to worship God.

Walking home late one night after having seen a war movie, Icksan remarked to me: "You know, Tarzie, you look for God for five years. Mr. B. he look for forty years. Icksan – he never look. All Icksan like before is fighting. Icksan fight in guerilla army. Not interested in spiritual life."

On my next visit to Indonesia I learned from my newspaper colleagues that Icksan – they knew him as "Captain" Muhammad Ahmad – was well-known as the youngest and one of the most resourceful leaders of the guerillas who fought for the liberation of Indonesia. One story is that Icksan had led a raid on a Japanese sub-headquarters and captured a huge sum of money which added substantially to the funds on which the Indonesian Army was founded.

Preparation for Subud apparently had many facets and possibilities.

5

It must out

"IT must out," was Icksan's constant advice to us. There was no point in suppressing or prohibiting the feelings, imagination or actions of people going through their initial period of purification. When he was leaving for Jakarta after completing his first visit to Ceylon, Icksan told some of us at the airport: "You will see many strange things in next few months. Horrible. I feel so sorry for you," and he laughed as though he couldn't imagine anything funnier.

The meaning of this cryptic remark became plainly evident before long when people, including those of us who had heard his warning, began showing ugly sides of their inner natures. The socially acceptable veneer which had previously covered over these qualities was ripped apart and the tenuous bonds of cordiality which had governed our former relationship was swiftly broken. To jumble the metaphor even further, Icksan had flipped open the lid of Pandora's box on the principle that "it must out".

And out it did with a vengeance. We went through a storm of pain and anguish, some suffering more than the others, but all suggestions to Icksan on his next visit to put an end to our troubles by issuing a peace fiat, were received with loud and prolonged laughter and the stock comment: "Yes, horrible. It must out."

The psychiatrists in the group marvelled at how deep into their own and other peoples' subconscious minds the latihan seemed to probe. A highly competent Freudian analyst in Ceylon who had moved from frank scepticism about God and worship to deep regard for the latihan within a year of entering Subud, once remarked: "As part of our training as psychiatrists we go through an intensive course of deep analysis. But till I had experience of the process of purification in the latihan I never realized how deep our strongest motivating influences lie." Icksan's response: "Yes, possible. It must out."

Willi Grillmayr, a Viennese neuro-psychiatrist working in Ceylon, came to Subud because it amused and intrigued him to see his friends like Vittachi and Collette – hard-boiled journalists – interested in such "unrational matters" as he called it. He tried his best to account for the post-opening manifestations he saw in himself and others by slapping on them the familiar labels of psychiatry – "autosuggestion", "auto-hypno-sis", "auto-irritation of the motor-function" and so on, but he was never quite satisfied. He was very doubtful of the healing properties of the lati-han and, in great good humour but undisguised disbelief, he chuckled Austrianly whenever he heard stories of Subud "cures".

But when he found that many people whose opinion he respected seemed to take a different attitude, he decided that he would test the curative power of Subud. He had a patient in an advanced state of para-lytic insanity, bedridden for nine years. He had tried every known remedy including a long course of Cobra-toxin and merion – the treatment advo-cated by Dr. Rottmann of Vienna. He asked Icksan whether he would test this patient. Icksan agreed to do the latihan with Willi at the patient's bedside. A minute or two after the latihan started the patient who had been immobile for so many years began to move and suddenly snatched an amulet which had been strung round his neck and flung it at Willi's feet. Willi described to the group his amazement at this phenomenon. Icksan had promptly rushed to the toilet to be violently sick. Then he had picked up the amulet and told Willi that the patient should improve from then on. We opened up the amulet and discovered a small clump of hair, a piece of bone and one or two other unrecognisable objects. "Lower forces," said Icksan. "Sick because influence of satanic forces. Now come out."

Willi was dumb with surprise, he tried his best to find a "scientific" explanation but it wasn't in the book.

A few weeks later, when Icksan and I were walking up the drive to the car which was taking him to the airport, we saw a stranger walk in. It was Willi's patient wanting to know how much Icksan's "fee" was. Icksan laughed in his magnificently unrestrained manner and said: "Practise lati-han. Amulets, charms, not necessary. It must out."

With definite patience and kindliness Icksan enabled us to see the kind of problem we would face as helpers and how we should deal with people who came to us. One of the ladies came to Icksan once in an acute state of excitement and reported: "Icksan, I had an experience last night which I must tell you about right now." I rose to leave them alone. Icksan said: "No, you stay. In Subud no secrets." I stayed and listened to a techni-colour dream in which satanic forces chased her down dark corridors and, when all seemed lost, an angel in the form of Icksan Ahmad came down to save her in the nick of time. Icksan heard it all through and said, "Nice dream. Nice experience."

Then when the lady had left, purring, he said to me: "You knew all imagination?" "Yes," I said. "It was obviously imagination." "Of course," agreed Icksan, "But would she have believe if I tell her so? It must out. By itself. That's it – by itself it must out."

And he advised me that as helpers we should never look caustic or frankly supercilious and disbelieving as I had, or tell anyone that the experiences they related were just imagination or plain lies – *even if we were sure they were.* People indulged in this kind of fantasy because they were at a stage of development in which they needed such supports to their spiritual worship. Eventually, he said, it would all come out as long as they did their latihan diligently. If they did not keep on with the latihan then it would be no longer our problem. This advice has been given to me over and over again by elder brothers in Subud, Sjafrudin, Prio Hartono, Anwar Zakir and Mas Sudarto but, I am afraid, to little avail. In my case it still must out.

6

The last days

BAPAK visited Ceylon in November 1958, and stayed nearly forty days. He brought with him Hardijati, Rahaju, his grand-daughter Indra and Icksan. As could have been expected, Bapak's visit caused great excitement in Ceylon – some of it pleasant, some inevitably unpleasant. I say inevitably because it was explained to us that when Bapak arrives in a new place the lower forces rally themselves to defend their domain and make things difficult for people to worship in the right way. After a day or two we found that Icksan was strangely subdued and different in his manner and even in his relationship with us. Nalini Jayatilaka and Sunetra often asked him why he seemed sad, and the only answer he gave was: "Not sad. Subud very hard," adding in a sardonic tone, "Tell your friends not to join if they think Subud easy."

He was referring, I think specifically, to the difficulties and burdens of Bapak's assistants in Subud. But every one of us learnt that Subud was not easy, whatever stage we were at. Sometimes understanding came so suddenly that it was difficult to bear with equanimity.

I had such an experience one day when Bapak was in Colombo. Icksan called me into his room and said: "Tarzie, Bapak want to do some personal shopping and has no money at all."

Instantly I reached for my cheque book in my hip pocket asking: "How much does he want, Icksan?"

Icksan looked at me very strangely and shook his head. "Never mind, not necessary now," he said.

I could not understand the note in his voice. "But Icksan, I have the money. How much does Bapak want?"

My pen was poised over the cheque book.

Icksan repeated: "No. Not necessary now."

I implored him to tell me why he spoke this way when I, as I thought, was willing to be generous.

Icksan said: "All right: I tell you . . . Did Bapak ever ask you how much you want of what he give you?"

Tears of mortification squirted into my eyes. I felt I had understood in a flash but it took me days to overcome the taste of my pettiness.

I was and am deeply grateful to Icksan for showing me this side of my nature so clearly and effectively.

Icksan and a few of us went late at night to sip a glass of beer and talk under the trees at my club. I told him that I had observed that his entire attitude was different from his previous visits and that even his explanations had not the force and clarity they'd had before.

"That is quite true," Icksan said, "Good reason." He was evidently bent on changing the subject but we pressed him to continue. After "receiving" for a minute he said he would try to explain:

"When Bapak give special assignment to helper – like transmitting contact to new group and giving necessary explanations – he also give him power to enable him to do the job. Like when King send Ambassador he give him credential – pleni, pleni, pleni – What? Yes, plenipotentiary authority. So he is different, stronger, though he may not realize it till he find himself able to do more than ordinarily. For instance, he find he suddenly give explanation he not know before or become more sensitive to state of Inner of other people. Then, when job is over, this power is taken away. So this period very dangerous. Place of power can fill with pride, self-love and he think his own power has grown. Must be very careful. This is time of great Test . . . This time Icksan come with Bapak. So special power not necessary. Maybe this difference you see."

As we all know now there was something else besides this which caused the change in Icksan during this visit. The first clue was given by Icksan himself.

"Bapak order me today to make ready to go to America with him. How can Icksan go? Funny. Why does Bapak tell Icksan to go? Very funny."

We asked why Icksan thought it was so funny that he should be asked to accompany Bapak to America. He looked at us for a long half-minute and replied: "He already asked Dr. Zakir to prepare to go."

But that was Icksan's sense of diplomacy.

A day or two later Icksan came to my house and looked around rather curiously. Eventually, he asked Sunetra: "Can Ismana (his wife) stay here if necessary?"

Sunetra said: "That would be wonderful. We'll have that room ready for both of you."

But Icksan replied: "Not, not Icksan. Icksan not come. For Ismana may be necessary."

Still the penny did not drop.

That afternoon I was in Icksan's room at Subud House when Bapak came in and sat down. I asked Bapak:

"Bapak, the Ceylon Group has been very lucky so far. We have had a great deal of help this year. Icksan came in December and March, Mr. Bennett came in June. Now Bapak himself has come. Icksan is also here. Can we expect more visits like this?"

Bapak did not reply immediately. He closed his eyes momentarily, then looked quizzically at Icksan. Icksan could not return the gaze and looked down at his feet, his face flushing with something like sadness. After a while Bapak turned to me and spoke in English, clear and deliberate: "Yes. But not Icksan."

After latihan that night the group gathered round Bapak in the sitting-room. There was a long silence. Bapak told me to repeat the question I had asked him in Icksan's room. I repeated my question in much the same words: Bapak repeated his answer: "Yes. But not Icksan." adding, "Another will come, but don't ask him so many questions as you asked Icksan." Hardijati interpreted this to the group.

Someone asked why Bapak had said this: the only answer: "Too heavy."

Not long after Bapak, his daughter and Icksan had left for Singapore en route to Jakarta, Sunetra telephoned me at the office one morning: "Are you standing up?" she asked. "If you are, sit down. I have something to read out to you."

I sat down and heard her read a telegram from Singapore.

ICKSAN DEAD FOLLOWING HEART ATTACK. CARMICHAEL.

Falil Caffoor, Lesly Jayatilake and I took the plane that afternoon to Jakarta. We arrived two days before Icksan's body, which was being shipped, arrived.

The first thing we noticed was that our inner confusion and reluctance to accept the enormity of what had happened, was not shared by the Subud members in Jakarta. They went about their business, courteous, hospitable and anxious to put us at our ease. They tried their best to console us although their sense of loss of a brother they had known much longer than we had must have been far deeper than ours.

We called at the house of Icksan's parents to pay our respects to them and to Ismana. We could hardly contain our sorrow and Lesly was overflowing with a sense of deprivation. Ismana, we were told, was in latihan and would see us soon. When she came out, young, translucently beautiful and completely self-composed, she said:

"Falil, Lesly, Tarzie, thank you very much for coming to Icksan's funeral. I know how much you love Icksan and how much he loves you. Will you excuse me?" and she returned to her latihan.

It was magnificent. But I could not understand how these people seemed to have so much detachment about the death of a young man, with a young wife and months old baby, who had died in the full prime of his life.

"Bapak, don't you feel ANYTHING? Is there no unhappiness in anyone here about the death of Icksan? Does no one feel the sense of loss we feel?"

Bapak smiled in great indulgence and replied (Prio Hartono interpreting): "Yes, of course, Bapak and your brothers and sisters here feel Icksan's death very much. See how Bapak has already lost several pounds in weight since Icksan died. But that is *this* Bapak, the Bapak you see. But the real Bapak is not sad. That Bapak is HAPPY for Icksan because Icksan has attained the peak of his spiritual possibilities in this world, so soon. His soul is now elsewhere, very high." And, in consolation to us he said to the Indonesians around:

"Icksan very close to Colombo Group. Icksan always walking about with these friends. Even drinking beer together! You will see Icksan again. He will visit you."*

Still, unappeased, I asked: "How? How does Bapak mean – 'see Icksan'? Like I see Bapak? Or in a dream?" Bapak said: "May be like a dream, but not a dream. You will know when you have the experience."

Riding in Suparto's Volkswagen minibus to the funeral a day later, we heard another strange conversation. Suparto, driving along cavalierly, said laughingly – but quite seriously – "Oh last night Icksan speak to me . . ."

I interjected: "How do you mean? Last night? Icksan spoke to you last night?"

This forecast came.true within a few weeks.

I "met" Icksan at my home in Colombo so surely and clearly that the thought of doubting it never entered my mind. A week later I had "external" proof of this when Ismana wrote to me to say that she had "received" one night that Icksan was with me. The date she gave was identical.

On another occasion, during the group latihan, I felt Icksan's presence once more and felt also that another member at the other end of the room was experiencing it. After latihan I dropped my wife home, and telling her that I had to go to the home of this other member, I drove up there. He opened the door at my knock and greeted me with these words: "You mean Icksan?"

Later Bapak tested these experiences and confirmed that they were the meetings with Icksan that he had foretold.

As though it was a commonplace happening Suparto replied, "Yes, we had big conversation."

I asked: "What did you talk about?"

Suparto: "I ask Icksan why not come back to stay here."

I asked: "And what did he say?"

Suparto: "Oh, he say: 'Too hot'. Much pleasanter where he is."

The night before I left Jakarta I sat in the garage of Bapak's house – used later as the Secretariat – and asked him more questions, mine, as well as those I was bearing from friends in Colombo.

Q. Did Bapak know in Colombo that Icksan was going to die so soon?

A. You should know. Bapak warned you about this.

Q. When?

A. When you asked Bapak about Icksan returning to help the group in Ceylon.

Suddenly I realized how opaque we had been.

Q. Bapak, Icksan was not an ordinary man. He was so helpful to thousands of people in Subud. His quality was extraordinary. Why did he have to die an ordinary death – from a heart attack, like an ordinary man?

A. How else would you have had him die? Every man must die either by ordinary means – by ill health – or by an accident. Icksan died of a heart attack because his heart was the weakest point in him. His body was too "thick", so this was the way through which he passed from this existence. Bapak will say one thing more about this. Had Icksan not died at that time by this means he would have died near that time by some other means. Icksan was a worker for Subud. He completed the work he could do on this earth and has gone elsewhere.

Q. The ladies in Colombo wanted me to ask Bapak whether Icksan knew he was going to die. If so, why did he not return to die near Ismana?

A. That would not have been surrendering, would it?

7
Questions, Questions

FOR some time I was known among Subud members in Jakarta as the man who had once taken ten written questions to Bapak. This reference provoked great merriment and Subud friends in Colombo and India frequently told me that I must not ask so many questions, that I should rather "accept". I am sure they were right in their advice but I found that I could begin to "accept" only when my questions had been answered. 1 found – and still find – it impossible to "accept" something that is confused or unresolved. If Bapak or any of the helpers could help sort out my problems for me I felt that I should go ahead and ask all the real questions I had. It must out, I told myself.

Besides, I also found that all those who protested at my asking questions from Bapak, or from Icksan or Prio Hartono, were very anxious to hear the answers. Sometimes they'd recoil with genteel horror when a question was put, but they always came forward eagerly when the answer was provided. I felt therefore that if I was to play the role of the caddie who tees the ball up for people to enjoy watching Bapak drive it off masterfully, I was gratefully prepared to accept my part. I too could share in the fun. After some experience as caddie I also came to a very rewarding conclusion: I did not have to judge whether my question was foolish or wise, juvenile or adult as long as it was real – that is, I really wanted to know the answer. So I asked all the foolish questions I had in the confident knowledge that I would not get a foolish answer.

There were others too – thank God – who were not afraid to ask questions that might sound too rudimentary or naive. Mohammed Siddeek of Colombo was one of these and the answers given to some of the questions he asked have helped me enormously to understand more. We were waiting to hear Bapak speak one evening, when Sideek who was seated on the carpet near Bapak's chair, turned his face up to Bapak and asked one of his supremely innocent questions:

"Bapak," he said, 'Where IS God?"

As the court reporters say, a titter ran round the room. When this subsided, we heard Bapak call out in a loud voice, "Siddeeeeeeeek!" Siddeek replied anxiously, "Yes, Bapak?" Bapak ignored this response and, turn-

ing his head to the ceiling called out – louder – "Siddeeeeeeeeeeek!" All
eyes in the room widened in amazement. Poor Siddeek responded again.
"Yes, Bapak?" Bapak ignored him once more and turning to the window,
called out really loud, "SIDDEEEEEEEEEK!" Now, excitedly rising to
his haunches and looking badly rattled Siddeek replied, "Yes, Bapak?"

Bapak smiled this time and after a pause, said: "You see. We look for
God in the clouds, in the mountain tops, in caves, in temples, churches
and mosques. We do not realize that God may be nearer to us than ourselves. So even when God responds to our call we do not hear him because
our attention is preoccupied with looking for him elsewhere."

The light that flashed in my mind – and I am sure, in the minds of
everyone present – was reflected in the obvious relief of instantaneous
comprehension that glowed on Siddeek's face.

∞∞∞∞

I asked: "Are there highly developed people living in the world today
who have reached spiritual eminence without the help of Subud? Is
Krishnamurti, for instance, such a man?"

Many Subud members who had listened to Krishnaji's talks and held
him in high regard, were very anxious to know Bapak's assessment of his
power.

Bapak said he would test this question himself. Standing up and clos-
ing his eyes, Bapak asked:

"Krishnamurti, where is his power from? It is from his heart?"

No.

"Is it from his mind?"

No.

"It is from God?"

No.

"Where is it from, then?"

Bapak explained the response he received: "It is his own human power.
He was born with true human power."

This clarification helped us to understand the reason for the tremendous strength we had all felt in the presence of Krishnamurti – a strength
and confidence which trickled away soon after we had left him.
Krishnaji's spiritual stature was evident to us who had sat at his feet but I
had found it impossible to use what he had imparted and to recreate its
power for practical guidance in my life. He was like a man on the river

bank who warns you that you are drowning and you realize that indeed you are. You splash about, trying to swim unavailingly against the current, but he does not give you a hand or throw you a rope. But he is already there. He was *born* on the banks of the river.

Another illuminating "test" was given by Bapak in India in response to my question about a man who had been many years in Subud and was still practising the latihan regularly, but whose actions showed that he was consumed by a feeling of being ill-used by people in Subud, a raw and ugly hostility which sometimes extended even to Bapak. Let us call him Hamsa for anonymity.

My question was: "Hamsa has been in Subud for many many years. He has great knowledge and intelligence. He has been very useful and active in Subud and still practises the latihan regularly. Yet he is capable of contempt and anger. What hope can people like me, who have not got so many of his talents and advantages, have of ridding ourselves of the influences of lower forces if he acts like this after so much experience?"

Bapak asked Anwar Zakir, Bomon-Behram and me to participate in testing this question:

"How much material force in Hamsa?"

The response was that it was very strong.

"How much vegetable force in Hamsa?"

Very strong.

"How much animal force in Hamsa?"

Very strong – but not as much as the other categories. "How much true human force in Hamsa?"

The response was a blank. None.

Then Bapak said: "Test Vittachi." The test started from the other end of the scale.

"How much human force?"

None.

"How much animal force?"

None.

"How much vegetable force?"

None – perhaps a slight, hardly noticeable amount.

"How much material force?"

The response was fairly strong.

"Already some progress," commented Bapak, smiling, "But very little yet."

Bapak explained: "In Hamsa's case the various forces necessary for a human being to live and work in this world have increased considerably but the true force which should be present to master and use these relatively lower forces has not yet been developed. Therefore, his mistakes could be greater than those which we, at the bottom of the ladder, are making."

When one has progressed much, the greater the possibility of error. Errors made by such people could be very dangerous to themselves and to others. They should, therefore, be more careful than those whose actions have less influence on other people.

8

New Valuations

THE idea that material, vegetable and animal forces were necessary for a human being's existence and spiritual progress was very revealing. I began to understand what Icksan must have meant when he asked us at the very beginning, "Are you sitting on that chair or is that chair sitting on you?"

Bapak explained this idea further from a different viewpoint. I had asked him a question about Buddhism, the religion into which I had been born: "Why did the Buddha advise us not to kill animals even for our food? Does this mean that people such as the Eskimos and others whose existence depends on hunting are excluded from the possibility of spiritual evolution?"

Bapak's reply was: "When did the Buddha instruct people not to kill animals? His words on this should be understood correctly. He said that animals should not be killed *wantonly* – for pleasure, for sport, from wickedness as people in his time did and even now do. This is one meaning. The other and deeper meaning is this: At that time many people were practising self-immolation, the mortification of the flesh – the animal side of a human being – in order to attain spiritual enlightenment. The Buddha himself experimented with this method for several weeks, fasting until his flesh shrivelled to practically nothing. Then the Buddha realized that killing the animal forces in oneself is not the true way to salvation. He realized that these animal forces also are necessary for man to live in this world even while seeking spiritual progress. It was then that enlightenment came to him – and, with it, his understanding of the way of moderation."

Since entering Subud I had become interested in reading the teachings in other faiths – Christianity, Islam (particularly Sufism) and Vedanta. I had never been able to become interested in the Gospels before I came to Subud. I was one of those unfortunate people who had been advised in school to read the Bible for its "good English", with the result that the spiritual meaning of the magnificently charged language of the Old Testament and the Authorized Version had never occurred to me. After Subud I found I was able to read the Gospels with a new understanding which I had been denied before.

Sooty Banda first opened my mind to the scintillating inner possibilities in the Gospels by his talent for fresh and significant analogy.

"Matthew," he used to say, "was a crack short-hand man. Mark was the pedestrian reporter. Luke was an interpretative reporter, and John was the poet."

We would read Matthew and John frequently together and discover new vistas of meaning at every reading.

The parables of Christ were a source of great delight and illumination when Sooty Banda cracked open a word or phrase big with meaning. But there were many stories which we found difficult to break through.

At the first opportunity, I asked Bapak to explain one or two of these difficulties, and ever since I have wished that Bapak had time to tell us more about his interpretations of some of these old teachings.

I requested Bapak to explain the meaning of the parable of loaves and fishes. I said: "Bapak, this story defeats me. It tells nothing except that Christ could work magic stunts when he felt like it. I cannot believe that this parable just wants to advertise Christ as a magician. Is there another meaning?"

Bapak (in English): "You not understand?"

I said no, I could not see any purpose in this parable.

Bapak (Icksan interpreting): "You remember you receive something when you come to Subud?"

Yes, I remembered.

Bapak: "And when you had received you were able to give something to others who asked for it?"

Yes, I remembered.

Bapak: "And what these others received was not different from what you receive in quality or quantity?"

Yes, it was like that.

Bapak: "And they, in turn, were able to give this to others who asked for it without diminution of quality or quantity?"

Yes, it was so.

Bapak: "Ah, now you know meaning of loaves and fishes. People who ask receive as much of loaves and fishes as they need and always one more loaf, one more fish remaining where it came from originally. Now you understand?"

Understand? I was delirious with joy and could hardly restrain my tears. No other meaning was even remotely possible.

On another occasion, Bapak explained the story of Abraham's sacrifice:
"Ibrahim," said Bapak, "received his son from God – a symbol of true
receiving of force or grace – when he was already past sixty. He was very
grateful to God and worshipped sincerely. But Ibrahim was still dominated by animal passions. So it was necessary for him to sacrifice these
lower forces. He was ordered to bring his growing son to the temple. But
the son was not killed. It was a wether that was killed – symbol of his
dominant animal passions. When these passions were subdued, Ibrahim's
son – his true self – was able to master the lower forces and grow to its
full possibilities of development."

Whenever I recall this clarification of the story of Abraham's ordeal, I
am conscious of a feeling of deep sympathy for sincere Christian people
who have not had the opportunity of listening to Bapak speak of Christ's
teachings. When Bapak explains these matters, it is not another of those
"interpretations" of the Bible produced by the thinking of so many com-
mentators and theologians. You receive a glimpse of the irreducible clarity of what the ancients meant when they spoke of Objective Knowledge.

Perhaps the best example in my experience of this way of direct
knowledge was provided by Bapak when I requested an explanation of
why so many of us whose religious tradition for generations had been
Buddhism or Christianity had began to say "Al-lah" instead of the names
of God which were more familiar to us.

Bapak said: "You also make the mistake of imagining that Allah is a
Mohammedan. He is God. The word Allah is older than language. Have
you not noticed that the first sound a new born baby utters – whether it
is American, Japanese, Indian or European is Al-lah. It comes out of the
new-born infant as Aw-wah, aw-wah, aw-wah. The tongue discovers the
palate – Al, Al, Al, and then from its raised position it must fall to rest –
lah, lah, lah . . . So the first sound a child utters is the name of God. Do
you see?"

I began to see that other names of God like Yahweh and Jehovah also
had come from a source "before language."

Sometimes, this direct knowledge from Bapak's clarifications is so
unexpected and even diametrically contrary to what is familiar to us, that
I put it away in a part of my mind reserved for stacking material for
future reference. For instance in March 1960, during a meeting in
Singapore, I asked Bapak to comment on Darwinism and its later devel-
opments.

Bapak said: "This theory is both right and wrong. For example it may explain physiological evolution but it does not explain the vital difference between man and animals – however highly evolved. That is, man has been given a soul with which he can make a choice between two alternatives. Even the most advanced ape does not have this choice. So the scientists interpolate a Missing Link. This link will always be missing."

Bapak went on to refer to "not one, but five different human races." He enumerated them on his fingers: "Black, Brown, White, Yellow and Red."

Were there five separate evolutions, then? Were there five Adams then and not just one? These were the questions I put by for future enquiry.*

* *In* Harper's Magazine *(December 1962) the lead article entitled "New Findings in the Origin of Races" by Carleton S Coon, the noted archaeologist, indicates that science is now beginning to believe that there were five distinct races – Caucasoids, Mongoloids, Australoids, Congoloids and Capoids (after the Cape of Good Hope) which evolved from a sub-human ancestor to man at five different times in human history in widely separated parts of the world.*

9

A Clean Ash Tray

A FRIEND in the Colombo group (let us call him Herbert) had a serious problem: drink. He had been in our old study group and was one of the first to join Subud. He was the manager of a growing company, had a fine family and considerable sensitiveness and intelligence. But he could not subdue his hankering for drink. Having heard Icksan say, "When inner say stop, it stop," Herbert was waiting for the word but it did not come. He observed changes in others and wondered about himself.

There was a young bachelor, rich, intelligent and personable who spent a small fortune on drink because he liked the taste of liquor and the feeling of boozy euphoria it gave him. Within a year of receiving the contact, he found that his body would not retain anything more than one or two small drinks. I once saw him defiantly drink down a bottle of beer and run to the verandah to spew it up immediately. One side of him wanted to stop drinking, but his mind could not obey his will, and he continued to drink. When I saw him disgorge the pint of beer I asked him what the matter was. His reply was memorable. Choking back the nausea he said laughingly: "This damn Subud!"

Herbert knew about his case and that of several others who had either stopped drinking or whose intake had been drastically reduced. When Bapak came to Ceylon, Herbert sought an interview to ask about his drinking.

"I know that I drink too much, and have been hoping the latihan would help me to stop drinking, but it is as bad as ever. Why is this so?" he asked.

"Because you do not want to stop it," was Bapak's answer.

I could not understand this. Bapak's answer seemed to contradict what we had been told at first. A year later, when I met Bapak in India I understood the beauty and simplicity of this explanation.

Bomon-Behram asked a question: "Should we not make an effort of will to stop certain practices and habits which we know are bad for our spiritual progress?"

Bapak agreed.

I intervened: "But, Bapak, when we came to Subud we were told that it is not necessary to try to use effort or will. In fact, Bapak said that we had NO will of our own or that it was too weak to be of much value ..."

Bapak: "Yes, this was so."

I went on: "But now Bapak says that we should use effort and will ..."

Bapak: "So you see a contradiction in Bapak's two statements?"

I: "Yes, it seems contradictory."

Bapak: "Why did you come to Subud? You came because you had tried various ways to help your spiritual life – Buddhism, Krishnamurti, Gurdjieff – all of which had required an effort of will. This will was not forthcoming or, if it was there at all, it had proved to be so feeble that it could not stand up against any opposition. Your life was blown this way and that according to the direction of the wind of circumstance. So you came to Subud. You were told that it was not necessary to use your will or make an effort except to practise the latihan as diligently as you could. This attracted you and you remained in Subud. Now, three years later, Bapak says: 'Use your will.' And you say that there is a contradiction. But do you not see that your experience between these two statements has resolved this contradiction?"

I replied that I could not see this.

Bapak: "It is like this. When you came to Subud there was nothing in you which could really be called Will. But as you practised your latihan, this Will became alive in you and has become stronger. You now have something that you can begin to recognize as Will. So now Bapak says: 'Use this Will, to the degree that it has grown in you, to stop these practices or habits which you say you *know* are holding up your spiritual progress.' To the extent that you do this, your latihan will improve, and to the extent that you do the latihan, your Will becomes stronger. In this way your Will and your latihan will react on one another and strengthen each other. If you leave it entirely to the latihan and deliberately continue bad habits, progress will naturally take a longer time. What you used to call your will before Subud was *wilfulness*. Now it is willingness." (Anwar Zakir interpreting).

Exultantly, I thanked Bapak for giving us this superbly illuminating explanation.

He continued: "Consider this ashtray. Bapak puts his ash in it. Servant comes in and cleans the tray. Bapak puts more ash in it. Servant cleans it out again. Bapak puts ash in it again. Servant cleans it out again. And so it goes on. Sometimes the ash will finish when the cigarette comes to an end. But if Bapak wants a clean ashtray *now*, he must stop putting ash into it."

Bomon-Behram had a supplementary question: "Why then should people in Subud not be given a code of conduct to guide them?"

Bapak: "Surely, the code of conduct has already been given?"

Bomon-Behram: "I have never seen it."

Bapak: "Why not? The code of conduct has already been given by the Buddha, Christ, Muhammad . . ."

BB and I laughed delightedly at the finished grace of Bapak as a dialectician. This is precisely what Bapak told us all from the very beginning: "Subud is not a new religion. Subud is not a teaching. All the teaching that we need has already been given by the founders of the Great Religions. Subud will provide the force which will help us to understand and follow our own religions better."

But we, with our canny talent for remembering what was convenient and relegating to limbo what was more difficult, had paid attention only to the first part of this explanation: "Subud is not a teaching . . ."

This clarification from Bapak put an end to my confusion about Subud and discipline. I heard some Subud members – usually those who had previously followed systems which impose a stern regimen of discipline – question the rightness of waiting for "inner" to say "stop". I myself had wondered on occasions about the absence of any rules in Subud and about the lack of any discipline imposed on us by Bapak to guide us through at least the stormy days of initial purification. I now realized that the only discipline that would be useful and effective was not one that came from outside, from a set of external rules to which we paid spurious lip service, but one that came from within us, as a deeply felt need of an *inner* self.

Someone present remarked that, all the same, it might be helpful if Bapak were to issue a code of rules for Subud.

Bapak (smiling broadly): "Bapak suggested only one rule and got into serious trouble on that occasion."

I: "What was that rule, Bapak?"

Bapak: "That ladies should not attend the latihan in slacks!"

10

Subud as Repair Shop

ONE of the most attractive features of the explanations and advice given by Bapak is its practical quality. Because the advice comes from inner experience and understanding there is no pulpit "moralizing" about good and evil or punishment and reward. I saw this very clearly when I asked him why he – through Ibu – had advised ladies in Subud not to wear slacks to latihan.

Bapak explained that the reason was very simple: "The latihan helps people to cast away the falseness they have acquired through social imitation and to develop their true selves to their full potential. A woman's true self is essentially feminine. The very fact that she chooses to wear slacks to worship indicates that there is something in her nature which wishes to be mannish. When she argues that slacks give her more freedom of movement than feminine clothes, what she means is that she wants to make masculine movements."

"If you have seen ladies in trousers doing latihan you will see what I mean," said Bapak and he proceeded to give us a demonstration in mime of this spectacle. The total impression was one of ridiculous gaucherie and unnatural falsity.

"Wearing trousers to latihan," said Bapak, "may help a woman to become a man but it would not help her to become a woman." It took only a quick imitation by me of Bapak's imitation of a woman in slacks at latihan to persuade Sunetra (an inveterate addict of slacks) to wear saris to latihan – despite the complications it involved.

We tended to obscure this marvellously practical aspect of what we learn in Subud experience by wrapping it up in mystical pseudo-religious explanations. At any rate, I did. This tendency appeared often in our attitude to illness. Here is an example from the experience of my own family. Our daughter "Cooch" used to suffer quite seriously from infected tonsils. At one time she had to absent herself from school two or three times a week because her tonsils troubled her. Her physical growth was retarded but ever since we had heard of Eva Bartok's experience and read all the varied (even contradictory) versions of her recovery we thought that there was something inherently wrong about surgery. Our impression that

Bapak was "against" surgery justified our fear of submitting our child to anaesthesia and the surgeon's knife – although she was frequently ill.

When Bapak visited Ceylon I took Cooch (then ten) to the Subud House because she wanted to pay her respects to Bapak. As soon as we entered Bapak's sitting room, he staggered us by pointing to Cooch and saying:

"Tarzie, better operate."

"Operate, Bapak?" I asked, feeling a little bit caught out.

"Yes, operate," said Bapak, pointing to his own throat.

"But I thought Bapak does not like operations?" I said.

"Bapak does not like *unnecessary* operations. This operation necessary. Soon."

Jati interpreted: "Doctor's skill also given by God. But some surgeons want to operate when it is not necessary as in Eva's case. Remember that Bapak's son also was a medical student."

What more evidence of the *practical* nature of Bapak's advice do we need? The only "mystic" element in this episode was how Bapak diagnosed Cooch's illness without hearing about it from us. But this sensitiveness to people's states we had already experienced with Icksan and other Indonesian helpers and it served only to reaffirm our conviction of the great practical power of the Subud force.

An experienced Indonesian helper once said: "Subud is as practical as a motor garage." This was said in answer to a member's question about how we should describe Subud when people asked whether Subud was a new religion. He said: "Imagine a beautiful park in the middle of a city. There are several excellent roads leading to the park from the city boundaries. One road is signposted "Buddhism", another "Islam", another "Christianity", another "Judaism" and so on. We are each given a vehicle to carry us to the park. But we find that this vehicle is defective: its tyres are flat, its body is dented, its transmission is choked and, above all, there is no fuel. So we take it to a motor garage to have it attended to. When this is done we can take any of the roads – they all take us to the park. Subud is a motor garage."

This same helper once interpreted Bapak's view of the relationship between latihan and sickness. He said that, broadly speaking, there were five kinds of sickness:

1. Ordinary or minor ailments.
2. Hereditary defects and weaknesses.
3. Sickness which comes as warning that one's life is not being lived in

the right way.

  4. Sickness given as punishment for a wrong way of living (too much thinking, worrying, is one of the causes of this category of illness).

  5. Sickness given to summon one to death ("As in Icksan's case," he said.)

Latihan done for the sick, if it is God's will, can relieve categories one and two. Latihan for three and four is to ask sincerely for forgiveness and receiving strength to change one's pattern of life. Latihan done in the case of number five helps in accepting God's will. The experienced helper would recognize this category when he encounters it.

He explained the way that the latihan acted on the first two categories: "Disease-carrying organisms live in and around us all the time. Many of them exist on our flesh and blood. But they do not get the upper hand over us until a condition such as what we call 'being run down' occurs. This condition of weakness may occur due to a variety of reasons and when it comes about, the disease-carrying organisms become dominant. We then become ill. What the latihan does, by God's will, is to remove this condition of weakness and strengthen the body to overcome the disease."

This explanation provided a highly practical clue for the understanding of what is usually labelled as "nerves", "general debility" or "psychosomatic illness". It also removed any basis for the widespread belief that Subud is a means of "faith healing".

People who came to Bapak in the express hope of being cured of their illnesses were advised to go to the hospital or to their doctor. When Bapak was in Colombo a woman telephoned me to ask whether it was true that we had "brought a famous faith healer to Ceylon".

I replied that we had done no such thing, but sensing the agitation in her voice, I asked what the trouble was.

Her husband was ill, she said. She was prepared "to try even faith healing".

She evidently wanted a cure from a "faith healer" but expected the faith also to come from the healer. She would provide only the patient. But on her plea to be allowed to meet Pak Subuh, an interview was arranged.

Bapak advised her to take her husband to the hospital.

All the same, it is difficult not to sympathise with those who look to Subud primarily as a means of receiving miraculous cures. There has been so much remarkable evidence of the therapeutic power of the latihan that people are bound to regard Subud as a clinic of last resort.

Of the many instances of this in my own experience one is worth recording here: A psychiatrist in Subud asked me one evening to help him solve a professional problem. He spoke of a patient who was highly educated and held a position of responsibility and authority, but had come to him a year before for analysis. This doctor, who was outstanding in his field of work, said that he had done what he could for his patient but he was now convinced that the only thing that would help any more was the latihan. But, as a doctor, he felt that it would be improper to advise his patient to come to Subud and, as a helper he knew that people should not be brought to Subud for cures. As he was talking to me, his voice suddenly tailed off and I saw his eyes fixed, surprised, at some point over my shoulder. The look of surprise turned to a smile of great relief and gratitude as he said:

"There he is!"

His patient, call it coincidence if you will, had come to receive the contact at that very moment. (Bapak being present, the rule about the probationary period had been suspended.) It was also extremely interesting to me that the man who was accompanying him and on whose advice he had decided to come to Subud was a Communist. The opening was spectacular – particularly in the case of the Communist. But, as it happened, the Communist stopped coming to latihan after a while but his friend continued. The improvement in him – not only in his mental state but his entire relationship with people – was remarkable to those of us who had known him before as a very intense and rather arrogant person. We have become close friends since then and the sincerity of his willing gratitude to God is truly astonishing from a man who had previously interpreted his role as a scientist in such a harsh manner that the very mentioning of the name of God had been sufficient to evoke his bitter scorn.

11
Subud and Politics

I ONCE asked Bapak about Subud in its relationship with current political events.

Q. "Bapak, it seems to me that never before in human history has there been so much organized hatred between people – religion against religion, race against race, nation against nation and ideology against ideology. What can put an end to this conflict?"

Bapak: "Maybe Subud..."

Q. "You mean people in Subud? People like us?"

Bapak: "May not be you. Maybe your children and their children."

Q. "But, Bapak, these forces are heavily organized. They have huge armies and armaments. And Subud has no organization to deal with this kind of force."

Bapak: "You are a Buddhist. You were born into the Buddhist organization. You are also born as a Ceylonese. But you came to Subud and you are still a Buddhist and a Ceylonese. Your understanding of what Buddhism is and what it is to be a Ceylonese has already changed. So with most of you. Your children – even without being formally opened are already different because you are different. Their children will also be different, and they also will be born into these ready made organizations. They will be more numerous than you are now. These organizations will therefore change in character because there will be many who are changed ... now do you see?"

What I did see was that the responsibility some of us had been assuming since we joined Subud had to be viewed in a fresh perspective. Some of us had fastened on to the possibilities of Subud as a mystic force which would change the world in the way we would like to see it within our lifetime, if not by 1960 or 1962. This eagerness, perhaps natural in those of us with an apocalyptic vision of our role in human history, had led us to expect revolutionary inner changes in large masses of humanity within a short time of Subud's spread round the world. We were exultantly preoccupied with counting heads in Subud and marvelling at how Subud had gained a hold in forty, fifty, sixty countries within two or three years of its emergence from Indonesia.

In this enthusiasm, some of us claimed ever increasing numbers for Subud in the world, choosing to ignore the glaring fact that, on an average, only fifteen per cent of the people who were opened continued regularly with the latihan. About 1,500 people were opened in Ceylon but only about one hundred and fifty (at best) practise the latihan. It is the same with Great Britain, Australia, America and even Indonesia, where one would ordinarily expect a higher proportion of stayers.

The psychological trick of recognising only facts which supported our premeditated thesis and pushing into a limbo of irrelevancy those which were inconvenient for our view of things to come, led to some of us even using the authority of Bapak's name to shore up our wishful thinking.

One such instance was the story that Bapak had predicted that by 1960, millions would be opened in India. This possibility excited me very much and I took the first opportunity, soon after I heard of it, to ask Bapak about it. But what Bapak said was: "In India very difficult."

And, together with the answer to my question about how Subud would affect the world, this altered my time-picture completely. Bapak said that we should "not try to go faster than God" in our own efforts at spiritual development or in our expectations for the world at large.

These expectations and highly charged hopes caused some of us great disappointment, particularly when we found that, like the British, we had "lost India".

∞∞∞∞

The truly practical quality of what we learn in Subud about the various forces which influence man is evident in what Bapak says about politics.

I once asked one of Bapak's oldest helpers in Indonesia for an explanation of a peculiar phenomenon I had noticed in the growth of Subud in the past few years.

Q. "In every group that I have visited I find that most of the members are middle class, relatively more educated and belonging to what is called the 'intelligentsia'. Why is it that Subud has not yet attracted larger numbers of working people and peasants?"

A. "Is this question important to you or is it only theory?"

Q. "No. Not theory. Most of our countries in the so-called democratic world are ruled by governments elected by people who are mostly workers and peasants. It stands to reason, does it not, that if these voters came to Subud, they would be able to bring a better judgement to bear on their choice of rulers and policies?"

A. "What you mean is that it would be better to start from the bottom, rather than the top – from this elite of educated people?"

Q. "It seems so."

A. "Is your view of the democratic process that power is passed on in a pyramidal order, the people at the bottom giving power to those immediately above them and they, in turn, passing it on upward and inward toward the centre, so that the centre finally derives its sovereign power from the people?"

Q. "That is as good a description of democracy as I've heard. Is that not the way it works?"

A. "Answer that yourself. Is not the reality different from this? Bapak says that what really happens is that an elite which calls itself professional politicians or party candidates goes out from the centre to the periphery, acquires power from the people and returns to the centre armed with this power. It is a movement from the top to the bottom rather than the other way about. People at the top decide what the people should want – this is called policy or planning or leadership – and the people have not much power to effect their decisions. When it becomes intolerable there are revolutions which are also engineered and captured by people belonging to this elite. Is that not how it goes?"

Q. "Yes, I agree that it is more like this in practice. But then, did not Christ walk among the poor?"

A. "He did. But when did Christianity spread among the people? Only after Emperor Constantine was converted. Then the teaching of Christ spread rapidly. It is always like that. Even Communism as a religion spread from above."

Q. "I see the point. But my observation, however, is that people in humbler circumstances are more inclined to be religious minded."

A. "True. But is it also not a fact that most people who are regarded as being 'religious minded' are interested in religion primarily as a protection against black magic, evil spells cast on them and their families, possible misfortunes in the future or to ask the gods for special favours?"

Q. "This explains why even in Buddhist temples the main attraction is the devales where vows are made and the various gods of the Hindu pantheon are constantly being propitiated and invoked to intercede in one misfortune or another."

A. "Bapak says that Subud is for discriminating or critical people who will be able to judge the truth of what they receive, without blindly accepting anything merely because Bapak or any of the helpers say it. When such people receive and progress spiritually then they will be able to help others who are not as fortunate as they are. Until they are able to help, their interest in the welfare of the 'poorer people' you refer to, is mostly sentimentality. Is it not?"

I accepted the justice of the rebuke without hesitation because although harsh, it was clear and administered without a trace of malice, clinically and disinterestedly as Bapak's judgements about people always are.

On another occasion, at the Subud Centre in Singapore, we were talking with Bapak who was in a very communicative mood about politics. He showed us the close connection that should exist between what we had learnt about the different forces which exist and the proper government of a country.

"A government need consist of only five ministers," Bapak said, "A Minister of Power, Industry and Commerce (Material), a Minister of Food and Agriculture (Vegetable), a Minister of Police and the Armed Forces (Animal), a Minister of Justice and Education (Human) and the Prime Minister." He concluded with a broad smile, "Not fifteen or thirty as many countries in the East now have."

In the course of the same conversation Bapak told us that there were, broadly speaking, four different types of people. He checked them off one by one: at the bottom, people who are Incorrigible (those who habitually prefer to do the wrong thing even if they know what is right); people who are Acquisitive (those who always want to acquire everything they encounter; even spiritual progress); people who want to DO good and, the rarest, people who want to BE good.

Bapak must have known that I, within myself, was rapidly estimating whether I belonged to category three or four or both because he smiled broadly at me and said: "All of us have all four levels in us, one or two more dominant than the others."

The best example in my knowledge of how Bapak, in his own life, practises the principles of Subud – in this case the basic principles of surrender, submission, sincerity and patience – took place in November 1958 in Colombo.

The Prime Minister of Ceylon at that time imagined that Subud was a subversive political organization in league with "American Imperialism", a secret society practising strange forms of magic and voodoo and intent on destroying his power by mystic means. Just before latihan one evening, the Chief of Police, who was a member of Subud, rushed in to report that he had just returned from the Prime Minister's office where he had been informed that his association with "a subversive group" was unforgivable and that Pak Subuh would be forcibly deported as an "undesirable alien" on the following day. He asked me to convey this information to Bapak and returned to his duties.

Heavy of heart, my mind buzzing with alarm and amorphous fears, I charged up the stairs to Bapak's quarters. Up the other flight of stairs panted Dr. Musa Djoemena, the Indonesian Ambassador to Ceylon, who had joined Subud in Ceylon, intent on the same doleful mission. He had also been summoned by the Prime Minister and told that this dangerous man, Pak Subuh, would be sent away from the country "at dawn". Bapak came out to his dining table and asked us to sit before we spoke our pieces.

"Receive," he said, and we closed our eyes and became quieter.

"Now you may tell Bapak what has happened," Icksan interpreted.

The story tumbled out from me and Dr. Djoemena gave his first hand description of his interview.

"What should we do now?" I asked, aching for action.

Bapak looked at us for a while and smiled as though at a private joke.

"Surrender," he replied in English.

"But Bapak," I appealed, "this man really believes that Subud is a dangerous organization and is determined to do what he says."

"Surrender," repeated Bapak.

"Is there nothing for us to do?" I asked.

"Yes. Surrender," Bapak repeated.

"How? What does it mean to surrender at a time like this?"

"If you oppose, his hostility becomes stronger. So surrender," Icksan interpreted.

"What will Bapak do now if the Prime Minister carries out his threat?" Dr. Djoemena asked.

"Bapak? Surrender. If Bapak has to go tomorrow, it is God's will. If not God's will, Bapak will stay. Best, after Bapak leaves, to meet for a while, in smaller groups – three or four groups at various houses, at different times, not to attract attention. That is one way to surrender. But now, best to do latihan."

As it happened, nothing was done about Bapak. He actually stayed with us two weeks longer than he had originally intended.

12
Virtues and Vices

ONE of the women in the Colombo group asked how we could know when we had progressed in our latihan.

Bapak replied that when we had progressed enough to make a difference we would not need to ask such a question. We would know. He added: "When a seed is planted and the plant starts growing, it has no knowledge of its growth. One day it is at one point, the next day at another point – but the process is gradual and the change is small. But later, when it begins to bear fruit, there is a distinct change. It now knows that it has fruit. One day it has one fruit, another day two and so on. The progress is now measurable. It is like this in Subud."

Another member said, rather dejectedly, that she felt she was not progressing at all because she had no unusual experiences to relate. This was a very common attitude, especially among those who read about other people's extraordinary experiences published in the *Chronicle* and other publications. Many of us never realize that only a tiny minority of people in Subud have unusual experiences and that only a very few of them ever write about them. It was inevitable therefore, that they should feel "left out" as this woman did.

Bapak's reply was: "When a stream is flowing peacefully to its destination it has no experience of movement. It is flowing as it should. But if some boulders are put in its path then the water swirls around them, and its flow is disturbed. Now it will have experience of something unusual. It is the same with the flow of the Subud force through us."

This explained why the oldest members in Subud made relatively few overt movements in latihan and spoke very little, if at all, about their experiences because their experience was already assimilated as an integral part of the flow of their lives. But, at our level, we are disappointed if we don't see spiritual fireworks.

I shall never forget the very proper looking gentleman in Ceylon who complained to Sooty Banda that he had experienced nothing since coming to Subud. Whipping out his closely annotated diary, he said, "Look here, one hundred twenty-eight latihans up to date and nothing to show for it!"

Sooty asked sympathetically: "Nothing? Nothing has changed?"

"No, nothing at all," the man answered, adding confidentially, "unless you count the fact that I was constipated for twenty years and I now have two motions a day."

∞∞∞∞

The advice given in Bapak's explanation to helpers when opening people: "Do not try to calm the mind yourself, the mind will become calm by itself," produced a plethora of questions. People who had practised – or at any rate heard of – Buddhist or Yogic meditation could hardly believe their ears when they heard that no effort was needed for the calming of the mind. Others who used their minds a great deal and found their thoughts careering along as usual during the latihan could not see how the mind would become calm "by itself" when its traffic of thought was incessant.

A helper sent by Bapak gave us a memorable explanation of this which helped me very much:

"Bapak asks you," he said, "to consider that you are sitting beside a pond, the surface of which is disturbed. If you try to press the water down to calm it with your hands you will disturb it more. If you blow on it intending to calm it – you will disturb it more. If you press it down with a board, you will disturb it still more. All you can do is to sit as quietly as possible and wait. Then the force of gravity, which is another manifestation of the force of God, will calm the pond. By itself!"

Another question which keeps constantly popping up is about Bapak's smoking. Everywhere there are well-meaning people who shake their heads sadly and wisely at this evident aberration of a "Holy Man". Regarding smoking as one of the more prominent of the deadly sins, they cannot understand how Bapak indulges in smoking.

One of them could not contain herself once when she saw Bapak smoking cigarette after cigarette at a meeting in England.

"What does Bapak get out of smoking so much?" she asked, rather caustically.

Bapak smiled when the question was interpreted to him. His smile stretched wider as he replied, almost confidentially:

"Nothing."

Soon after Bapak visited Coombe Springs for the first time they asked him what more they could do for his comfort. Was there anything he needed, perhaps, in his apartment?

"Yes," said Bapak, "a television set."

One of the ladies hastened to explain that television wasn't quite the thing; that, culturally speaking, it was a bit low-brow and that she herself had a set at home but had placed it in the kitchen – for the maid and the children. Bapak said: "But Bapak *likes* television."

One might say – ah, but that is Bapak. What about the influence of such things on others?

An experience with Icksan in Colombo helped to resolve that kind of doubt for me. Icksan and I had gone swimming one afternoon when we hoped that the hotel pool would be deserted and we could have a quiet talk. We were sitting sipping a drink, when the hotel cabaret star, a brassy, blonde bomb-shell for whom I had written some topical lyrics, came over to join us. As she spoke, gesticulating theatrically, her body bursting out of her bikini, I felt very bad that I had brought Icksan there and exposed him to this "impurity". I sat silent while she entertained us with story after story of her connubial disasters and casual conquests in the hot spots of the world. I was becoming more and more angry that she wouldn't leave us, but I noticed that Icksan seemed not to be troubled at all. In fact, he seemed to be having a whale of a time. He was nodding his head, saying: "Yah? Yah? Yah?" and wagging his head alternately saying: "Really? No! Really? Funny! Funny!" and so on.

When she had left eventually, I hastened to apologise to Icksan for having brought him there and subjected him to all that "heaviness".

Icksan said: "I do not feel heffy. You feel heffy. You make yourself feel heffy."

I asked him what he meant.

"You think all the time how heffy for Icksan and you feel headache. But Icksan say, Yah! Yah! Yah! and Funny! Funny! You remember? Ah! Latihan. Icksan ask protection. So no headache!"

This incident also gave point and clarity to what another helper had told us once: "We now practise the latihan twice or three times a week. As we progress we will be oftener in a state of latihan. We will be in conscious touch with our soul more constantly. Much later we can hope to reach a stage when, without latihan, we will not be able to live at all, like a fish gasping for breath out of the water. The state of latihan is the proper medium for a human being to exist in – as he progresses toward the true human level."

It also showed me that because we were in Subud there was no reason to run away from the things that make up our ordinary life. At the beginning, I, like some of my friends, thought that I should not blunt the edge of my new-found spiritual interest by exposing it to the world I lived and worked in. It was something precious to be burnished and made finer in solitude. I spoke about this to one of the helpers from Indonesia who said: "It is easy to imagine you are strong when there is no opposition. It is easy to imagine you are virtuous when there is no temptation." This rang a true bell but not for me. I became increasingly convinced that I could not continue in my profession of journalism — with its minute by minute preoccupation with the ugliness of human relationships.

My wife's family owned a small island in a large, rather isolated lake. It had a house and the minimum necessary comforts. It provided all the vegetables, rice and coconuts that a family needed.

I told Bapak that I had decided to resign my job and take my family with me and seclude ourselves in that island. I said that I was fed up with journalism and the "power of the press", and all that went with it.

Bapak listened, smiling, and remarked:

"In six months' time you will be king of the island!"

∞∞∞∞∞

Bapak's answer reminded me of another glorious moment of brilliant clarity which occurred during a session with Krishnamurti. A German industrialist who had "renounced" the material life had come out East and was living in the jungles of Ceylon as a "swami". In his white robes and beard he came to one of Krishnamurti's meetings. At the end of the talk he offered a comment: "I do not think that it is possible to reach the point of 'choiceless awareness' you speak of as long as one remains in the material world. It is essential to renounce the material world. It is essential to renounce everything in life if we wish to attain enlightenment."

Krishnamurti: "What have you renounced, sir?"

Swami: "I was an industrial magnate in Germany. I had great wealth and power. I renounced my wealth and the power it gave me. I had many women. I used to drink. I had many vices. I renounced my vices."

Krishnamurti: "Ah – but sir, have you renounced your virtues?"

13

The dark times

IN my fourth year in Subud I went through an extremely unpleasant experience. Suddenly I ceased to feel any movement, outer or inner, during the latihan. I attended latihans as regularly as I could but there was no experiencing of the state of latihan as I had known it before. There was no difference between the ordinary state in which I lived my life and my state during the half hour in latihan. The same thoughts and feelings which dominated me in my ordinary existence persisted in the latihan.

I also felt I might have lost something that had been very precious to me. Icksan had shown me how to "feel inner" frequently during my working day. Whenever I felt tense or had a moment's break from the day's chores I would collect my attention and sense the existence of the force which had been lodging within me. As soon as I became aware that it was still there, alive and moving, there was a spontaneous and pleasurable response, an inner acknowledgement of its presence: "Ahhh, yes!" That was all. When this happened, the tensions vanished and my inner state became calmer.

This faculty, too, had become dimmer.

Week after week, month after month I sought to regain my familiar sense of the force of the latihan. But it eluded me. At one stage I even concluded that I was the unique case of a man who had to be "re-opened". However, even the distinction of being unique did not lift my spirits.

Finding myself in Zurich during this period, I flew to London to consult an experienced helper. He was very sympathetic and suggested that I was passing through a period which the Christian mystics referred to as "the dark night of the soul." I returned home still dejected. I felt that this explanation was inapplicable to me. Ideas like "dark night of the soul" were much too rich for me. In my state I felt that my soul did not deserve even a dark night because it must be minuscule, if it existed at all.

The worst aspect of the spell was that gradually I was sheering away from latihan. I had begun travelling a great deal and I found that, unlike during my previous journeys, I was not so anxious to seek out Subud groups on the chance of joining them at latihan. And when this happened, the misery would pile up within me so intensely that after a while

I would feel I needed a latihan desperately. On one occasion I arrived in Calcutta in this state to discover, to my acute disappointment, that the Subud group had scattered for the vacation and that my closest friends in India, Ian and Mariani Arnold, had left for a beach resort named Puri. I asked my professional colleagues in Calcutta to get me a return rail ticket to Puri that very night. Till I arrived there I did not realize that Puri was two hundred and fifty miles away. We had time for one latihan that night and I took the next train back. I had travelled five hundred miles for a latihan but I still felt empty and deserted by the inner force that had sustained my state for four years.

This inner depression inevitably spoiled my personal relationships as I went about like a bear with ten sore teeth in his head. But when I reached the point of feeling that I was irredeemable, I got another opportunity of visiting Bapak in Indonesia and asking him to help me out of my despondency.

Bapak heard me through and said (Prio Hartono interpreting): "In school there is class for physical exercise and class for mathematics. You like physical exercise. So you like always to be in class for physical exercise. But sometimes necessary to go to mathematics class also."

One of the oldest helpers in Indonesia explained further how this process occurs. "The latihan acts on various parts of the being of man as it is deemed necessary by the will of God. Sometimes it is the physical body, at other times it is the feelings, at still other times it is the mind and so on. People who receive the first manifestation of the working of the Subud force in their bodies are, therefore, lucky. At the very start they have overt *proof* of something new taking place. They can see and sense it in external movements. Those in whom the force first starts working in the brain, are not so lucky. They cannot see any external manifestation of a force at work. The purification of the brain, however, may be going on while the man himself may declare that he has not felt anything at all. The real difficulty in such a case is that the purification of the brain means the cleansing of the psychological content of the brain – which are a man's thoughts. What are these thoughts except the ordinary things that he thinks about? So, in the latihan he finds that he continues to think the same ordinary thoughts as he does out of latihan. He sees no difference between the state of being in latihan and his ordinary state. So he is disappointed. *What he does not realize is that in the state of latihan he actually is sufficiently conscious of these thoughts to discover that they are commonplace thoughts.* In his ordinary state he is not usually conscious of his thoughts. He *is* his thoughts. This is the difference between the two states in such a man. But he himself may not realize this."

These explanations brought me instantaneous mental relief from the sense of despair I had endured for many months. But they did not bring back the taste of the latihan. I now knew I should not worry about it, but I still wished to experience distinctly once again the working of the latihan in me.

One evening at a latihan in Karachi, to my enormous gratitude, it returned. The small group there asked me to participate in the opening of a new member. Before the latihan began we sat awhile and talked. The probationer told us he was a member of various other spiritual systems and described his experiences. I was thinking: "Heavens! I am in a low enough state as it is. Why should I be afflicted with this man's heaviness also?" I had not helped in opening anyone for nearly a year. I was unhappy that this should be the first experience after this long break.

Twenty minutes after the latihan started he broke into a loud spell of sobbing and, suddenly, Bill Smith, the other helper in the room and I began to sing. I felt the latihan strongly within me for the first time in almost a year. As soon as the latihan was over the new member came up to express his thanks. But I told him that I should thank him instead for helping me to feel the latihan so clearly after a long time. I felt I had learnt what Bapak meant when he told us that a newly opened man may really help someone who had been in Subud longer because the new man might have a much older soul. I also believe that there was another lesson for me in this experience: a helper must help if he is to receive help.

14

Personal Epilogue

I HAVE one more story to tell. It is a very personal story which I feel I must write as a record of my profound gratitude to Subud, and to Bapak in person, for granting me incontrovertible proof of the mercy of God. Some of the events I am about to describe are still beyond the comprehension of my mind but my inner feelings understand them very well and have no questions. No logic can possibly explain to me, for instance, how I – by no stretch of imagination a model of spiritual or moral rectitude – should have been the beneficiary of such attention, but I know that my being is suffused by a warm sense of thankfulness whenever I recall it.

My wife was being delivered of our youngest son, Adil, on January 21, 1960. I was on the hospital verandah, not pacing as an expectant father is supposed to do, but writing an editorial for the evening newspaper of which I was the Editor. I remember the heading of this piece: DANGER. This was a part of my editorial efforts to warn the country that the new Prime Minister who had succeeded the man who had been assassinated a few months previously, was planning to subvert the democratic process and establish a police state in Ceylon. After my wife was taken to the operating theatre I went home to see about the children. Ed Kerner, who was staying with us on his home leave from his job in New York, showed me a telegram which had just arrived. It said: "Bapak wishes to see you here immediately," and it was signed by Bomon-Behram around whom the Subud group in Bombay had grown. I requested Ed to make the necessary arrangements for me with the airlines, the Indian consulate, the exchange control, health and immigration departments and all the other authorities involved. I packed my bag and went back to the hospital to take my leave of my wife. The baby had been born and she was just coming out of the ether. I read the telegram to her and she nodded agreement that I should go.

At the airport I remembered that I had not taken leave from my employers and telephoned the managing director to say that I would be away in Bombay for a few days. All he asked was "Subud?" I replied: "Yes, Subud," and off I went.

I arrived in Bombay at midnight, spent the early morning hours at the airport and went along to BB's apartment where Bapak was living, soon after daybreak. Bapak came out in his dressing gown and greeted me as though there was nothing at all unusual in my presence there that morning. He inquired about Sunetra, whether the baby was a boy or girl – named the boy ADIL – but said nothing about his summons. After a few minutes of this, he returned to his room saying: "Better wait here."

After an hour Rochanawati came out to greet me but, suddenly she stopped, covered her face, turned about, and fled as though she had seen an apparition.

Now I was really rattled, as you can imagine.

I sat and waited. I really learned for the first time how to wait. There were no newspapers, radio or cigarettes about – the customary supports of people like me who had never really experienced quietness. The only comfort I had was to try to "receive" whenever my thoughts built up into a dam of apprehensive tension.

After several hours Bapak came out again with Anwar Zakir. He said: "Better not go back to Ceylon now." I raised an enquiring eyebrow.

"When Sunetra is well, better bring her and the children also and stay with Bapak."

I said nothing, waiting for an explanation. None was forthcoming. Bapak asked me to return again the next day and I left him.

On the following morning Bapak said: "Maybe not necessary to bring Sunetra and the family. You can go back, but not for ten days more."

I was about to burst into a flurry of questions when Bapak said: "Danger now past. But better wait for about ten days."

"What danger, Bapak?" I asked.

Bapak paused for a while and said almost casually but in a tone of great kindness toward me:

"Politics. If you had been in Ceylon yesterday you would have been killed."

"By whom Bapak? How?" I asked.

He then proceeded to describe this man in such acute detail that I was able to identify him immediately. Bapak said that this man had been watching my house for two weeks for a suitable opportunity and had decided on the previous day as the right time.

At this point Rochanawati appeared, asked me to stay to lunch and explained her strange behaviour the previous morning. She said that she felt that she had actually seen an apparition – hence her hasty flight.

Later Bapak said: "Better leave your job."

I asked how I should earn my living.

"You have been good journalist, but this journalism now finished. Now better write books," he advised.

I said that writing books for an Eastern market would not bring enough to live on, that I had already written a book which my publishers had said was a best seller in Asia, but it had brought in very little money.

"Also better take job that takes you from place to place. You courier," Bapak said. "Take job so you can visit many Subud centres."

I asked who would give me such a job. There had been some talk about the possibility of a job with the International Press Institute but my company had refused to release me and I had not even sent in an application for the post. I could not see how I could get a job which would require me to travel.

"If job offered, better accept," Bapak advised, adding with a smile: "If terms unsatisfactory, ask what you need."

My mind refused to see any sense in all this but my inner feeling was convinced that it was right. I wrote out my resignation and mailed it to my directors, giving no explanations.

In the course of the next few days Bapak again referred to my immediate future.

"Your home, Malaya," he said, "Ceylon now not good for you and family."

This seemed even more unlikely.

∞∞∞∞

I returned home shortly after and went directly to my friends in the Criminal Investigation Department to ask whether they were aware of the recent activities of the man that Bapak had described. They smiled very knowingly and asked what my special interest in this man was. I too smiled knowingly but said nothing further. They then said that they had been on this man's trail for several weeks and had observed his activities near my home for a period of thirteen days. He had then "lost interest".

When I returned to my office, the Managing Director, who was an old friend of mine said: "What is all this about resigning your job?"

I said I had no explanation to give, but that I was through working in Ceylon. He was a little upset at my failure to provide even a meagre explanation of my decision to leave a job in which I had been treated extremely decently.

"This Subud business seems to have gone to your head," he remarked rather sharply.

He had no idea how close he was to the truth.

"What are you going to do? You have no job offers from elsewhere, have you?" he asked.

I said that I had no notion of what I was going to do. Just then, the peon brought in an urgent telegram for me. It said: "Executive Board International Press Institute have decided offer you post Asian Representative stop. Please cable response in principle."

The terms they were offering were stated further down. They were unacceptable as the salary was a little less than I was earning in Ceylon and would have been insufficient for a post of this nature.

I cabled back to Zurich stating my terms which they accepted the same day by international telephone. And so, within a few weeks, I was doing a new job which has been taking me from place to place all over the world during the past three years.

The International Press Institute had decided that my base should be Colombo. But very soon Colombo became impossible as headquarters because of the new Ceylon Government's attitude to such concepts as the freedom of the press. The Institute thought I should move to India – but the Pakistan Press protested and threatened to quit the Institute if its Asian Representative was based in India. India did not like the idea of my being based in Pakistan. Burma was out of the question as the Press was muzzled. Singapore was impracticable since the Singapore Prime Minister and the press were hardly on speaking terms. The Indonesian Press was coerced by President Sukarno to surrender all its liberties just at this time and all the Indonesian members of the International Press Institute had their newspapers confiscated. Farther East was impractical as an Asian base because the bulk of my work was in South Asia. My range stretched from Karachi to Tokyo so it was decided that Malaya, which was a half-way point and still enjoyed a great measure of democratic freedom, should be the Institute's Asian Headquarters. We moved to Kuala Lumpur in 1961 and have been supremely free of the sense of political oppression that had burdened us in Colombo. So, the last part of Bapak's advice to me was obeyed under the ineluctable compulsion of circumstances.

In March 1962, I went to Jakarta to pay my respects to Bapak. I asked him a question which had been nibbling at my thoughts for two years. I said: "I have seen Bapak's attitude to death – even the death of people very close to Bapak like Icksan. It is not what I am used to. Bapak does not regard death in the way we do. Yet Bapak interceded with events to save my life. Why did Bapak do this?"

Bapak's reply was very terse: "There is right time to die and wrong time to die. That was wrong time for you to die."

And he spoke about other things.

∞∞∞∞

I still do not understand, but perhaps I will one day before it is the right time for me to die.

BOOK 2

ASSIGNMENT
SUBUD

CONTENTS

1

Ballads, Songs and Snatches

WHEN the last page of this book has been written, a part of my life will have come to an end. For the past five years I have lived the life of a twentieth century gypsy, pitching my two-day camp in Calcutta, Bangkok, Singapore, Jakarta, Hong Kong, Manila, Tokyo, Cairo, Zurich, Paris, London, New York, or San Francisco. Bapak had told me in January 1960 that I should leave Ceylon and get a job that would take me "from place to place to place" (*A Reporter in Subud*). And he had added, seemingly by way of consolation for recommending this nomadic existence: "Visit Subud groups. You are courier." It so happened that I was then given the kind of professional job that necessarily took me from place to place to place and, necessarily also, made me and my family exiles from our home in Ceylon.

In the past 30 months I have spent a total of four months at home — made up out of bits and pieces of four days, one week, ten days, or a fortnight. Once, recently, I was able to spend a longer time at home — 40 whole days and 40 nights. It was the strangest thing. I felt as awkward as a stockbroker at a boys' camp. My little sons stopped treating me as a peripatetic uncle who dropped by to deposit a bag full of toys, disrupt their lives for a few days and vanish into the clouds. They discovered they had a father.

It has been fun, it has been lonely, exhilarating, depressing, boring, rewarding, sometimes pointless, sometimes wonderfully meaningful — all these, simultaneously and separately. I have learned and unlearned many things, about myself and other people.

As to being a "courier", I have discovered that there was less to this than met the eye. I have never seen any special aptitude in me that qualified me for such a function. I had a job that enabled me to visit Jakarta and other Subud centres oftener than most people could and, because of this, I had the opportunity to carry and deliver messages from group to group and, on occasion, to and from Bapak. That was it.

But, there was something else: I noticed that people in Subud had a role to play — some an active role, some a passive role, some a role extended in time and space, some a series of brief roles, some were hard roles, some easy.

Husein Rofé had a role to play – to take the Subud contact to Europe. Meredith (now Roland) Starr, Ronimund von Bissing, Aubrey Walton, Reginald Hoare, Douglas Kibble, their wives, and a few others, whose names I do not know, had their role to play – to prepare the ground for Subud's first major step outside Indonesia. John Bennett had a role to play: he was the man who brought to Subud the hosts he had baptized and gave Bapak his first home and tabernacle outside Indonesia. Pierre Elliot had his role – his organizing skill was taxed to the limit in London and Paris. Margaret Wichman, June Sawrey-Cookson, Sheila Ross, Maria (then Olive) Kibble, Olga de Nottbeck and many others played their roles in the early years of Subud in England. John Ross had his brief and brilliant role. Eva (now Ilaina) Bartok had the finest role she has ever played in her life – and without a trace of make-believe. Bob Prestie had his role – to start Subud in the United States. Victor Gebers played his role in South Africa, Ian and Mariani (then Bulbul) Arnold in India and Ceylon, Isaac Gerson and Sooty Banda had their respective roles in Ceylon – one prepared the nucleus of people who were able to receive Subud and the other kept alive in them the sense of miracle which sustained them, keyed up and expectant for the coming of Subud. Icksan Ahmad played his brief, scintillating role and left the scene,* Dan Cahill was given a Robinson Crusoe role, toiling bearded and alone in his island atop Manhattan with the world outside.

But that was long ago. Only seven years ago – but already, long, long ago. Since then there have been new players and new roles. Every Subud member of our generation has his role. And, looking back over five years, mine has been the role of the wandering minstrel, clad in my spiritual shreds and patches, always moving from country to country, group to group, telling stories about Subud experiences and Subud people. Some of these stories are still new and leave the taste of newly minted coins on my tongue. Some of them already have the patina of age. Some I have told over and over again, often to the same listeners. But they never seem to pall either on me or on the people who hear them – not because of the quality of the telling, but possibly because as we grow older in Subud there are new meanings and richer connections.

When *A Reporter in Subud* had been written, I thought I had told all my stories. But I was wrong. There is more to tell and here it is. This is

---

In Sooty Banda's characteristic cricketing metaphor: "A hundred before lunch."

possibly my last appearance as a story teller. I have learned from the experience of others in Subud that it is essential to recognize one's role, play it, and, when it is done, to be willing to leave it. There is nothing more pathetic than an actor clinging to his role after the theatre is closed, declaiming Hamlet in a pub. In Subud it is the same. We must surrender our costumes and be ready to play a new role if called – even if it is only a passive walk-on part.

Bapak has indicated to me that it is now time to stay home although home will be in another country. When the last page of this book has been written, my role will have changed. And by the time this book is published, you will probably find, if you knock on my door, that I am at home.

2

Safety in Numbers

AT first, most of us were desperately keen on increasing the numbers in our groups. When I received the contact I felt as though I had won a sweepstake and, like the spendthrift I am, set off on a big splurge, scattering my winnings wherever I went. Another man described his reactions differently: he felt he had discovered a mountain of gold big enough to satisfy the needs of all and he saw it as his duty to share his secret with everyone he met. A group of Moslems in Ceylon had a different response. Each year for several years they had met a Moslem "messenger" – as they put it – who appeared every year, unannounced, in the jungle lands of the South, to tell them of the coming of a new Messiah and vanished as suddenly – no one knew where. The year that Subud came to Ceylon, this messenger did not appear in his customary haunts. They took this as a sign that they were to carry his message to other Moslems. But when they had been opened in Subud, they found to their astonishment that, for the first time in their experience, they could talk about spiritual matters to non-Moslems as well.

They carried their message to their friends, acquaintances, their customers in the bazaar and, within a week of Subud being started in Ceylon, Moslems, Buddhists, Christians, and Hindus of a vast variety of interests and occupations received the contact. One early enthusiast in a crowded bus was trying to persuade a friend to come to Subud. The friend put up a stout and very vocal resistance. But a stranger sitting across heard it all and came over to be opened next day.

Some of our oldest friends avoided my wife and me like the plague because we were trying to sell Subud as hard as we could. We declaimed, we swore, we begged and pleaded, we cajoled and threatened and argued with fire in our eyes and dazzling words on our tongues. Some came just to keep us quiet. My parents, for instance, listened in silence as I spoke. They must have wondered what had happened to their ever loving son whom they had known as one of the most bellicose anti-religionists of their time; their son (who at 16 had declared himself an agnostic, at 17 an atheist, at 18 a nihilist, between 19 and 24 a Trotskyist) seemed, for the first time in his life, to be in *favour* of something. This must have touched and amused them vastly. A few days later I found my father in the latihan room waiting to be opened and heard that my mother had gone upstairs to receive the contact from Mariani Arnold. After many years I was able to cry that evening. I felt real remorse and a sense of gratitude that I had been allowed to make some recompense to my parents who had tolerated my erratic enthusiasms in magnificent patience mixed, perhaps, with amused scepticism. My father had tried to make me see that before I set out to reconstitute the world in my image, my image should be reconstituted, but he had not got very far. A few days later, my friend Mohammed Sideek told me that my father had said: "I still know nothing about Subud, but I feel certain that if Subud has been able to penetrate Tarzie it must be something to be reckoned with."

Our zealous proselytizing, we realised later, had much simpler motivations than we would admit at the time. There was safety in numbers. Big organizations give small people a feeling of bigness and security. As individuals we were exposed to ridicule and even political persecution. The bigger we were in numbers though not in soul, the less vulnerable we would be.

We were all seated around in the living room of Lesly (now Ronald) Jayatilaka's house in Colombo listening to Icksan Ahmad – the first of Bapak's assistants to visit Ceylon – giving clarifications about Subud experience when I realized that I had an appointment with a group of people who, if they could be persuaded or browbeaten into joining us, would strengthen our organization financially, if not spiritually. As I was making my way out, Icksan called out: "Tarzie, where are you off to now?" I told him my mission. "Better sit down," he said. "Relax. Can meet them later. Tomorrow or next week." I was straining at the leash. "Not necessary to work so hard for Subud," Icksan added. My enthusiasm thus deflated, I sat down and sulked.

In the evening, seated under the trees at my club, Icksan asked us to receive for a while. Then when the sediment of disappointment had been removed from inside me, Icksan explained why we should not be overanxious about bringing in new members:

"There is a right time to come to Subud. There is also wrong time. If you bring someone at wrong time he comes to see miracle or receive cure or to see Icksan hypnotize with smoke from Dunhill pipe! Then because no miracle, no cure, no hypnotize, he go and not come back. Inner open, but plant remain stunted. One day it become right time for him to receive spiritual gift. Then he need. But he not come to Subud then because he say to himself: 'Agh! I already know Subud. Useless. I go else-where.' So you lose one customer!" We laughed loud with new under-standing. The Subud press gangs ceased to prowl or, at any rate, not as enthusiastically.

We began to sense when we should speak about Subud and when we should not. Bapak had told us once that we would know when and to whom to speak. "No propaganda," Bapak said. "Propaganda only for pol-itics. God does not need propaganda."

But, Bapak said it was also our duty to speak about Subud so that more people could receive the contact. How could we do this, we asked, unless we sought people out and spoke about Subud?

"People will seek you out," Bapak said.

And ask about Subud?

"No. About other things, About house for rent, or about children, or about marriage, or (turning to me) about some news. If you speak to them rightly about these things then, if it is God's Will, you will find them speaking about things which will *naturally* enable you to tell them about Subud."

Sooty Banda understood this first among the people with whom I was intimate in Colombo. He could sense when to put the heat on and when to turn it off. He would say: "If a man has a stomach ache and goes to a doctor he may be advised to eat a banana. If he *has* a stomach ache he will eat the banana and ask questions afterwards. But if he has *no* stomach ache but asks the doctor: "Tell me, doctor, what is good for stomach aches?" And the doctor says: "Eat a banana," he will say: "Now, doctor, why is a banana better than a pineapple for stomach aches?" And then all hell breaks loose. Arguments, arguments and counter-arguments. So we should speak about Subud only if the man feels he has a stomach ache. Then he might be willing to have a banana and ask questions afterwards."

3

The Pot and the Plant

ONE day the Government of Ceylon sent its auditor to the Colombo Zoo to check the inventory. The investigating officer reported that one item – a box containing a culture of meal-worms used for feeding the birds – had not been listed and, with the crassness of bureaucracies, sent a clerk to count the meal-worms for the inventory. The Director of the zoo stood by and watched the performance in vast amusement. The counted worms were put on one side as the checking proceeded. After a while, the Director asked the clerk to recheck the lot already counted. To the clerk's consternation, there were several more worms than he had accounted for before. Then, understanding dawned on his face as he realised that the worms were multiplying almost before his very eyes. The exercise was obviously pointless and the audit clerk went away a sadder but wiser man who had realised that there were more things in heaven and earth than were dreamt of in the Government's financial regulations.

I often think of those meal-worms and that frustrated audit clerk when I encounter the continual change in understanding of Subud experience and Bapak's clarifications in myself and among my brothers and sisters in Subud.

For instance, for a long time, I, like many others around me, regarded Bapak as a guide to success and security in this world, a sort of spiritual Dale Carnegie. Latihan was a kind of Pelmanism-without-tears, and testing was a do-it-yourself Aladdin's lamp. I would ask Bapak every imaginable kind of question (what Mohammed Usman aptly called "spiritual questions from the mind") about my job, about the political situation in relation to my worldly prospects, about economic security, about my physical health, all questions designed to produce reassurance from Bapak that my condition in this world would not be too uncomfortable, if not actually sumptuous. I suppose I still do but not with the same insouciance ever since I discussed this with one of Bapak's older helpers in Indonesia the evening after Icksan's funeral.

He said: "I am surprised that so many people ask questions about their worldly life, their physical body, and other material things. Bapak is only interested in our spiritual growth. In our soul, not in our material being.

He is interested in the plant growing in us, not the pot. In fact, it may become necessary for the pot to be smashed to make it possible for the plant to grow as it should ... Like Icksan."

Bapak said the next day: "Icksan's soul grew to its maximum possibility in this world in four years of Subud. His soul was still a little boy when he lived here but now it can grow."

And, perhaps because he saw me still looking sad, added in indulgent amusement: "Icksan is now free of this world. He can now visit you without a BOAC ticket."

This sort of concept, I find, is still difficult to understand and we will still make such remarks as "Mr. X was in Subud. But he lost his job quite inexplicably." Or: "Mr. and Mrs. A. are both in Subud but they are seeking a divorce." Or: "I have been in Subud for five years but I am still as broke as I was before." Or: "Mr. Y was doing the latihan diligently. But he had that nasty accident recently."

I too have found it very difficult indeed to accept the notion that the pot is less valuable than the plant. The pot is here and now, tangible, solid and utterly real. And the plant? The plant is still in the realms of poetry. But through our own and other people's experience, many of us are beginning to understand the relative significance of the plant and the pot.

Jim Dawson (this is not his real name) was a foreign expert working for the Government of an Asian country. It became apparent to their new associates that the Dawsons were not very happy – within themselves or with each other. Jim was a master at his job and did it painstakingly and meticulously. But he was addicted to gin. At every party he drank – not much, but far too much for him. His friends were appalled at the difference in Jim at the office and Jim after a few drinks. He was a highly cultivated man and conscientious about his work, but gin turned him into an inchoate jelly of self-pity and maudlin sentiment.

His wife Pam was of a very different mould. She winced visibly whenever she noticed that Jim was drinking. She was contemptuous of what she called his "effeminate nature" but never dreamt that she was intimidating him with her masculinity. She scorned and abused him for his drinking and lamented the fact that it was "dragging her down", never realising that the gin haze was his only refuge against her abuse. Jim began drinking in the office too. He hid a bottle of gin in his desk drawer and, as he put it, "sneaked a snootful every half hour."

He had tried to join Alcoholics Anonymous and a Gurdjieff group in

Europe but Pam had stopped this with a well-directed whiff of verbal grape-shot. Anything not strictly church was a lot of mumbo-jumbo in her view. One morning Jim telephoned an acquaintance and made an appointment to see him at once. "I need help," he said. "I have come to see you because I heard you were in Subud. Tell me about it."

He listened attentively and said:

"I'd like to receive the contact. But I am terrified that Pam will disapprove. I will have to do this without her knowledge." The friend offered to speak to Pam about Subud. Jim was aghast at the thought. He was sure that this would be disastrous. He was told that it would be better if they both joined Subud together. It was out of the question. The friend suggested that Jim should wait, as Pak Subuh was coming there in a few weeks. He sneaked out during office hours and had an interview with Bapak who advised him to attend the latihan that evening when he could receive the contact. Jim said that his wife would be angry and that it would be better if he waited until his wife would be willing to accept Subud. Bapak said that in his case it would be advisable to receive the contact immediately and that his wife might change her attitude later.

That evening he was opened and felt the action of the latihan immediately. He attended latihans whenever he could. His main preoccupation now was how to get to the latihan and not how to hide himself in the seductive security of the bottle. He became accustomed to being without gin for longer stretches. One day he found himself, quite confidently, announcing to Pam that he was going to the Subud House for latihan. He answered Pam's questions forthrightly and heard her say: "I think it's a jolly good thing you have become interested in something other than booze." After that he attended the latihan regularly and quite openly.

A few months later Jim and Pam were motoring along a lonely road on their way to a vacation resort. It was a hot, muggy afternoon and Pam, who was driving, fell asleep at the wheel. The car shot off the road and into the scrub jungle below. Seriously injured, they both lost consciousness. A few minutes later the doctor of the hospital at the vacation resort about 80 miles away, happened to pass by and saw the over-turned car. He rescued them and took them to the hospital where, after attention, they revived. Pam had broken a hand and was badly bruised. Jim had multiple fractures in both legs and in one of his arms. They were moved to the hospital for surgery.

When Jim's friend went to the hospital to visit him, Jim said, rather ruefully: "Isn't it fortunate that the good Lord sent the doctor along just at that time?" The friend nodded in sympathy and murmured something about protection in Subud. "But can you explain why the Lord didn't take a protective look at us five minutes earlier?" asked Jim and lapsed into bitter silence.

The friend made some wise-crack about the need for Heaven and Earth synchronizing watches but it fell with a dull thud.

Pam left the hospital within a fortnight but Jim had to have several operations and stayed in the hospital for many months. The friend came as often as possible and did the latihan by his bedside. Eventually Jim was able to walk with the aid of crutches and had to go through the painful process of getting his muscles – including the steel muscles in his hip – to carry him with the aid of a stick. The accident did nothing to improve his relationship with Pam. She became increasingly irritated by his physical helplessness and her contempt for him turned into a burning resentment at being saddled with a cripple.

During Jim's long stay in hospital Pam became romantically interested in another man. When eventually they returned home to Europe, they tried to make a go of their marriage but it would not work. She returned to Asia and her romantic interest. Suddenly Jim felt free. He had never taken any steps to free himself of his wife. His sense of liberation had a deeper source. He had none of the stock responses of a man whose wife leaves him for another man. There was no sense of wounded vanity or the customary antagonism toward the other man or resentment that his wife was leaving him when he was physically handicapped. He was able to accept this new situation in his life, and acceptance had brought freedom.

He was able to take his new state with equanimity and even considerable nobility. His only concern was for her state and future.

As for him, he had the latihan, he had returned to his old job and was doing satisfactory work and, most wonderful of all, for the first time in his experience, he found that his son and daughter were able to communicate with him without pretence and false notions imposed by society. Jim no longer drank. He was clear inwardly and outwardly, for the first time in his life. His letters said that he was consciously and positively happy. He even joined Alcoholics Anonymous in order to help other frightened people hiding away in bottles as he had been. His old friends find that meeting Jim is an exhilarating experience. They have never before seen such a consistently happy human being.

Jim remarked recently: "I now have some idea of the mysterious ways of the good Lord," and his eyes twinkled merrily.

To Jim Dawson the meaning of the story of the pot and the plant must be very clear indeed.

But it would be a mistake, I think, to imagine, like the fakirs and the human sacrificers of old, that God's will for us is necessarily harsh. I have seen something since I came to Subud that I would never have been able to appreciate before: that there is an obligato of God's mercy accompanying the cruelty and harshness that we experience in our lives.

To balance the story of Jim and Pamela Dawson let me tell you another which happened very recently – a few days before the World Congress in New York.

I had arrived a few days before the Congress and was staying with Sherman and Laura Labby in their loft apartment in West 22nd Street. One morning they both left the apartment together on some professional call. I was still being lazy in bed when the telephone rang. A woman's voice said: "Is your name Tarzie? Hurry up and get over here to 22nd and 5th. There's been a terrible accident."

I asked: "What? Who ..." but she had rung off. I drew on a pair of slacks and ran to the intersection. There was a large crowd in the middle of the street, the traffic jammed on either side of it, and a checker cab, with its front dented, stopped in the middle of the street. A woman came up to me and told me that Laura had asked her to call me. My heart in my mouth, I asked her what had happened. She burst into hysterical tears, sobbing: "Oh, oh, oh, that poor boy, that poor boy..." She was obviously not going to be much help so I shouldered my way through the crowd and asked the policeman what had happened.

"He ran across the street and was hit by this cab. Went seven feet up in the air and fell right here."

"How badly was he hurt?" I asked.

"Look at the cab, man. Just look at the cab. He was barely conscious when I sent him to St. Vincent's hospital. If you hurry you might find him. In the taxi I prayed all the way to the hospital that Sherman had had enough time to receive the latihan before he died. The nurse refused to let me go into the examining room, "Serious accident," she said, "the doctors are now with him. His wife is there in the waiting room. You wait there. I'll let you know."

I found Laura sitting, straight-backed, in a deep state of shock. I sat beside her and, after a while, tried to receive. I felt a dull pain on my left hip but, inside, it seemed to be light and fine. I told her this. But the moment I had said it, I became frightened at the sudden thought that this might mean that Sherman had been hit on the left side, and that his inner was light and feeling fine, but that he was dead. I called Whitmore Ovington's house where Bapak, who had arrived a few days before, was staying and asked Usman to tell Bapak what had happened.

Bapak advised: "Ask Laura to remain quiet. You do your latihan for ten minutes. Don't think about Sherman. Just do your latihan. Tell Laura that Bapak will pray for Sherman. He will be all right." Relieved, I told Laura my news.

Again, horror rushed through my head. I figured, Bapak is only interested in our souls, not in our physical bodies. Perhaps what Bapak meant was that though Sherman would die, his Inner would be all right. But, just as Laura must have felt, I preferred Sherman tangible and around in this world where I lived than light and free in the next world. I did the latihan. A few minutes later the nurse came in and solemnly asked us to go into the casualty room.

And there was Sherman *sitting* on the bed in his underpants and shirt, smiling incredibly. "Hi," he greeted us. "Just look at them pictures!" The doctor showed us the X-ray photographs. "Not a bone broken," the doctor said, still astonished. I looked at Sherman's body. Not a scratch. Not a drop of blood. Laura was still speechless, crying and laughing like rain through the sunshine. Sherman was actually able to walk to a cab. We went back home and did a latihan.

Sherman told us later that the moment he was hit, he was aware of his being thrown up in the air and that he was in a state of latihan. When he fell on the asphalt he was speaking in latihan. Laura who had by then rushed up to him realised this but everyone else was sure this was delirium.

The next evening the three of us walked to the Subud House, a few blocks away. Bapak and Ibu passed by in a car on their way to the latihan. We stood by on the sidewalk, Sherman and Laura barely able to keep their gratitude from flowing out in tears. Bapak was pointing Sherman out to Ibu and laughing as though the whole thing was tickling him pink.

The cop on the beat recognised me the next day and asked after Sherman. I told him he was all right and that he had gone back home directly from the hospital.

"Yaw kiddin'," he exclaimed. "It jes' can't be. Seven feet up there. It jes' canNOT be."

I mused on my way home that if God could do, he could also undo, if it was His Will.

4

Faster than God

THE continuing difference in our understanding of Subud became evident in many departments of our life as time went by. At the start we were all in a hurry. We felt we had hit the spiritual jackpot but it took us time to realize that the results would take time to appear. Bapak and his helpers spoke of how the latihan would purify our bodies inwardly and outwardly and how our limbs would "become alive and responsible".

Icksan once said, "When body has life, our seeing, hearing, smelling, tasting, touching, all become worship of God. When sex organs become alive, sexual activity becomes worship. Even bodily functions become worship."

Many of us expected changes to take place in a year or two or at the most four, which we had cannily set as the deadline, since Icksan was then only four years old in Subud. I hope I shall not give offence to anyone if I tell a story here that has amused many people wherever it has been told before. In 1958 when John Bennett visited us in Ceylon, some of us took him and his wife Elizabeth to visit Anuradhapura and Sigiriya, the ruined monuments of the ancient Sinhalese kingdoms. That night we stayed at the Sigiriya Rest House which stands in the shadow of the magnificent "Lion Rock" – the fortress-palace-in-the-sky built by King Kasyapa. John Bennett, who had just spent a week in Jakarta with Bapak, regaled us after dinner with accounts of what Bapak had told him about the action of the latihan. We heard of Bapak's assurance that our bodies – our limbs and our inner and outer organs would become "alive and responsible" as we developed in our spiritual life through the practice of the latihan. We retired to bed late that night, tired but exhilarated with what we had heard. Sooty Banda and Mohammed Sideek shared a room. At breakfast next morning, Sooty who always had a great deal of bantering fun with Sideek, caused a burst of laughter with his story of the "experience" Sideek had "received" after they had gone to bed. At about two o'clock in the morning Sooty thought he heard Sideek whisper his name. Figuring that he must have imagined it, he went back to sleep. Then he heard Sideek whisper again – this time a little hoarse.

"Shut up," said Sooty in the customarily endearing terms he used with his friend Sideek.

Silence for a while.

Then, again, Sideek's whisper came through, hoarser now and even a little excited.

"What is the matter?" asked Sooty. "Seen ghosts?"

"Sooty," whispered Sideek in a strange voice. "My sex!"

"What is the matter with it?" Sooty asked.

"It's alive!" breathed Sideek. The wonderful truth was out at last.

"What do you mean it's 'alive'?" Sooty asked, his voice edged with scepticism and alarmed that Sideek might be taking him for a ride.

"Yes, it's alive," said Sideek. "I can *feel* the vibration."

"Yeah?" said Sooty. "So you can feel the vibration?"

"Yes, I can even *hear* it," panted Sideek.

This intimation was startling enough to impress even doubting Sooty. He reached across and switched on the light and, from the tangle of bed-clothes, something leapt off the bed and out of the window. The rest-house cat had been warming itself against Sideek's body.

Gamely joining in the laughter, Sideek protested that Sooty had exaggerated the story but his face showed us that he had learnt that we would have to wait awhile before our bodies would become "alive and responsible".

The eagerness to progress fast persisted in all of us. In Bapak's words, we were trying to "go faster than God". Some of us wanted to see progress in ourselves, others looked for signs of the efficacy of the latihan in rapid changes in the political situation of the world.

This concern for the immediate transformation of the world had, at least partly, arisen from our reading more than we perhaps ought to have into an early clarification about the pace of Subud. Someone had asked Bapak the reason for the fact that none of the older spiritual traditions had spread by such easy means as seemed possible in Subud. In Subud a man who had been opened for only a short while was able to transmit the spiritual contact to many others and they, in turn, to many more. Bapak replied, smiling, "This is the Atomic Age. Therefore God has provided a means of progressing at atomic speed."

One evening Bapak was giving us a friendly talk in Colombo on the spiritual possibilities of the beings in this world. He said that every man and woman in this world had a different limit to the spiritual develop-ment possible in his or her life. Through the sincere practice of the lati-han we were trying to reach this limit. Certain souls, he said, might reach their potential as soon as they were opened, some within a few years, others within 32 years, and still others within 42 years. Vadic Siriwardana, who had a naturally precise mind, could not bear this vagueness and asked in a voice drenched with anxiety:

"Bapak, can I be *certain* in 42 years?"

Bapak's laughter was spontaneous and unrestrained and his face was wreathed in compassionate amusement. Vadic told us later that he needed no further answer to his question.

In this respect the difference between us and the Indonesian Subud members who had the advantage of living near Bapak was remarkable. Vivienne Pope who lived at Tjilandak for over a year had noticed this very clearly. Meeting her there once, I asked her what had impressed her most about her Indonesian colleagues. Her reply was that the most outstanding difference that she had observed in their behaviour was that no one asked questions about how much they had progressed in their spiritual life. Most of us are continually concerned about what changes (for the better, of course) there were in us between five years ago and now, between last year and this. We were always making internal balance sheets. But in the case of the Indonesian members Subud had become integrated with their lives and they seemed to grow without the self-conscious stock-taking with which we troubled ourselves. If in their testing they showed deeper sensitivity and inner development, they thanked God for His blessings. If they committed a mistake, they thanked God that they had the means for cleansing themselves. There was no heavy breast-beating or public remorse. Win, lose or draw, they did the latihan and went about their ordinary lives.

This observation helped me to understand something that Bapak once said to me in a very reflective mood as we stood on the top of Mount Faber one mellow tropical evening, looking out over the city of Singapore.

"Truly Subud people are lucky. When they receive good fortune they are grateful to God and when they are not fortunate they are mindful of God."

I thank God that I had sufficient sense to refrain from making the moment hideous with questions.

5

Off with our heads

I HAVE heard some Subud members lament that they have not observed any marked change in themselves after three or four years in Subud. This always surprises me because it seems to me that those of us who indulge in what we have called spiritual stock-taking are bound to find some differences. From the simple fact that those who complain about their static state have persisted in the latihan for three or four years, can we not justifiably conclude that something must be taking place within them to make them return again and again? Otherwise why should they come to latihan? Subud houses, particularly in the first few years, are not the gayest and most attractive places in which to spend two evenings a week. Continued shoulder-rubbing with Subud people has never led anyone up the social ladder or to advancement in business. On the contrary, Subud members have often become regarded as social pariahs or political outcasts and, on the whole, Subud groups are notoriously impecunious. Attending latihans and banging one's head on the floor – as I did for several months – or swinging one's arms or body about, week after week, month after month, year after year, cannot be described as fun. Unlike in traditional churches and temples there is no "holy" music, no massed choirs, or throbbing of drums at the latihan. There is neither grand decor nor antiquity in latihan halls. There are no set pieces, no feast days, no moving commemorative orations, no elevating and eloquent sermons. The latihan does not "take us out of ourselves" – rather does it put us back into ourselves – hardly ever a pleasant prospect.

Why then do we go on and on unless some value is being received? And does it seem possible to receive any value without experiencing some change which makes it worth our while to continue?

Carmen de Silva of the Colombo group asked Bapak one morning how she could be certain that she was progressing. From the eagerness with which all of us craned forward to hear Bapak's response it became evident that the same problem was present in everyone. Bapak said: "When a seed is planted and begins to grow, its appearance above the ground may be an 'experience'. From then on its growth does not give it evidence of change. From outside it can be observed to be at this height one day, at this height the next week, at that height a month later, and so on. But, for a long time, the plant has no knowledge of its own growth. Later when it begins to bear one fruit, then another, and another, then it may find measurable change in its life. Bapak advises patience."

By their fruits they shall know themselves.

But I feel that the difficulty arises often because, unlike a plant, the changes in us are, more often than not, inner changes. Only outward change is easily noticeable and sometimes even spectacular. Inner change is relatively subtle. And, as Bapak has explained, our senses and our minds and hearts – encrusted with the influence of lower than appropriately human forces – are too insensitive to feel and measure spiritual development. We seem to require an inner instrument to assess inner change.

Prio Hartono once gave us an analogous clarification: "When you are driving a car your attention is focused outside, in front of you. You are unable to see what is happening immediately behind or around you. For this purpose we are given a rear-view mirror which reflects what was previously concealed from our awareness. The latihan kedjiwaan, if it is God's Will, will give us a spiritual mirror to enable us to feel what is happening inside. The more sincerely we do our latihan the clearer the reflection will be."

When I heard this explanation I rejoiced in its lucidity and was sure that the nagging questions within me would cease. But of course it was not that easy. The yearning for certainty returned shriller and more insistent. The mind said: "All that is very well – but it is all in the future, some day, in never-never land. What is the good of that for me here and now?"

When I told Prio Hartono these reactions he was helpful again when he said: "Bapak says modern people want proof. They can have proof even now if they will look!"

And of course there was proof when one looked. Part of the trouble had been that we were looking too hard, too deep, and too close.

When I look at my Subud life I recognize certain small but distinct changes that may not be easily visible to the naked eye.

I see for instance, that there has been a revolution in my mental attitudes towards political problems, society, human relationships, traditional values, and money. I realize that my early militant non-conformism had made me as rigid and bigoted as the forms and people I had been rebelling against. I realize that my revolutionary political ardour – like that of most revolutionaries or liberal reformists – had trapped me like a squirrel in a revolving cage. I realize that there can be no political solution to any significant human problem unless there is a significant change in human beings.[1]

I realized that I had been wearing a cloak of hard urban values which had prevented me from being sensitive to the feelings and needs of simple people. Only intellectual brilliance and bloodless verbalisms could excite me. I realize that our life training has been to regard the mind as the most exquisite phenomenon in the universe and to look upon feelings and emotions with suspicion and contempt unless they could be frozen into high art. I saw that I had been terrified of showing or accepting love – the word itself embarrassed me to the quick.

When a Fleet Street colleague once remarked to a group of us drinking beer at The Feathers, that we seemed to be incapable of talking about anything except gin and sex, I countered with bland certitude: "Is there anything else?" Urbane laughter. Clever. Cynical. Brittle. This was the life, Koestler, Kafka, Kierkegaard. In the beginning was the Mind and the Mind was God ...

And here we were, only a few years later, beginning to trust our emotions and even the sensitiveness of the physical body more than the subtle argument of the mind. After the 1963 Briarcliff Congress at which 350 people from all over the world had relied more and more sincerely on inner guidance from testing in latihan, John Lake of Los Angeles remarked in loud dejection: "Oh God! I suppose I shall now have to screw my head back on."

I saw then how it was for me and most other Subud members who had been trained and nurtured in the religion of the mind – how much more willing we had become to give our minds their proper place as relatively inefficient computers for calculating our way through our worldly lives, but no more.

What more convincing proof of change could we need? But I expect many of us will continue, as I will, to demand more and more proof until the latihan becomes indistinguishably integrated with our daily lives.[2]

[1] *Bapak once asked us: "Can a carpenter make a table better than himself?"*

[2] *Bapak's words are: "Until the Outer and Inner come together".*

6

Life in Subud

WHEN will it be possible for us to say that Subud has been integrally woven into our daily lives? One quick answer is: When we don't need to say it. But like all such answers, it illuminates quickly but the light it gives vanishes as fast. I like to think that for most of us it will not be an impossible achievement in this lifetime.

There is some evidence for supposing that this wish of mine may not be entirely fatuous or impertinent. Let me say straightway that this evidence is not from my own experience but from one or two hints that I have heard Bapak drop, and from my observation of the lives of a few Subud people in Jakarta as well as outside Indonesia.

Bapak remarked at the Briarcliff Congress that the fact that so many Subud members participating in it had been able to conduct all the business of the Congress without rancour, bitterness or anger or "desire to misunderstand" showed that the practice of the latihan had already had some influence on their inner lives.

But, of course, we can damage ourselves by making the mistake of letting our imagination blow it up out of due proportion. We could, for instance, commit the hideous error of ignoring the evidence in our individual lives which reveals the chasm between what we are and what we hope we shall be, and how far we have yet to go to bridge it. Such self-delusion is bound to cause us traumatic disappointment when, inevitably, these unpleasant facts thrust themselves into our awareness at critical moments in our relationship with ourselves, with others and with God.

Bapak once said to us: "You practise the latihan twice a week for half an hour each time. Later you will need three latihans and, later still, you will feel the need for doing the latihan more often. When progress is made you may reach the time when being out of the receiving state will be as uncomfortable as being out of water is to fish. The latihan state is the proper medium for a real human being whose Inner and Outer are in constant touch with each other."

This impressed me so deeply that at the first opportunity I told Bapak that I wanted to stop being a journalist.

Why? asked Bapak.

"Because in my job I have to criticize people every day, sometimes very harshly. An editor must believe passionately in certain standards and opinions and to defend them he has to attack others. Doing this every day of my life makes it very hard for me in Subud. I collect more dirt in my job than I seem to be able to throw away in latihan. This is a losing battle unless I change my profession." Bapak answered: "Your profession is journalism and it is right that you should criticize others according to the policy of your newspaper. But the trouble arises not because you criticize but because of your passion. It is not necessary to leave journalism to progress in your spiritual life. Bapak will put it another way. A man may be a butcher by profession because his grandfather and his father before him were butchers. Circumstances have made him a butcher*. But this need not prevent him from receiving the Grace of God and from progressing in the latihan although it may be more difficult for him. He does not need to stop being a butcher. He needs to become a *good* butcher. He should learn to cut efficiently and neatly and he can do this only if he does it without passion. His Inner should not be involved in this activity. Only his skill."

I wish I could claim that Bapak's advice effected an immediate and profound transformation in my professional performance. The truth is that I went on in much the same way as before and still continue to be involved in what I write. As a matter of fact, things got so bad that a year later I asked Bapak again how we could be expected to progress spiritually if we did not hide ourselves away from the dust and grime of material life.

Bapak is the only human being in my experience who can really chortle: amused, detached and indulgent. He chortled:

"If God had intended that you should be a hermit, He would have put you in a cave."

We keep coming back to the old Subud question: Are you sitting on that chair or is that chair sitting on you? Are you eating that food or is the food eating you? Are you drinking that whisky or is the whisky drinking you? Are you running a newspaper or is the newspaper running you?

Since that time I have been living a different kind of journalistic life:

*During his visit to Paris in July 1964 Bapak advised Laurence Petric of Chile who has a meat business to breed his own cattle so that he could control the supply and quality. One of the ladies present said that she had thought being a butcher and being in Subud would go ill together. Bapak's reply was: "Better a good butcher than a bad priest."

working in newsrooms in Madras, Bangalore, Kerala, Orissa, Lahore, Dacca, Karachi, Chittagong, Kuala Lumpur, Manila, Hong Kong, and holding journalistic workshops and seminars from Karachi to Tokyo. Mercifully, I have been away from Colombo and journalism in Ceylon where I was not strong enough to practise my profession without passion and have now been given a job to do in which only such skill as I have is involved.

In the process, I have been privileged to observe Subud members here and there whose lives have been increasingly infused with the strength they derive from the latihan and guided by their inner spiritual understanding.

It has been a rewarding experience to meet Subud brothers in Indonesia who live their daily lives deprived of many of the creature comforts which most of us take for granted. I know one Subud family with six children whose income is no more than the true equivalent of $4 a month* and they are regarded as relatively well-to-do. Their real sustenance is derived from the latihan. The guidance through their lives is their receiving through testing.

I was present, one day, when a Subud member in Jakarta came to Bapak with a serious life problem, the solution to which would have affected the entire future of his family. All he asked was: "Bapak, is the indication I have received correct?"

Bapak nodded. Nothing more was said and, apparently, nothing more was needed. I know that the indication was obediently followed without prevarication or any interpretation calculated to soften the pain it caused in the human heart of this Subud brother. It was the simplicity of faith that I found most impressive.

On a recent visit to Jakarta I discovered Sjafrudin busy studying for his law examination. I asked him whether it was not difficult to concentrate on a heavy law book after a six year lapse. Sjaf said that it was easier than he had imagined it would be. He had found that his mind "closed" when he read an unimportant passage and "opened" when it had to remember a significant passage for the purpose of the examination. He simply accepted this as inner guidance to his preparation. Our old teachers would be horrified if they heard of this strange approach to sacred matters like examinations and the law. But I am sure we need have no

*At the time of writing the official exchange rate is 45 Rupiah to one US dollar. The open market (no one calls it the black market) offers 1800 Rupiah to the dollar. Rp 6000 a month is the salary of a senior government official. (March 1964)

worries that Sjaf will get by.*

This simplicity of faith was best exemplified – in my experience – by Icksan's life. He had a small import business which he had started on a bank loan. This was his family's sole means of existence. But when Bapak wanted him as his assistant on his first visit to England and Europe, without any hesitation Icksan put a padlock on his door and went away to London. For nearly two years he was engaged in opening new members and guiding groups for Bapak in London, Holland, Germany, Switzerland, California, Ceylon and Singapore and by the time he returned, his business was a wreck. He was preparing to resurrect it when Bapak took him again to Colombo and Singapore, where he died.

Subud members who were very close to Icksan asked Bapak what they could do to help Ismana, Icksan's young widowed wife.

Bapak said: "Ismana is Bapak's daughter. It is Icksan who needs help. The debts he had in this world should not be allowed to burden him where he is now."

In a matter of weeks all this was settled; Icksan's simple direct faith, thank God, had been justified even in material terms.

There were other Subud members elsewhere who, because they have not had the opportunity of living near Bapak's physical presence, have probably given me even more reason to hope that my life too could be more and more inner-directed by Subud. Such families I have encountered in the United States, England, Germany, India and Ceylon. They go about their normal life occupations – commerce, medicine, accountancy, industry – but their inner attitudes, to the people they meet and to the circumstances of their life work, have undergone a remarkable transformation. Their reliance on the guidance they receive through their testing and the resolution with which they obey inner indications – even when it seems disastrous to the mind – constantly fills me with admiration. I often think how marvellous for them that they are becoming as little children.

But what is most impressive is that like little children, they have not found it necessary to withdraw from life or society in a way which attracts undue attention to themselves or jeopardizes their professional position.

They participate in the social activities that convention and business thrust at them, and even contrive to enjoy themselves much more thoroughly and conscientiously than they ever did before – always returning

He did.

from a state of diffusion to the sanctuary of receiving. These are the truly "sly people" who have discovered the secret of renunciation – that the ascetic's cave and the devotee's temple may be found within themselves. They may have found the key to the words of the Lama who, asked by a newspaper reporter whether it was true that he could fly into the clouds, replied,

"I can refrain from flying into the clouds." *

*During Bapak's most recent visit to Calcutta he was asked this question: "A Superman may prefer to create rather than to procreate might he not?" Bapak replied in English: "Superman normal. God is normal."

7

The philosopher's stone

DURING one of my recent visits to Jakarta, Bapak said that a group in Germany had asked whether testing was not the heart of Subud experience. "This is indeed so," Bapak commented. "Without the experience of testing it is not possible to gain faith in our inner development."

Later, I discussed this with Sudarto, Brodjo and Prio whose experience and faith in testing is phenomenal. They would test at the drop of a hat. Brodjo told us how at the start he could not convince himself that the indications he received were reliable – except when he was testing in the presence of Bapak. Brodjo said: "So I practised even in small things. If I wanted to go to meet a friend I would test 'Is he at home or not?' And, even if I received 'no', I would go to his house to check my testing. In Jakarta this is not easy. We have no telephone or motor cars. And *betjas* (cycle-rickshaws) are expensive for us. Like this I became more and more sure that the Inner had a means of receiving direct knowledge that the mind had not."

For people like myself who have been taught from the time we were babies to regard the human mind as the ultimate refinement in the Universe, this has been a very difficult attitude to accept even as a working hypothesis. How was it possible that the truth came to us only when the mind had stopped? And how can there be "knowledge" – direct or indirect – without cerebration?

I remember a Subud member whose mental equipment is undoubtedly impressive, telling me five years ago: "This testing thing. This is the one thing in Subud that I cannot accept. If testing is true then we have at last found the Philosopher's Stone. The ultimate secret which was denied to the Alchemist has been handed over to us for the asking. It is patently absurd."

I must say that I was inclined at that time to agree with him. My difficulty was to understand why a spiritual loafer like me should be given this fantastic gift while people who had devoted their lives to a spiritual search had been passed over. And how could we be sure that the mind was not interfering in the process of testing from within and dictating to the Inner what answer it should provide?

I remember one early occasion when Bapak was testing one of the women in the Colombo Group. She closed her eyes and made some extremely fluent movements of her hands and body signifying, it seemed, that the answer to the question posed was "good" or "light" or "yes". I whispered to Icksan: "Good Subud actress". Icksan whispered back: "Are you sure it is acting?"

I shut up discreetly but I could not accept this "performance" as evidence of this woman's having received the truth.

Icksan often used me as the guinea-pig for many of the early exercises in testing we were put through. I "let go" as sincerely as I was capable of and responded to the tests. But my mind was ticking away like a time bomb ready to burst into hot denunciations of all this as sham and superstition.

When Bapak visited us in Ceylon someone asked him about the present state of the soul of a celebrated spiritual teacher whom some of us had followed for many years. Bapak asked me to stand up and test this. I closed my eyes, relaxed, and suddenly felt an enormous overpowering weight upon me. I fell like a log. There was no choice or pretence about it. My fall was heavy and sincere. Bapak said, rather sadly it seemed to me, "Still here, in this world."

Then my mind began to grow. Did I or didn't I? Did I fake it or was it real? If I had failed deliberately, surely it would have been more fluent, more graceful. But perhaps my mind was being cleverer than that. It could have skipped one step and played it more subtly. But surely that wasn't the answer I *wanted?* And so on. All the while something deep inside me was certain about the reality of the overwhelming force that had borne me down and about the spontaneity of the movement, of the feeling of sadness and torment that had coursed through me. But the mind denied all this evidence. It refused to acknowledge as truth an answer that was completely unpalatable to its tastes and values and its notions of fundamental justice.

This intellectual doubt seemed to be supported by a conversation that took place in Singapore some time later.

I asked: "Bapak, would I be right in thinking that none of us can test correctly?"

Bapak smiled and nodded agreement. I went on: "Then why does Bapak test with us at all?"

Bapak's smile became broader: "Injection," he said laconically, making a prodding gesture with his finger.

From then on I felt I was justified in refusing to test individually or as part of a group. For a long time I actively scoffed at people practising testing. I would submit to testing only with Bapak or with one of his authorized assistants. All the while, however, there was a deep, persistent, nagging suspicion that it was essential to practise testing without such an injection of force which would not be always available when something important had to be submitted for testing. Since the most attractive feature of Subud as a way of life was, for me, its concern with individual growth and responsibility, it was necessary to learn to rely on one's own inner capacity. Therefore, whenever I did latihan with the Arnolds in Calcutta or with New York members who placed a great deal of value on testing, I participated. Such experiences, supported by an occasional shot in the arm from Bapak, eventually convinced me that it was necessary to test and equally important to learn to follow the inner answers I received. Let me hastily add here that I have never been capable of as much submission in this respect – following the indications given by the test – as many others I know or as much as I myself often wish.

It was a tremendous relief to have got over the phase of believing that one should test perfectly or not at all. It is like writing. Many people who want to write, never write anything because they wait till they can write a masterpiece. The result, of course, is that they never write anything at all.

Not long ago we received an object lesson testing from one of the members in the Kuala Lumpur group. Peter Knibble – very young in years but old in Subud (he had been opened six years before when he was barely 18) submitted a problem for testing. It seemed a trivial or rather an "unspiritual" kind of question, but since it was very important for him, the group agreed to participate in testing it. Peter is in charge of a department in a large commercial house in Malaysia. That morning he had received a cable from Bangkok instructing him to meet a plane bringing two of his bosses to Kuala Lumpur on the following day. Peter found that there were two planes due from Bangkok – one in the morning, the other in the afternoon. He had so much work to do that he had time to meet only one plane – not both. He wished to know which he should meet. We "tested" the first plane. It was a unanimous NO. Then, instead of logically assuming that he should meet the other, we tested that too. Everyone seemed to receive a confused response. (We realized later that this was because our minds which were convinced that it had to be the second plane, were interfering). We suggested that Peter should submit to the test alone while the rest of us received the force within us.

Peter's test showed that he should NOT meet even the second plane. It was so clear to him that he determined that he would not meet either plane.

I must admit I was afraid that Peter was taking a serious risk since young executives like him are not permitted mistakes based on what would be regarded in the commercial world as mere whimsicality.

On the next evening Peter came in looking like a cat who had swallowed a brace of canaries. He had received another cable informing him that the visit had been postponed.

I single out this experience for relating not to show that our testing was right but to record our gratitude that Peter Kibble had shown that one of us was capable of that degree of faith in Subud testing – done, let us mark, without the help of Bapak's presence or even one of his assistants.

My certainty about the validity of testing really came to me during a session with the New York group. There were 15 helpers present, and a moderator read out written questions put to the group. The helpers would receive for a while and then put it to the vote. How many Ayes, how many Noes and how many Indifferent? The Ayes had it or the Noes had it as the test went on. I had to choke on the protests that arose inside me. This idea of majority decisions on such matters horrified me. In my ordinary experience, the majority has generally been wrong – the minority was more likely to be right in arriving at critical decisions. Instead of protesting, I decided to participate in the next test and check the response in myself.

A Catholic Bishop had written to ask the group to test his question. He had applied for Subud membership not long before. He was a Ban-the-Bomb demonstrator and had been charged with obstructing the police, endangering the public peace etc. etc. He had decided to plead guilty at the trial and would certainly be sentenced to a term in prison. He now realized that peace could not come through such action but from submission within and he was anxious to join Subud. Would the group waive the three month probationary period and open him at once so that he could "have the solace of the latihan in prison?"

My mind said, "Why bother to test this? It is obviously right that a concession should be made in this case."

My heart said, "What a fine human being. Of course he must be opened immediately."

But when I submitted to the test, the Inner said No. It was firm and definite – No.

The answer itself did not concern me much. It was the clarity of the response and the fact that it overrode the wishes of the heart and mind that made an impact on me.

Thereafter, all my criticisms of the democratic methods of the New York group lay down and died. I realized that, at our level of receiving, such rough and ready methods as the counting of heads were the only means available to us just now. Later, God willing, there would be sharper indications and unison of response within a helper's group as there is among the older helpers in Jakarta.

My experience received profound confirmation at the World Congress when the members of the Executive Committee of the Subud International Services organization were being chosen by testing. From the ten names nominated by the Congress I had privately marked out five as the most effective group for the work ahead. One of those I had rejected was a friend of mine who agreed with me that he was the last man to be on such a committee. At the testing session my mental judgment received two major blows: Four of the five I had picked were eliminated. And I was called upon by Bapak as one of those who were to test the candidature of my friend. Again my head said No, my feelings said No, but as soon as I began to receive, my body reached upward and my hands rose high in profound acceptance of this man as being right for this task.

I learned two valuable lessons from this experience: It gave me an explanation of the continuing failure in the world of politics to find the right people for the right tasks. It also showed me, without room for any doubt, that we now had a real possibility of making value judgments from a more reliable instrument than our hearts and minds had so far proved themselves to be.

One more testing story. A friend who, I feel, would prefer to be nameless here, related to us a spiritual experience he had received before he came to Subud. He was in a state of great nervous tension and sadness one night when he decided to pray. When he was deep in prayer he saw a clear, bright greenish-blue light above his head. It came nearer and nearer and seemed to spill over his head and bathe his shoulders. He said he felt that it was "like Heaven!"

Soon after he came to Subud, he told Icksan about this incident and asked whether it was a "true experience".

Icksan told him that he could test it for himself.

First Icksan tested my friend's response for "light" and "heffy" which, in Icksan's connotation, stood respectively for Yes and No. Then Icksan asked him to receive whether it was a true experience.

The answer was "light" – Yes.

"Yah, yah. True experience," said Icksan. But something in the tone of his voice may have seemed odd, for my friend asked:

"Icksan, what is it?"

Icksan: "You wish to test whether this experience is from God or not?"

Yes, he would like to test this.

He received. The answer was a resolute No. He protested, "But Icksan, it says No! How can that be? The experience was like Heaven!"

Icksan: "You test again."

Again it was a clear No. My friend's heart and mind wanted the answer to be Yes but his Inner said No.

Then Icksan asked him to test whether the experience was from the human level.

No.

Was it an experience from the animal level?

No.

Was it from the vegetable level?

Yes. It was from the vegetable level.

Then Icksan explained that human beings should, if they are purified, live at the proper human level. But we live at the material level. The symbolic colours associated with the vegetable level are blue and green. Thus, when we receive an experience from the vegetable level we are receiving it from a level actually higher than we are at. Even an experience from the vegetable level is "already like Heaven" when we are living at the material level.

Since then I have been less inclined to talk as glibly as I used to about "lower forces". Even in Subud the Law of Relativity applies.

(photo courtesy of Harijanti Vittachi)

Varindra with his first wife Sunetra (now Harijanti) and daughter Anuradha

Icksan Achmed, Coombe Springs, 1957

Bapak with John Bennett and Dr. Zhakir (translator), Coombe Springs, 1959

(photo Ilaine Lennard)

Varindra at The 9th Subud World Congress held at Amanecer, Colombia 1993

(photo Sachlan Cherpitel)

Varindra at The Seventh Subud World Congress held at Anugraha, England, 1983

8

Not teaching but learning

ICKSAN touched my hand during one of the mass latihans held in the first week of his visit to Colombo where some three hundred people were opened in three weeks. Icksan was introducing us into the simple mysteries of the helpers' function. He pointed to a young man who had just been opened. With his eyes tightly closed he was reciting words from the Koran, punctuating them with loud affirmations of Allah, Allah, Allah!

Very gravely, Icksan whispered, "Notice how easily he speaks name of God. Funny! You see him next week. Maybe not so easy!"

A few days later, Icksan indicated the young man again. All he could do in his latihan now was to utter a rasping sound like Augh, Augh, Augh as though he was in pain within. There was no sign of triumphant vindication on Icksan's face. It was still grave as he said, "Now better. Now real. Not so nice as Allah, Allah, Allah as in beginning. Now ugly, but true. From inner, not from teaching."

We learnt much from Icksan's refusal to compromise with the value of truth learnt from experience. Gently, but firmly he thwarted every attempt by some of the helpers who, following the old traditions of priestcraft, couldn't resist the temptation of teaching.

Icksan said to us:

"Subud not teaching. Subud receiving. If people progress through latihan Bapak happy. Icksan not jealous. In Subud only experience. Bapak say, 'If Bapak is teacher and he know ten things he teach only nine. Because if he teach ten, then – no pupils. No pupils, no teacher! Funny'!"

I had often heard Icksan, Sjafrudin, Asikin and Prio say, "Bapak says that the only sin is teaching." I felt I understood, but the old mind was asking for appeasement and at the first opportunity I asked Bapak why he considered teaching such a deadly sin.

Bapak explained (Anwar Zakir interpreting): "Through the practice of the latihan we are made more and more sensitive to receive directly, by each individual – according to his special needs as seen by Almighty God. Each man thus receives the guidance proper to him at the time he needs it. A teacher can teach only from his mind. He can give information and guidance of a kind that can be generally applicable to everybody.

It is like the difference between 'special' medicine and patent medicine. But in 'special' medicine what is good for one man might be bad for another. So in Subud each man receives what he requires, and anyone who *teaches* Subud goes against the Will of God because what he teaches may not be what is truly indicated for a particular man or woman."

But, continually, the falseness embedded within us would burst through in our actions and thinking. For instance, we used the word "Brotherhood" without any real content of feeling. Even at the time when our group was going through its first massive spell of purification, when we could hardly pass each other on the stairs without bristling, when rival cliques, freed from the spurious decorum of society would abuse each other roundly – we still liked to refer to ourselves as a Brotherhood. The Brotherhood idea was great but the trouble arose when some of us wanted to be elder brothers.

It was ugly. But now we can look back on it and realize that it was nevertheless real. We were like that within us, and out it came: heavy gobbets of undigested learning, twisted hates which had previously been covered over by a thin veneer of social propriety, lumps of malformed egoism suppressed under the lid of social mores, bits and pieces of meaningless relationships – all these were disgorged in an extended spiritual Bacchanalia.

When I went to Bapak's house to take my leave of him on my first visit to Indonesia, Bapak asked me, "What is the chief impression you carry away with you from Jakarta?"

"Brotherhood, Bapak", I replied. "I have just had a glimpse of what real Brotherhood means. Our group is not a brotherhood. There is so much quarrelling. I don't know what is happening to us. I am one of the worst!"

Bapak laughed as he said: "There is no reason to worry or to envy the group in Jakarta. You should have been here to observe this group a few years ago – at the start. Much worse than you in Colombo!"

Bapak's explanation of this process which nearly every group in the world has experienced was translucently simple and clear: "Consider a well of water with plenty of mud and dirt at the bottom. You begin to clean it. You scoop a handful of mud off the bottom and throw it on the bank. The water, which seemed clear before, is now disturbed and muddy. But the well is already a little cleaner."

The experience of cleaning out the well has taken many and strange forms from which it is possible to learn a great deal about ourselves and the people around us.

A life-long friend – let me call him Anil – had come to Subud. His life had seemed impeccable. He was a model student and a spectacularly proficient athlete. He never had a harsh word for anyone and people used to refer to him – in the stuffy public school phrase – as a 'Real Gentleman'. Anil was married when he came to Subud and his wife joined at the same time. A few months later he came to me with a story which surprised me because it was contrary to his nature as it had appeared to us. He had fallen in love with another girl, and was determined to divorce his wife and marry again. He wanted advice about how he could do this without hurting his wife for whom he had a deep regard.

Fortunately, Bapak was with us at the time. I suggested that he should tell Bapak about his predicament but he recoiled in horror. I was able, however, to persuade him to tell his story to Icksan. Anil sat on Icksan's bed and Icksan and I sat on the chairs as the story was told. When Anil was nearing the end of his story, we heard Bapak walking down the corridor towards Icksan's room.

Anil stopped mid-word and breezed rapidly out of the room.

Bapak entered smoking a cheroot and sat on the chair I offered him. I sat on the floor. There was a long silence during which Icksan and I looked deliberately away from each other. Bapak raised an enquiring eyebrow at us. We tried to avoid his gaze. Bapak then asked us what the problem was. I murmured that we were just passing the time of day. Icksan looked as bland as he could. Then Bapak, pointing with his cigar at the depression left on the bed clothes by Anil, said:

"Tell him that it is necessary to understand this situation. People before they are opened, get married from passion and wanting. People may therefore get the wrong partners. Later the man comes to Subud. His inner begins to grow. Then he feels: 'Hm, A is not my real wife. B should be my wife.' So he divorces A and marries B. His inner continues to grow. He may feel later that B is not his real wife, and so he divorces B and marries C who, he now feels, is nearer his ideal. Later he feels that C too is not his real wife and may even feel that, after all, he might have remained with A. He may have married A from passion and they may be the wrong partners. But when both come to Subud they may be able, if it is God's Will, to change in such a way that they *become* the right partners for each other."

In a state of semi-stupefaction, I told Bapak about Anil's problem. Bapak said, "Tell him to speak to this girl about Subud."

A few days later she was opened in the same room in which Anil's wife was doing the latihan. Some weeks later Anil found that he was no longer interested in divorce and decided to break off his new relationship. He said to her, "You may think badly of me but I wish you will not stop going to the latihan."

The girl's reply astonished Anil:

"Why should you advise me to continue with the latihan? Subud is not your property. It is mine also. Of course, I will continue with my latihan."

I have lost track of them now and have no idea of how they are doing. But I shall always be grateful to them for what I have learnt from their experience.

9

Symbolism in Subud

I REMEMBER reading recently a celebrated Protestant theologian lamenting what he called "The Lost Dimension of Religion". He was referring to the meaning of the symbols of Christianity. He said that the modern church was losing the battle against atheism because it was trying to explain on a horizontal plane ideas which could only stand up on a vertical plane. In other words, it was futile and even ridiculous to try to explain religious symbols at a factual level. For instance, he said if one tried to explain the noblest Christian myth – the story of the Fall of Man – factually one would, in effect, be saying that about 6000 years ago a young couple named Adam and Eve who lived in Iraq were exiled for petty larceny and they were terribly embarrassed. Since then their descendants have never been able to live down the social stigma ...

Late one night in Bapak's flat in Paris I asked for the true symbolic meaning of the story of the expulsion of Adam and Eve from the Garden of Eden. Bapak asked: "You mean about snake and apple?" He closed his eyes briefly, tuning in for the answer. Then he leant forward and in a confidential stage whisper said: "Top Secret". We burst out laughing at the glorious notion that a story which had been bandied about in so many faiths for thousands of years should still be a top secret. That none of us know the meaning of the story nor, evidently, were ready yet to understand it, was only tolerable because of the laughter and the dexterity with which Bapak had parried the question. But there have been redeeming moments over the past seven years when Bapak has shared with us his understanding of the symbols and myths of spiritual experience. I have never ceased to be astonished by the fact that Bapak's experience is not confined to Islam alone but ranges freely over nuances of symbolic meanings also in Christianity, Buddhism, Hinduism and Judaism. I shall probably never cease to be astonished, and delighted, at the feeling of dead-centre accuracy and clarity that Bapak's evaluations of symbols and his use of analogies arouse in me. It is like a magnesium flare, illuminating brilliantly and quickly.

My understanding of Bapak's explanations of some of the parables in the Christian gospels have already been recorded (*A Reporter in Subud*).

There have been other moments when Bapak's words have opened up the truths locked in the symbols of other faiths. And when they are shown to us, we also see that the great myths and symbols which have sustained humanity for centuries have many terraces of meaning, each perfectly valid and satisfying at its level. When Bapak is travelling about he speaks in the metaphor familiar to his audience: of Christian or Jewish symbols in the West, Buddhist or Hindu symbols in Japan or India, and Islamic symbols in Indonesia.

During Bapak's visit to New Delhi in September, 1964, Bapak showed us how we had misunderstood the symbols of Buddhism and Hinduism. Even those who used these symbols every day had lost sight of the original meanings which gave them validity and life.

For instance, the statue of Buddha representing him either naked or clad very lightly, symbolised that he was in a state of surrender. Depicting him in a state of *samadhi* or tranquillity did not mean "concentration" or "meditation" which needed effort, but rather total surrender and submission to the Will of God, because *samadhi* or tranquillity is possible only when one's will is submitted to God's Will, when they become one.

On another enormously profitable day Bapak told the Delhi group in one of his fireside chats about the meaning of the yellow robe worn by the Buddhist monks and fakirs.

The yellow robe, Bapak said, symbolized the fact that its wearer had received the highest value, God's Grace. This value, in its turn, was symbolized by gold which, in its turn, was symbolized by the colour yellow. One who had received God's Grace was symbolically entitled to wear the yellow robe. Since he had received the highest value there was no need for him to display it or draw external attention to himself. He could afford to be "normal". He could now live among ordinary people and wear ordinary clothes. But unfortunately, the symbolic meaning had been lost long ago, so that people still clung to the rags of the symbol and lived apart from other human beings, in poverty, rejecting the world into which God had put them.

A woman in Delhi who said she wished to come to Subud brought along a *Swamiji* – her guru – to appraise Bapak spiritually before she would join the group. Apparently, Bapak did not pass the test for she never returned. But Bapak had noticed the *Swamiji* carrying a *japamala* or rosary with which he prayed during the *Darshan* (or sight-audience) that Bapak gave to him and his spiritual protégé. I, for one, am grateful to her and the *Swamiji* for paying Bapak that visit because it provided the opportunity for an incandescent clarification of another religious symbol – the bead rosary.

The original and true meaning of the rosary was that each bead represented an inner organ which had been touched by the latihan, the Power of God. As we feel the vibration of this Power in one of these organs, we should count one bead. When the vibration is felt in another organ, another bead is counted – and so on. So, prayer is the receiving of God's Power from within, not set patterns of words. The organs are linked together by the Power of God that courses through them, one by one, hence the *mala* or necklace of beads.

Those of us whose education has trained us to think in categories and competitiveness never get the answers we want from Bapak. It seems to me that Bapak being a channel for the Great Life Force which precedes everything in this Universe, is incapable of categorical thinking or feelings which exclude one thing in order to accept the other. Everything is given its due place when Bapak speaks. One thing flows into another.

Once, many years ago, when Bapak was in Colombo, Coombe Springs sent for his approval the proof of the cover page of the *Chronicle* that was due to be published. It featured the seven-circle Subud symbol and in the centre they had printed a monogram of Subud, SBD. Bapak asked me to write to Coombe Springs and suggest that the monogram should be removed. "Subud has no monopoly of God," Bapak said.

I also remember that at that time someone asked Bapak whether the fact that Muhammad came after Jesus meant that he was "higher than Jesus". Bapak smiled at this and replied: "There is no question of higher or lower. It is only earlier and later. It is more like this: the symbol of Abraham was water – white water. This symbolised semen. White water flows and is channelised through Moses, the law giver. Then the infant Jesus is born. Always Jesus is referred to as the lamb, the infant son of Maria. The baby grows into Muhammad. Muhammad means Man. Now man must grow his soul."

I felt I had seen a glimpse of the true possibilities of evolution for Man. I began to sense that the next stage of Man's evolution did not lie in adapting his body to technological changes but in developing his inner possibilities.

Bapak has often spoken of the symbolic significance of the Cross. The Cross has many facets of meaning. Bapak asked me to "receive Christ" in me one evening when he was testing with us. I demurred. "How is that possible?" I asked. The idea of Christ within me was preposterous even to my healthy ego. "Never mind. Relax and receive," said Bapak. As soon as I closed my eyes and became "open", I felt a strong sensation in my breast and my hands began to indicate this. "Yah," said Bapak. "Now receive Muhammad in you." At once I sensed a strong surge of power in my genitals, so strong that I clutched them in the atavistic attitude of protection.

I heard Bapak laugh and say, "Yah, Yah, finish". Bapak explained (Icksan interpreting), "Jesus Christ represents female principle among the prophets. That is why Jesus is always referred to as the son of Maria, the 'meek and gentle' Jesus. Muhammad represents male principle. The word 'Muhammad' means Man. In perfect Man both these principles are balanced."

At other times Bapak has said that the Cross existed long before Jesus and that it symbolized Man. Recently he told us that Christ or the Cross represented absolute surrender and submission to God.

Wherever Bapak moves the symbols give up their secrets. Driving Bapak through Delhi, I pointed out the cyanose-blue domes on the new Pakistan Embassy and the Moghul tombs of the Safdarjang and Tughlak eras, always featuring the domes and the minarets. Bapak remarked (Usman translating), "Symbols. Domes symbolized breasts. The minarets are phallic symbols. They are fertility images indicating that the inner, the soul, should be fertile and must grow even after death. That is why they used symbols on tombs."

In Calcutta, seated in the shade of a mango tree, Bapak answered questions about the Hindu pantheon. Krishna, Parvati, Viswakarma, Kali and other deities were not actual beings but symbolic personifications of certain human characteristics and virtues.

One morning during Bapak's visit to Delhi I drove him to see the famous Qtub Minar, the 80 metre-high medieval tower built by the Moghul kings. It is supposed to commemorate a military victory. But there is an old legend that tells a more interesting story. I related this to Bapak: The Emperor's daughter was very ill and the physicians could not diagnose her trouble. Her mother advised her to bathe seven times in the River Jumna. She was cured. She vowed that she would in future cast her eyes on the river every morning in gratitude. But, because the river was too far away for her to visit it daily, the Emperor built a tower from which she could view the river and fulfil her vow.

The symbolic meaning of this legend delighted me. The illness of the

Princess was her need for marriage. The river is the symbol of fertility, the water that brings fertility and makes new life grow. When she was married she was "cured". The tower is the symbol of the phallus which was the instrument of her cure.

In 1960 Carl Jung asked many questions about Subud. He was too ill to see visitors, particularly journalists. So the questions came through an intermediary – one of his pupils in Zurich. He was most interested in the process of opening in Subud and in the explanations given by Bapak about religious myths and symbols. I provided whatever answers I could. After several remote "interviews" of this nature Dr. Jung made this comment: "These people seem to have arrived emotionally at the same place which we have reached intellectually."

I know nothing about that. But I have often speculated upon what a fiesta of myth and legend and symbols there could have been if Carl Jung had been able to meet Bapak.

Much more recently Bapak made another reference to the world of spirits. During his visit to Paris in July, 1964, Bapak said: "This earth is the domain of the Satanic creatures. This is the Alam Saitonia, the Satanic world."

I remarked that Western people had often asked me about this kind of supernatural or spirit experiences of Subud members in the East. For instance, Mas Sudarto's story, reported in the *Pewarta*, of a woman in Jakarta who had vomited black snakes during a latihan, had provoked widespread comment, mostly incredulous, in America and Europe. Many people seemed mortified that Subud was getting mixed up with what they felt certain was fantasy and spiritist irrelevancies. One world, the familiar world of streets, buildings, automobiles, airplanes and government regulations, was quite enough for them to handle without burdening their experience with another world where they could cope even less efficiently. But because they respected Subud and the experiences of older helpers like Sudarto they tried to explain away the snakes as being "merely symbolic" or "metaphysical". It was difficult, if not impossible, to take the story literally, as Sudarto had apparently intended. Bapak's comment on all this was: "These were indeed real snakes. Real snakes that could be seen and touched." He then added: "Real spiritual snakes." Then, seeing the film of confusion on all our faces, Bapak explained (Usman interpreting): "These snakes were real external manifestations of the lower forces which had dominated this woman's inner. They took the form of real live snakes in order to give her proof of the nature of the lower forces which had controlled her. They could be seen and touched by other people too. But they soon disappeared by themselves, because they were spiritual."

Mercifully, there are other supernatural creatures too in this world, creatures of a different and more benignant nature. During Bapak's last general talk in Paris he suddenly interrupted himself to remark: "You may be surprised to know that there are many angels present in this hall. There are many more of them than there are of you. Bapak can see them. You may not be able to, yet."

10
The ghosts go west

WHENEVER Sudarto or Brodjo or Prio referred to "Satanic beings" or "spirits of the lower forces" I used to wince with embarrassment. But because I loved and admired them I would put such statements in my mental "suspense account". Having been brought up to regard the "scientific attitude" as the only proper stance for the 20th century intelligentsia – of which I had no doubt I was one! – my mind revolted against accepting such notions which seemed to be more proper for the life and times of our grandmothers than for moderns like us. These references to a co-existent netherworld seemed to me irrelevant and even harmful to our understanding of Subud. I was inclined to explain such talk as part of the essential Indonesianness of the Indonesian helpers – like their inexplicable preference for beancurd, Pat Boone and Coca Cola.

But I was never sure. And when Bapak himself said one day: "When a man is opened he immediately receives a means of protection against black magic," I realized that there might be more to it than the Indonesian concern with hexes and bomos or voodoo merchants.

Two years before we left Ceylon, we moved from the little house we had built ourselves to a much larger place near the Subud House. My wife and I did our latihan in the main bedroom. After a few days, we noticed that a strange smell pervaded the room between five and seven o'clock in the afternoon. It was indescribable – a compound of decomposition, faeces, and much more than we could identify. The children, the servants, and visitors to the house all encountered it. We had the roof and the ceiling cleaned, the floor polished immaculately, the surroundings attended to by the Municipal health people. But the smell persisted.

One evening when Prio Hartono was in Colombo, he came home with me, Joe Perera and Vadic Siriwardene, late after latihan, to sit around with a coke and listen to some Pat Boone records. Sunetra, who had retired early, did not know that Prio had come home. She came down the stairs and, halfway, she said, "I can't sleep in that room. That awful smell has come back."

Prio immediately stiffened like a pointer.

"Smell?" he asked, pointing to the ceiling below our bedroom. "That room?"

We were surprised at what we thought was an accurate guess.

"Come, Tarzie, Joe, Vadic. Suné, you stay here," Prio said, and off we went to investigate. The room was thick with the smell – it was almost palpable, like smoke. Prio at once signalled to us to start our latihan. After a minute or two, the smell disappeared. Not a trace of it was left.

Prio said, "There is a spirit in this room. Don't tell Suné because she is pregnant. But this room is the home of this spirit. Maybe the man who built this house. Because you do the latihan here, he feels insecure. The latihan makes him uncomfortable. So he tries to smell you out of this room. He is a very weak spirit and can do nothing more dangerous than try to stink you out of here. Perhaps it will not return now for a few days but it may reappear. If it does, just do the latihan like tonight and it will vanish."

I promptly put this in my suspense account. But the speed with which the smell vanished when we did the latihan was not easily accountable. We christened this phenomenon "Stinker" and watched for its return. Sure enough, three days later, when I had returned from work and was hanging up my jacket, I smelt Stinker's presence in the room. I started my latihan and, within half a minute, Stinker disappeared. It reappeared many times after that, but the knowledge that we now had a force within us which could overpower such a phenomenon without effort, removed all sense of concern and fear. I was even able to tell my wife about it without alarming her. I questioned the previous tenants of the house and those who followed us after we moved again, but none of them had encountered Stinker. He must be snug again in his favourite room without those terrible Vittachis and their unorthodox prayers.

Further confirmation of the existence of certain forces which seemed to be disturbed by the latihan was given to us at the same time. Vadic Siriwardene used to complain that he could never fall asleep on latihan nights. He often told me that the latihan would persist in him and prevent him from sleeping. On other nights he would ensure his sleep by drinking one or two glasses of beer. He told Prio about his problem: on latihan nights, whenever he was about to doze off in bed, a flash of something like an electric current would course through his mind and he would awake, startled, and until the early hours of the morning, this battle would rage. And Vadic would be tired and miserable the whole of the next day. We labelled this phenomenon "Flash".

The explanation amazed us. Flash, said Prio, was a very clever Satanic being which had marked Vadic out for his very own. But Vadic's joining Subud had upset Flash's plans. Flash was so clever that he had figured out a way to make Vadic leave Subud. On latihan nights when Vadic's "inner dust" had been thrown away, Flash would disturb his sleep in an unpleasant and painful way. But on other nights when there were some alcohol fumes in Vadic's head, Flash loved it, this was more like home. Flash too curled up and went to sleep with Vadic. But, over a period of time, Vadic would almost inevitably have been led to believe that it was the latihan that was making him sick and miserable and that he should abandon this dangerous practice and take refuge in the familiar beer haze.

Vadic's quick understanding of this explanation served to weaken the force of Flash at once and, after a prescribed "course" of daily latihans. Flash left in search of a new habitat.

Another Subud member at the same time, was fighting a running battle with a phenomenon we called "The Strangler". Young Raman lived alone in a cottage not far from the Subud House. He had been asked by one of Bapak's visiting assistants to do a latihan every night around midnight before he went to bed in order to help him overcome the terrifying fears he was experiencing since his opening. We used to sit up with Raman at the Subud House to help him stay awake until just before midnight when he could walk home for his latihan and sleep.

He was getting along fine but, half-way through his "course", he reported one morning that on the previous night when he had been about to enter his house, he had been "forcibly put to sleep on the doorstep," where he had spent the night without being able to do his latihan. One evening he had gone to bed early, expecting to wake up before midnight and do his prescribed latihan before resuming his sleep. He woke up with a choking sensation, heavy pressure on his chest and a distinct feeling that something was trying to strangle him. He asked for the protection of the latihan and was later able to sleep peacefully. Raman too, by God's Will, got rid of his familiar, The Strangler. He became engaged to be married, brought his fiancée to Subud, married soon after and now lives freed from the unseen perils which were trying to put him under their thrall.

I asked Prio why people in the East seemed to be more conscious of spiritual phenomena than people in the West.

Facetiously I wondered whether there were fewer spirits in the West that they were not so evident. Prio's explanation was:

"There was knowledge in the East as well as in the West. People in the

East directed this knowledge toward a study of spiritual matters while people in the West directed theirs towards making discoveries in the material world. The study and harnessing of material forces became their special concern. This is called Science and Technology. By spiritual practices, Eastern people were able to make discoveries in the spiritual world and to experience spiritual phenomena. By scientific practices Western people made discoveries such as about the qualities of small particles and the atom. For instance, this table here looks and feels solid to us, but they will tell you that it is not solid. That it is nothing but particles moving rapidly in space. We do not *see* this. And they do not *see* the spiritual phenomena we speak about. The quality of the two is different and the way of experiencing the reality of the two is also very different."

A few months after these episodes I met Bapak during his visit to Bombay. I told him about Stinker, Flash and The Strangler and about the ghost stories Prio had told us. "Prio specialist in these things," Bapak chuckled. I said that I was surprised at the frequency with which we seemed to be encountering the world of "spirits". Bapak's face became grave as he said (Anwar Zakir interpreting): "What we should realize is that there are many more of them than there are of us. Satanic beings far outnumber human beings in this world. This is the world of Satanic forces. The proper world for true human beings is not here. Elsewhere."

A glimmering of understanding of what Purgatory might mean, appeared. Perhaps Purgatory and Hell are right here and now – in this world and not in another dimension, in another life. If this is so, many of the events in this life which seem impossible to understand by a process of reason could be explained. I feel I have begun to see that it is unreason, improbability and the logic of the Satanic forces that really direct the material world of politics and commerce in which we live – the world in which man's inhumanity to man is the familiar experience, where tyranny thrives and crooks succeed, where gentleness, humanism and considerateness are regarded as weakness and are doomed to failure.

I remember, for instance, my reactions on the day that John F. Kennedy was killed. I was in Manila that morning when the news broke. I was full of horror rather than sadness. It was so irrational, illogical and improbable that the situation of human beings in this world could be altered so easily and swiftly by a single act of paranoia. How could it be God's wish that a man of peace and humanity, a man of courage and cultivation, the most powerful and the most secure man in the world, should be shot down like a dog at the first attempt, while tyrants who

had caused misery among millions, and whose power was causing constant threats to the peace of this world, were given the relative immortal-
ity of nine lives?

On my way back to Kuala Lumpur that day I saw the same un-under-
standing in the faces of people in Vietnam, Singapore and Malaya, even
people who had no special love for Kennedy's policies. People were stupe-
fied by the sudden revelation that there was no security for anyone in this
world. For Asian people it was the death of the father of a family – a rich
family, a religious family, an intelligent family, a good-looking family
and, above all, a secure family that was beyond comprehension.
Everywhere I heard the word "meaningless".

That night I re-read Mark van Doren's play on the death of Lincoln.
On the first page, the word again appears – "meaningless".

A day or two later, during the group latihan, Bapak's words came back
to me: "This is the world of Satanic forces. The proper world for true
human beings is not here. Elsewhere. We have been sent here to get to
know God's creatures – from the very lowest category – just as a cadet
officer must learn and experience the nature and functions of the lowest
rank in the army before he is confirmed. Thus we must know and experience the nature of the lower forces before we can approach the grace and
greatness of God."

11

What's in a name?

ONE of the features of Subud experience that I once relegated to the suspense account as an essentially Indonesian thing with no direct bearing on our lives was the practice of changing names. The first name change that I had heard of was Eva Bartok to Ilaina Bartok. Oh well, film stars were always doing things like that, so it did not impress me much. The next was Margaret Wichman who informed Icksan of the change of her name by signing a letter to him, "Margaret (formerly Edith)". Icksan, chuckling merrily, wrote back: "Dear formerly Edith".*

When I returned to Coombe for the 1959 World Congress I met Asikin – once Imran – on the landing leading to Bapak's quarters. I greeted him warmly: "Hello, Imran. How are you?" But he said, in his gentle way, "Not Imran. Asikin. Bapak has given me my name. Asikin."

I said, "What on earth does all this mean? Does it have any meaning?"

He started to explain when Bapak suddenly appeared at the door and called, "Imran!" We both burst out laughing. Bapak, interested, inquired what was so amusing. Asikin reported our conversation. Bapak smiled when he had come to the end. I asked Bapak about the significance of this name changing. Bapak laughingly gave me an explanation but I have never decided whether it was serious or not:

"Before we are sent down here," Bapak said, "they register our names up there. We are expected to do our business here and return to where we came from. When we return, they ask, 'What is your name?' We reply John or Peter or Maria. They look through the register and say, 'But your name is not here. Why not try elsewhere?' So, better to find your right name when you are here!"

I never could figure what the form was; whether, assuming there was some significance in name changes, one should ask Bapak for a "Subud name"; whether it was right to wait until one felt that the name one bore was wrong or uncomfortable and then ask Bapak for the right name; or whether it was best to wait patiently until Bapak himself gave one the right name. So I have done nothing about it.

Margaret swears she never received this letter. I wonder what happened to it?

Bapak himself always called me Vitarzie. transposing and telescoping the two names I am known by and this seems as right as any. In Calcutta I woke up one morning distinctly remembering a dream in which I was called by another name. I remembered the name very clearly. Part of me was inclined to ask Bapak whether this was my right name but another part has shirked doing this because Bapak might say that it IS the right name and then I would have to adopt it. I think the name sounds dreadful and I shudder at the prospect of having to inform 1500 editors all over the world – trained sceptics with whom I have professional contacts, that I shall henceforth be known by another name.

But every now and then, my attitude about this receives a sharp sideways jolt. Driving in Bapak's car in Tokyo on his return from America in 1963 I told him about a scientific discovery which a Subud brother had made through definite inner guidance from his latihan. Bapak's comment was interpreted by Usman: "That is why Bapak gave him his right name which means Pathfinder." *

We have a son, born just before we came to Subud, who was one of the most restless children I have known. We took him with us on one of our gypsy journeys through Italy, Britain, New York, Washington D.C. and Nashville, Tennessee, when he was barely five months old – during which he had a varied succession of baby-sitters and different surroundings. He would do nothing for himself – eat, drink his milk or sleep without intense coaxing. When Prio Hartono was staying with us in 1963, my wife who had a feeling that his name – Nilu – was wrong, suggested that we test this and we got a definite indication that it was the wrong name for him. At the Briarcliff Congress I asked Bapak about this. Bapak asked me where the name Nilu had come from. I replied that it came from out of my head. Bapak's look read, "H'm... bound to have been." He said that the name was very bad for the child and a day or two later he gave him the name Roosman. I wrote home informing them about the new name. By the time I returned, Roosman had already accepted the name and if anyone called him by his old name he would firmly point out that he was Roosman, not Nilu. His teachers and school friends too accepted the change without the questioning that I had expected. But what was most remarkable was how he seemed to have changed from a wild creature to a gentle and relatively responsible boy. He has by no means lost

*I forbear to mention the name because the man referred to is inordinately modest about his work, and besides, I feel that this is his story, not mine.

his zest for life and he still seems to be powered by some high octane fuel but the inner transformation is unmistakeable.

I used to dread that Bapak would give me my true name. But during one of the all-Saturday-night sessions at Tjilandak during a recent visit (March 1964), Bapak began speaking about names. He spoke about Selamat, the one surviving witness to Bapak's revelation. "Selamat knows his name is wrong. But he will NOT ask for his true name, he thinks he is safe," Bapak said. I knew, of course, that he was not talking about Selamat at all but about me. The old will still held out. But Prio who sat beside me and was also aware that Bapak was talking about me, said, "Bapak, Tarzie says the name Bapak gave to his son has already helped the boy. But Tarzie himself has never asked for his name." Bapak turned toward me and said in English: "Yes. Your right name with a V. Like Victory." This explained why Bapak had always called me Vitarzie. The next day Bapak gave me my Subud name – Varindra.

I remember Prio telling us one of Bapak's clarifications which possibly has a bearing on this dilemma of mine: We come to Subud because we are tired of the old house in which we have lived up to that time. The house is crumbling, unsafe, the roof is leaking, the floors are damp, it is badly ventilated and dark. So we want a new house. But we don't want the old house demolished. We would like the new house to be built on top of the old house, although neither the foundations nor the walls will stand the weight of the new structure. We want to hold on to both houses at the same time.

12

Postscript

THERE are more stories left at the bottom of the barrel. They have been left out of this book deliberately. Some stories are better told than written. Some stories have the peculiar characteristic of turning into their opposites as soon as they are set in print. Some others, I fear, might actually do some harm if they are stretched to suit someone's fancy or regarded as "authority" because they refer to conversations with Bapak or with some of the older helpers. Even the quotation marks I have used are intended more as a dramatic device to convey something of the tone, pace and colour of the conversation, rather than as indications of verbatim accuracy. Of course, I have had to rely on my memory and on scraps of notes made after the event. I am sure that there are as many shortcomings in this writing here as there are in any reporter's copy. Words are a notoriously imperfect means of communication.

I remember once, during the Suez crisis, asking my professional colleague Aubrey Collette what the word "world" connoted for him. He said: "I see long streets, tall buildings and people clad in overcoats. It's in black and white." The March of Time film series had possibly provided him with this picture of the World. I asked Sooty Banda what the word "world" meant to him. He stroked his beard with his right hand and made a "googly" bowler's movement with his left. "Globe," he said, and dismissed the subject. I asked Aubrey Walpola, another colleague who worked on the copy desk, what the word "world" conveyed to him. "Big map with large countries like Egypt marked on it," he said. He was handling Suez copy at the time.

I asked another the same question: What does the word "world" mean to you?

"Getting dressed in a clean white suit and sitting in a waiting room to be interviewed for a job," was his astonishing reply. Where in the world – there we go again – had he got this meaning? Probably he had been admonished at school "to study hard to be equipped to go out into the world and succeed," which meant, very simply, to get a good job.

All these were Subud members and all of them, especially as journalists, must have used the word "world" half a dozen times a day, when talking to one another, writing for the newspaper. Yet, there was a variety of connotations in their response to this common word. How then can we expect to communicate through words except very imperfectly?

Why then do I, or any of the others who have written of their Subud experiences, try to communicate in words at all? Perhaps, because we must. In Icksan's immortal epigram – It must out. It seems to me that this is the reason for Bapak's reply to the question when the first Subud books came out: "Why do people write about Subud experience?"

"Purification," said Bapak and did not stop for any supplementary questions.

I therefore ask for forgiveness for having inflicted my purification on you.

BOOK 3

A
MEMOIR
OF
SUBUD

CONTENTS

PREFACE

BAPAK often encouraged me to tell stories. He himself was the best storyteller I have ever known. He told stories to Ibu, to his children and grandchildren and to his sons and daughters in Subud. His stories illuminated the allegorical mysteries of the Ramayana and the holy books of West Asia, they opened our minds to new meanings of seemingly impenetrable assertions, and to the mysteries and events in our traditional lore, giving them a freshness and richness far beyond their literal value. Arjuna, Bima, the Pandavas, Ibrahim and Sarah, Abu Bakr and Ali took on palpable substance and character to which we, in our own life and time, could relate. Knotty symbols, which we had inherited from our ancestors and acknowledged as being important without necessarily understanding their significance, opened up like sunflowers yielding new colours and patterns.

But Bapak's stories and explanations never let us make the mistake of assuming that the new insights we had been given were exclusive of other and older meanings, however superficial and even 'wrong' they may have seemed to us. This taught me one of the most valuable lessons we need in order to understand the world: life is not about either/or but about and/and.

Bapak as storyteller was like a master diamond-cutter revealing hidden facets of the material he worked on, so that the value of the whole gem was enhanced and our appreciation was enriched. His stories never entrapped our minds in narrow dogma. Rather, they freed us from rigidity and from the stereotypes which divide us within and without and prevent true comprehension of reality.

Storytelling, he said, was a good way to convey truths without preaching or teaching. They served to calm the turbulence in our heads so that a fresh aspect of reality could be accepted without it adding to the turmoil in the mind. He advised me to give myself two inner 'tests' before I told a story. I was to ask myself; 'Does this story put me in front?' If it seemed likely to, it was clearly an ego trip which, rather than calming peoples' minds and communicating something of value, would only create distrust and hostility and enhance the turbulence. And, Bapak said, when I was about to tell a story, I should spread out my inner antennae (and he splayed the fingers of his right hand, directing them at an imaginary group) and sense whether it might cause offence to someone out there, either because it went against a deeply held prejudice which the listener wished to protect or because he or she was not then in a state to hear it, however 'true' and interesting it seemed to me.

Often, while telling a series of stories, I have been so caught up in them that I have failed to make this precautionary test or my antennae have been insufficiently sensitive so that I have wounded someone unintentionally. As for the first test, when I speak in front of Subud members I am really careful to say that nothing I am about to say has any authority whatever, but that I will only try to convey my own understanding of what I heard Bapak say. If anyone understands it differently, they are free to reject my version and say so without offending me in the slightest.

But speaking in front of an audience is always a perilous experience. Especially when people seem to like what is being said, the speaker is in danger. I have often felt my ego, even seen it inside my head, like a monstrous little lizard flicking its tongue out at me to taste the adulation it is receiving, puffing itself up in self-congratulation. When I become aware of this – it takes a while because the lizard and I are one – I look it straight in the eye and say, 'Drop dead, my friend', and it obliges. At any rate, for a while. I recall Bapak summoning Sudarto, Brodjo, Prio – the three musketeers of the Old Secretariat – and me to do a latihan in the early days of Cilandak (when we used to spell it Tjilandak). I had a shattering half hour. I 'saw' many ugly aspects of my nature which were very different from the perceptions I had about myself:

When the latihan was over I wanted to slink quietly away to my cubicle in the guest house, put my head under the pillow and die. I was making for the nearest door when I heard Bapak calling my name from the other end of the hall. As I approached, Bapak asked, 'Why are you frightened? You are very lucky to see yourself as you are. You see that Varindra is brave, but that Varindra is also a coward. You see that Varindra is honest, but also not honest. You see that Varindra likes the truth, but also tells lies. When you see yourself; you must look and not be frightened. If you are frightened and do not look, these bad things will hide in your heart and grow like toads under stones.' So I learned to look my lizard in the eye, to acknowledge its existence, so that it would not grow into a dinosaur.

Bapak's advice is in the front of my consciousness as I begin writing this third collection of Subud stories. The possibility that my egotism will rear its head in these words is all too real. And the possibility that some of these tales, or some feature in them, might offend a reader is even more real. All I can do is to ask for pardon ahead and try to be as true as I am capable of being, hoping that what is true for me might also be true for everyone.

Why do I write these stories at all? Obviously not for the usual reason: money. No-one ever made money in the Subud book market. In my mind there is a portrait of the Subud writer as a thin man. If one of us were able to communicate our assimilated Subud experience through the medium of a popular novel as John Bunyan, CS Lewis and Doris Lessing have done with their own spiritual experiences, we might. But no one has done so until now. I tell stories because I must. That is how I express myself; how I bring forth what is in me. In that sense it is a sort of latihan for me.

Bapak used to say that writing was my purification. You may well ask why I should inflict my purification on others, especially my brothers and sisters. What shall I say to that except that no one is obliged to turn this page over and go on reading as Georges Gurdjieff's Transcaucasian Kurd did when he went on eating the burning chilli peppers he had bought, thinking they were succulent fruit, and suffering because he was determined to get his money's worth. Besides, isn't it the fate of family members to have to cope constantly with one anothers' effluence?

Once when the month of Ramadan was over I went to bid goodbye to Bapak early in the morning. It had been a month of rich experience of ourselves. Bapak said (Muhammad Usman translating), 'Varindra, you have been through a long fast from which you have learned much. You will now be travelling in many countries and meeting Subud members. Tell them the story of this Ramadan.' As I often did when I was in Bapak's presence, I asked a stupid question. 'Bapak, what shall I tell them?' Bapak looked at me rather surprised it seemed to me, then smiled that familiar tolerant grin, and said, 'When you sit in front of them, be quiet. Then open your mouth and wait for Bapak."

That, brothers and sisters, is what I propose to do until this book is completed. I shall sit quietly and wait for Bapak. These stories are mostly from and about Bapak. I am humbled by this thought and I am aware that though writing is my business, the blocks and stones in my mind and in the channels of my memory will not let the stories flow as clear and true as they should. But I hope that I shall be able to convey something of the rich experience of more than 32 years in Subud. These are parables of and for our time. They are my way of understanding and remembering.

1
The training of a journalist

BAPAK sometimes used me as a butt to make a point obliquely for the benefit of everyone present.

He once asked, 'Varindra, what is the difference between you and an animal?' By then I had learned to sense when he expected a response and when he was asking a rhetorical question, so I kept my mouth shut. He went on (Prio Hartono translating), 'An animal is controlled by its instinct, by the rules within. A tiger will never eat vegetables. An elephant will never eat meat. That is because a tiger cannot eat vegetables and an elephant cannot eat meat. But you can decide for yourself whether and when you want to eat vegetables or meat, or neither, or both. It is up to you. This is God's gift to man. Man has freedom to choose between vegetables and meat, right and wrong, good and evil. But this freedom you have been given also means responsibility. You are responsible for the consequences of your freedom.'

Unfortunately, Bapak explained, the sub-human forces in our nature, to which we are in thrall at most times, obscure this human capacity to choose between right and wrong, so that we do not use this gift of freedom. Nor are we always conscious of the responsibility of choosing what is right rather than wrong. The latihan frees us gradually from the thraldom of the lower forces and trains us to become increasingly aware of our freedom to choose, and of our responsibility to choose the right course of behaviour and action. 'This,' Bapak added with a smile, 'is testing. Inner testing.' The smile, it occurred to me, signified Bapak's indulgent awareness of the possibility, indeed, likelihood, that we would grab at this phrase 'inner testing' to justify our propensity for doing what comes natcherly.

I was delighted by Bapak's description of the latihan as a way of attaining conscientious freedom. As a young journalist raised in colonial times to think British, and *be* British, I had been sent for what was called 'training' in Fleet Street. For a short spell I was 'trained' at *The Times*. The acting editor, Donald Tyerman (who later edited *The Economist*) sent me to Mr Robbins, the new editor, and Mr Deakin (they were never referred to by their first names according to the mores of *The Times*), the foreign news editor. 'They have seventy years of experience between them,' he told me. I learned absolutely no journalism at *The Times* but I learned what it was to be an English gentleman. From there I was sent to Lord Beaverbrook's *Daily Express* and the *Evening Standard* where I learned all the journalistic skills I ever knew and forgot how to be an English gentleman. In that process I absorbed a skinful of spurious self-serving values.

The most self-serving of them, largely because it seemed beguilingly self-evident and therefore apparently true, was the 'freedom of the press.' I was guiltily aware even at the time that this freedom was limited at the *Express* by an uncanny and pervasive tendency among my colleagues to pander to the Beaver's pet prejudices. His Lordship had some curious hatreds. Louis Mountbatten was one of them. Noel Coward was another. The British Council still another. It seemed we were not allowed to refer to the Commonwealth. His Lordship, a colonial himself out of Canada, preferred the good old-fashioned 'Empire'.

One afternoon a messenger from upstairs arrived at the picture desk where I was training to select and crop photographs for publication, and announced that His Lordship wished to see me. My colleagues gave me a long sad look which, I later learned, signified that I was tagged for instant dismissal. I entered a huge room and approached a huge desk behind which appeared a large head on a little man to whom I was introduced by a man called Robertson who was, I was told, His Lordship's managing director.

'How is Nehru treating little Ceylon?' was Lord Beaverbrook's opening gambit. I gawped and spluttered, 'What do you mean, Sir?' 'Well? How badly is he bullying your country?' the Beaver asked. I said that Jawaharlal Nehru was not bullying us at all and that, on the contrary, he was very fond of our little island and its people.

'Do you think he'll feel upstaged if we sent the Duke of Windsor to be your Governor General?' was the next dramatic move.

I said I didn't think so but, my sense of patriotism bristling a bit, I wondered aloud about Dudley Senanayake, our young Prime Minister's reaction to the idea since he was not likely to take kindly to our country being used as a dumping ground for banished members of the British royal family. 'Dumping ground? Dumping ground!' his Lordship exclaimed and Mr Robertson intervened to say that all this was off the record and hurried me out of the room. I had learnt that Nehru, because of his friendship with Mountbatten, was another limitation to the freedom of the press in the *Daily Express*.

But this was only one aspect of the real nature of press freedom. My training gave me many useful professional skills and also bred in me an intense loathing of any form of imposed censorship, characteristics of permanent benefit to me. But it also turned my mind away from any attention to the other side of the coin of press freedom: responsibility. The only responsibility my colleagues and I acknowledged was to stay clear of the laws of libel, contempt of court and Parliament – not because they embodied important social values, but because it was expensive to violate them.

And, now Bapak had solved that conundrum for me. Freedom and responsibility were not opposed to one another but apposed aspects of the same value. One had no meaning without the other. In fact, they were the same thing. I realized at that moment that this recognition was the fountainhead of human morality, the source of the wisdom essential to social progress. Without it, all human activity – political, military, cultural or commercial – was determined by sub-human forces 'free' from responsibility. But my mind whose perpetual questing caused enormous amusement among my Indonesian brothers – like Icksan Achmed, Shafruddin Achmed, Pak Sudarto and, even more, the intellectual, Prio Hartono – had produced another clever problem out of Bapak's explanation.

'But aren't right and wrong different in different times and places?' I asked. Bapak gave me that long-suffering gaze which he had bestowed on me often since the early days of Coombe Springs when I had first displayed my Doubting Thomas traits.

'God's will does not depend on time and place,' he said softly. 'It is man's will that is changeable. Man's will is influenced by the *nafsu* which change according to changes in the material world. The latihan is a training given by God to help us distinguish God's will from that of the lower forces.'

I began to see the meaning of 'Thy will be done'. When we prayed and beseeched God to do this or that for us, all of us most of the time, and most of us all of the time, were petitioning for *our* will to be granted. What we were saying, in effect, is 'God, Thy will be done, but please let it accord with mine.' It became clear to me that human freedom lay in the willingness to see and accept God's will. God's will was responsible choice. Our will was the freedom of the wild ass to kick up its heels. Wilfulness.

As I grew older and saw how my profession was being practised in

Asia, Europe, Africa, Latin America and the United States I became more
and more concerned with our preoccupation with our right to enjoy that
sort of unbridled freedom and ignore other people's freedoms. Two of
those that interested me as a journalist were the right to privacy and the
right of Africans and Arabs and Asians to be reported as they saw themselves, rather than as stereotypes viewed through lenses pre-set by centuries of imperialism when colonial people were looked upon as 'lesser
breeds without the law' – exotic, quaint but, alas, quite malformed,
uncivilised and uncouth. Prospero had thought of Caliban, the early pro-
totype of the colonial 'savage', in these terms:

> *Abhorred slave,*
> *Which any print of goodness wilt not take,*
> *Being capable of all ill! I pitied thee,*
> *Took pains to make thee speak, taught thee each hour*
> *One thing or other: when thou didst not, savage,*
> *Know thine own meaning, but would gabble like*
> *A thing most brutish.*

There are more recent examples of this lofty imperial attitude. Henry
M Stanley of the *New York Tribune* had been sent on a circulation-raising
gimmick to look for Dr Livingstone in the jungles of Nyasaland (now
Tanzania). Having 'found' the old man – who, evidently was quite resentful at being found – Stanley won fame as a great explorer and empire
builder. On his way back to New York he was invited to address the
Manchester Chamber of Commerce. In that extraordinary speech this
paragraph stands out, embossed in my memory as a classic example of
stereotyping the 'other', the stranger:

> *'There are fifty millions of people beyond the Gateway to the Congo, and*
> *the cotton spinners of Manchester are waiting to clothe them. Birmingham*
> *foundries are glowing with the red metal that will presently be made into*
> *ironwork for them and the trinkets that shall adorn these dusky bosoms,*
> *and the Ministers of Christ are zealous to bring them, the poor benighted*
> *heathen, into the Christian fold.'*

There you have it: the people of Africa seen from a zoological viewpoint – primitive millions waiting passively for the boons of the Empire
to drop from above to redeem them from barbarism. As far as we know,

they, were the first to evolve from the Ape to Man but, evidently, they had no history of their own, no civilisation, no redeeming qualities to distinguish them from the animals of the Serengeti plains. It made a better story for the readers of the *Tribune*, for the industrialists of Lancashire and for the missionaries who, from the time the Imperial age began, had deracinated Jesus in their minds and recast him in the mould of a blonde European come to save the heathen Chinee and other assorted non-Christians from eternal perdition.

Victor Hugo, sitting on the pier at the port of Oran in Algeria wrote about a big crate he saw being unloaded. It contained a guillotine imported from France. 'Civilisation has arrived at last,' he reported ecstatically.

The scales were falling rapidly from my Fleet Street trained eyes. The latihan was making me increasingly willing to drop the stereotypes in my own head which had narrowed my view of the world and distorted reality for many years. The freedom of the press that I had advocated and defended vehemently now seemed meretricious and even dangerous unless it was modulated by the recognition of other people's rights and by the obligation of the journalist to be responsible.

As this change came about I realized that many old shibboleths were still present in my mind and I asked myself ruefully – as, Ogden Nash had done:

Am I just maturing late,
Or, simply, rotting early?

Often I asked myself how this sense of responsibility was manifesting itself in others in Subud. I saw many instances of irresponsibility among brothers and sisters – as they, no doubt, saw in me – irresponsibility towards their families, towards others in Subud, towards society as a whole, and towards themselves. The freedom which we had been let out into when we joined Subud often went to our heads. Some of us even left our jobs without securing any alternative means of sustenance for ourselves or our families. Some seemed to cancel their precious responsibilities when they acquired a Subud name on the grounds that they were now 'different' people. Some of us had already experienced the changes in us which the practice of the latihan had wrought – changes particularly in attitude, habits, points of view, in value scales, judgements we made – even in our physical behaviour.

But, if we were being honest with ourselves, we also recognized that 'progress' was not a steady movement forward, that we often lapsed into the old habitual modes, and that there were many faults so deeply embedded in our character that they were persistent and difficult to eradicate. In my case I could recognize the Varindra in me co-existing uneasily with the old durable Tarzie. I learned gradually that this 'twin-effect' was a reality and that it would take a long time – perhaps a lifetime – for me to grow into Varindra, if I ever did. I also learned over the years that Tarzie was the journalist whom my colleagues in the press knew and with whom they felt comfortable because he was familiar to them. So I called myself Varindra Tarzie Vittachi as my byline as a *Newsweek* columnist because both aspects were present in my writing. I could only hope that the first would become increasingly predominant in my work, making it more responsible and therefore more worthwhile. There were times when I doubted that this was happening but there were also occasions when there was encouraging proof of the effects of the latihan.

A particular incident of this proof stands out in my mind. The editor of *Newsweek International* called me one morning and said he wanted to have lunch with me that very day. He had cancelled a date he had for lunch and urged me to put off anything I had on my calendar. I asked, 'What's up Bob? Am I being fired?' He said no, not at all. On the contrary. At lunch he opened with an interesting question. 'In response to our columns we usually receive seven or eight letters from our readers. You scarcely write about anything that is topical. But we have been getting more than 20 letters for nearly all your columns. Your last piece on your meeting with Mahatma Gandhi in 1946 – I can't imagine anything less topical than that – has brought in several hundred letters. Can you explain why? What do you think?'

I thought for a while and said, 'Bob, I don't suppose it is because my columns are better than anyone else's. Perhaps you have already given the answer. Isn't it possible that there are thousands of people out there who are sick and tired of the tyranny of topicality? They may be looking for something they can reflect on. Could that be the answer?'

I tell this story not as a piece of self-puffery but as an illustration of how the latihan changes the very nature of our activity, whatever innate talent we have, to more humane purposes than they were being put to before. The Fleet-Street-trained Sri Lankan journalist who had specialised in the breathless ephemera of life that consumed his professional energies had been 'trained' from within to interest himself in subjects of more durable value and be able to interest others in something more valuable than the day's topical news.

Fleet Street gave me an outer training in the craft of journalism. I am grateful to Subud for the inner training the latihan has given me. It has shown me how to concern myself more with the responsibility of being a journalist and with eternal human values than with my rights as a journalist and with the daily trivia of the passing scene that vanishes from our awareness like soap bubbles in a gale.

2

New cages for old

THE liberating force of the latihan has been a consistent underlying theme of Bapak's explanations and stories. His insistence on the importance of Subud enterprises was clearly motivated by his wish that Subud members as individuals and people responsible for the raising of families, as well as the Subud brotherhood as an organisation, should be free of the importunate pressures of money and other material needs. He accepted the reality that most Subud members were salary earners with the same indulgence with which he accepted our sins against ourselves and against one another, but he always urged us to use what entrepreneurial talents we had, to become free of dependency on a salary, through enterprises.

Several times he asked me, 'Varindra, are you not sad to see your brothers and sisters living poor lives – earning inadequate salaries or having no work at all? Bapak is sad when he sees this. That is why Bapak urges enterprises. Subud members should not be so dependent. Subud should be able to research and develop Subud medicine, to have Subud teachers in schools who can educate children for life guided by Subud principles. For this Subud enterprises are necessary.'

Behind the vision of the future 'products' of enterprises was the principle of increasing freedom from material dependency. When Bapak first advised me to observe the Ramadan fast he explained that one of its main purposes was to help me recognize the extent of my dependency on certain habitual appetites. Recognition of these would help to free myself of excessive, earthly influences that control all of our lives.

I recall Bapak's reply when in the first week after I received the latihan at Coombe Springs in 1957, I asked what Subud was about. Bapak's eyes took on that amused glint as he said, 'Are you sitting in that chair or is that chair sitting on you?' When I looked befuddled Bapak went on, 'Are you smoking that cigarette or is it smoking you?' Then I understood. I wasn't enjoying the cigarette. It had habituated me to its demands of being lit and smoked.

Freedom from habit was only one aspect of the process of liberation. Bapak once pointed to a small rock and observed that it couldn't move left or right, or up or down, or roll over. Many 'laws', Bapak said, controlled its existence. Plants were controlled by fewer 'laws'. They could at least wave about and grow. Animals, by still fewer laws. They could move in one place, turn about in a circle as dogs do, climb and move around. They were more free. Human beings should be the freest from control by earthly laws because they had the capacity to choose and even to be aware of choosing. They are controlled by fewer material laws. But, alas, Bapak said, with that glint growing into a smile, they make thousands of laws of their own, to bind themselves. And, he added, they spend much of the time breaking the laws they themselves made! They have even made a special class of people called 'birocrats' (this, with a quick glance at an Indonesian brother from the Bank of Indonesia) whose business is to say 'NO'. If they said 'yes' they'd have no job!

We all broke into laughter but understood that Bapak was not encouraging us to break the law. He was commenting on the absurdly complex social mechanisms in which we have entrapped ourselves to limit human freedom, contrary to our claim of being human beings progressing to perfection along an evolutionary path.

Freedom and the promise of increasing freedom was what first encouraged me to persist in the latihan. I imagine it was the same with many other Subud members. We had escaped from the restrictive bonds of doctrine, dogma and the repetitive ritual of our own traditions and welcomed a way of worship which had no strings to it. 'You can even say no to God in the middle of the latihan and leave the room and you will not be struck by lightning,' Bapak told us in Colombo (Icksan Ahmed interpreting).

This, I told myself, was what freedom of worship should mean. Worship that increases human freedom.

But some of us, it appeared over the years, wanted Bapak to give us new rules to regulate our lives and relationships. To these demands Bapak's frequent reaction was that all the teaching and regulations – the commandments – we needed had already been spelled out by the founders of the great religions. In the case of Islam they were to be found in the *shariat* and the *tarekat*. What we received in the Subud latihan was the *hakekat*, the receiving necessary for each one of us.

During the third international congress held in Tokyo in 1967 a very prominent and vocal delegate popped up several times insisting that I, as chairman, should appoint a sub-committee to record what he called the Guiding Principles that were being enunciated by Bapak in his explanatory interventions. Knowing this member's military background and his liking for regulations, I deflected his persistence by not hearing him or by giving the floor to someone else. But, after a while, I began wondering whether he might be right after all: whether, since Bapak was indeed our spiritual guide, there might be some purpose in producing a guide book of principles gleaned from his statements. So I adjourned the meeting for half an hour and went to Bapak's quarters to seek his advice.

'Bapak,' I said, 'Mr X has been proposing several times that I should appoint a committee to prepare a record of Guiding Principles from Bapak's explanations. What is Bapak's opinion?' Bapak's reply was (Pak Usman translating), 'Guiding Principles? *Allahu Akbar*. That is the Guiding Principle. Not rules on paper.' I was leaving the room to transmit this gem of an explanation when Bapak called out to me and said (in English), 'Varindra . . . be clever!'

When the meeting restarted, my persistent Subud brother stood up and asked, 'Varindra, are you serious or not about the need for a record of Guiding Principles?' My reply was, 'My dear brother, your proposal is such a serious matter that as chairman I charge you with carrying out this task with the help of any others who are as concerned as you are about Guiding Principles.'

A titter, as the saying goes, ran around the house. As it happened, nothing ever came of the proposal because the mover himself got the message and lost all interest in the idea. And the brotherhood was spared a new Manual of Discipline to supersede the one produced by the ancient Essenes. Allah indeed works in mysterious ways.*

On a later occasion, a delegation of helpers from a European country visiting Cilandak to observe Ramadan decided to improve the shining hour by asking Bapak whether they should codify 'Subud Rules' for the benefit of future generations in Subud. Bapak took this in and was silent for a full minute as though he had decided to let that one go unanswered. Then he turned towards me and Pak Usman who had come on some other business and asked, 'Varindra, how high is the floor on which you live in New York?' I said 22nd. Bapak asked 'Can the windows be opened?' I said they could. Bapak went on, 'Varindra's wife. Lestari. opens the window and looks out. Varindra looks over his newspaper and says to himself; "Hmm, Lestari is at the open window. Interesting!" And he returns his attention to his newspaper. His eldest son, who is nineteen,

*John Bennett, another who deplored the 'indiscipline' which he detected among his pupils who had come with Subud, had done this in the back of the book of the first international congress.

looks out of the window. Varindra looks over his newspaper and says, "Roosman, better be careful." His youngest son, aged eight goes to the window. Varindra says in a sharp voice, "Imran you must never again go to the open window."' Then Bapak turned to the delegation and said, 'Rules are for children.'

But we were children who felt insecure without a railing of rules to hold on to, though – as children do – we often resented being regulated. We would often take the advice and explanations given to us and harden them into unintended rigidity and, in the process, distort Bapak's meaning. This tendency was sometimes abetted by poor – even wrong – English translations from the Indonesian. I came across a classic instance of this in the United States several years ago. Walking into the latihan hall at a sizeable centre I found three or four men huddling among the boots and the coats in the narrow anteroom. I wondered what they were up to but decided that it was none of my business how people got their kicks. Leaving the room after the latihan I saw they were still there, but now with their ears intently pressed against the partition abutting the wall. My curiosity got the better of me and I asked the helpers what all that was about. They enlightened me. It seemed that Bapak had proclaimed 'a new rule' that candidate members should 'hear' the latihan being done during their three-month probation.

I said nothing but on my next visit to Jakarta I told Bapak about these extraordinary goings-on. Bapak looked very amused by my story and turned to Usman with a look of bewilderment. Usman recalled that during Bapak's last visit to America Bapak had explained the importance of candidates getting to 'hear about' the Subud latihan so that by the time they came to their opening they would know that it was not meditation or any other form of 'training'. I realized that 'hear about the latihan' had been turned into 'hear the latihan'.

I was greatly relieved to learn this because one of the most appealing features of Bapak's explanations had always been their clear common sense. I asked Bapak what should be done to correct this mistake – whether he would make a statement in *Subud News*. Bapak said it would be better to leave it alone. The practice was not likely to spread, he said with a chuckle, because people would realize that the number of candidates at the beginning of the probationary period and the number listening at the wall at the end would sharply differ. Boots and socks, Bapak observed, don't smell too good!

As a journalist and long-time student of political theory and practice I was frequently astonished and always fascinated by Bapak's advice on regulations and organisation in Subud. He constantly reminded us that the latihan, the essence of Subud, could not be organised. But, since everything and everybody has an outer as well as an inner dimension, some organisation and 'administration' was necessary. This principle was enunciated clearly at the first world congress, 'All matters of administration are to be regarded as a service to facilitate the spread and orderly development of Subud throughout the world.' Bapak emphasised that 'in Subud, administration is based not on authority but on consent, because the orderly development of Subud is the concern of all Subud members.'

Those were the first glimmerings of what Bapak later called 'Subud social democracy'. The lesson was clear: organisation was a service, subservient to the purpose of Subud, its form and action deriving legitimacy from the consent of men and women practising the latihan. Organisation was for Subud members, not for the organisers. Organisation, he told me many times, was necessary but it should be kept to the minimum needed for good order. Like William Blake did, Bapak reminded us that freedom without order is meaningless chaos, but freedom restrained by regulations and bureaucratic rigidities devised for the sake of 'order' is nothing but slavery, depriving human beings of their essential faculty to choose and the 'space' in which to grow.

> *A robin redbreast in a cage*
> *Puts all heaven in a rage*

This was a renewed clarification of the ancient question of the opposition between individual freedom and social order. And Bapak resolved it by pointing out that freedom and order were not opposed but apposed aspects of responsible behaviour, the responsibility arising from the inner guidance of the latihan. Not one of us in Subud, whether we were called chairman or helper, whether we were in a committee or a *dewan*, had any authority over any other member. But we had responsibilities. The political challenge to us was how to carry out our responsibility without authority. Referring to the functions of the chairman at the Wolfsburg congress Bapak said, 'You must not say that it is Varindra who holds the authority or that the people who hold the authority are the helpers' *dewan* or the organisation. No; the one who holds the authority is Bapak.' And he went on to explain that he was only the conduit for the authority of God.

This advice shone through as a new vision of the political function of office holders. but, like all eternal verities, it was a restatement of a very old truth which has been crucial to the growth and spread of all spiritual movements in history. The Sabbath is for Man, not Man for the Sabbath.

3
Holier than thou

ANOTHER tendency similar to our penchant for rules became evident as time passed. Some of us wanted to carry over not only the rules we were raised on – even though most of the time they had been observed in the breach – but also the rituals and practices which seemed appropriate to 'spiritual' behaviour. For instance, the ancient practice of saying grace before meals was widely adopted and adapted as proper Subud conduct. The meaning of saying grace of course is to express conscious gratitude for the food about to be eaten and for the opportunity given to share it with others; the moment of silence was a good and simple reminder of this obligation. Especially in a world of fast food and stand-up meals it was salutary to give ourselves a break in breathlessness.

But some of us overdid it, insisting on observing the practice even when having a meal with people outside Subud who were not accustomed to saying grace. While the others were helping themselves to the food we would close our eyes and go into our silence routine causing the adults around the table to draw back in embarrassment and the children to go into a fit of ill-suppressed giggles. It took us a while to understand that it was plain bad manners to make other people feel ill at ease and attract attention to ourselves as a breed apart. It took us even longer to understand that it was possible to observe the silence with our eyes open and without making a scene while leaving others to go about their business in their own way.

Some of us stretched the eyes-closed silence longer and longer on the principle that the longer the grace the holier it was. When I laughingly told Bapak that I had spent as much as five minutes on this pre-prandial ritual at a meal with a certain group Bapak's laconic response was, 'Cooked food is better eaten hot.'

One of Bapak's most earnest pleas to us was *'Biasa, biasa'*. Be normal. Be normal. One evening during Bapak's birthday a Subud member from Sri Lanka waited in line observing the others kneeling to place their hands on Bapak's knee in the customary Javanese way of *sunkum*. Our friend thought he'd do a bit of Subudmanship and fell flat on the floor, picked up Bapak's foot and placed it on his own head. Bapak looked mortified in embarrassment but only said '*biasa, biasa*'.

The lesson was simple and clear. We all have ways of expressing our feelings of love, devotion, loyalty, respect and reverence. Some of us, trained in the best British public school tradition of not wearing our hearts on our sleeves (though it is OK to wear our spleens on our sleeves) are awkward and afraid to show such feelings and will not go beyond a stiff-necked bow or a firm man-to-man handshake when expressing gratitude or respect. As a well-brought-up colonial I too was at first squeamish about showing Bapak the profoundness of my gratitude and love for him for bringing us the ability to feel God's grace in our bones. But that passed with years of emotional decalcification brought about by the latihan. Don't we all remember how Bapak, in those mass testing sessions would ask us to cry and laugh from the depths of our being?

On one occasion when Bapak asked me to test my feelings about a question I had taken to him, the emotional dams, put up in me by my education and training, burst and I wept uncontrollably for possibly five full minutes. And, when it abated, I felt cleansed but, out of the latihan, I felt shame at my display of 'weakness'. Bapak noticed my wet grin of embarrassment and explained (Prio Hartono translating) that it was kosher for a man to cry and show his feelings. He said that what was bad was to suppress the feelings in us. Just as the physical body must evacuate its residues through defecation, urination and sweat to be healthy, the emotional residues in us too should be evacuated through laughter and tears. The mind which amasses enormous quantities of rubbish is evacuated by everyday dreams. The latihan, Bapak said laughingly, is therefore 'a sort of laxative', a process of intensive purification. It was normal.

Excessive public shows of feeling, however, were offensive, I realized, to ourselves as well as to others observing *because* they were excessive, not 'normal'. It was plain to all except the actors that they were not purificatory but histrionic displays intended to draw public attention and lay claim to being special. It is the old pharisaical fallacy that being the first to fall on one's knees in the congregation at the temple, and the last to rise, was proof of a special relationship with the Almighty.

I recall with great amusement how a group of Subud brothers in England once decided to adopt the Indonesian *petchi* – the black cap that Bapak, as a Javanese, wore – as *their* 'normal' headwear. Bapak was arriving in London from the United States. They chartered a small bus to go to Heathrow, *en masse*, to welcome Bapak as he came through the customs doors – a guard of honour of *petchi* wearers, distinctive from the common

or garden Subud members around who were mostly hatless. The amusement of the welcoming crowd at this special devotion turned to loud
laughter when Bapak appeared around the corner wearing a new fedora
he had bought in America, which he wore with the insouciant rakishness
of Cary Grant. The *petchis* soon went out of fashion. The *petchi* pack
became hatless according to current norms of young men and women.

The leader of these *petchi* wearers used to play another game of
Subudmanship to impress others. Whenever someone had returned from
a visit to Cilandak or from a meeting with Bapak, he would take the
trouble to go to the group where the man was doing his first latihan following his trip. Since I was the most frequent visitor to Cilandak in those
days I was often the target of his attention. Bapak had advised me to
avoid 'belonging' to any particular Subud group as long as I was international chairman so that I would not be embroiled in the parochial politics, (thus saving my energies, presumably, to deal with international politics!) So I used to go from group to group in London to do my latihan.
But our friend exercised some curious ESP and always managed to turn
up at the group I had picked. Soon after the latihan began he would cross
the room and stand in front of me making hand gestures of collecting the
spiritual sustenance he imagined I had brought with me from my journey. When he felt he had amassed enough to go round, he would move to
the next member, stand in front of him and make the reverse gestures of
doling out the goodies he had collected.

This bothered me at first since his standing before me disturbed my
latihan but my annoyance soon turned to amusement and I said and did
nothing about what I thought was a harmless piece of spiritual buffoon-
ery. But one evening when he tried to deliver his goodies to Philip
Bentin he found himself grabbed by his necktie and taken outside. The
scuffle made me open my eyes and seeing what was happening, I moved
out to prevent any untoward damage. I heard Philip, still hanging on to
the tie, saying in impeccable Etonian tones. 'Dear brother. I have a lousy
latihan. But it is mine. I like my own latihan the way it is. The next time
you bother me or anyone else in our group I will send those teeth
through your throat. Got that?' The poor fellow pleaded that he was only
doing his own latihan, that was how his own latihan was, he explained.
But, *mirabile dictu*, his latihan changed at once and there was no more collection and distribution done. Tough treatment for a spiritual brotherhood, we may say. But whoever said that we must be milktoasts in
Subud?

At about the same time a helper in New York had developed an extraordinary form of latihan. He would go from one to another in the latihan and make a grab at people's testicles. The grunt which followed each grab evidently satisfied his need and he would go on to the next man. There seemed to be nothing homosexual about this. The guy was only indulging in some schoolboyish 'spiritual' prank. When this treatment was given to me at a helpers' latihan and I protested, another helper, a gentle giant of a man who earned his living as a greengrocer, picked up my attacker by his collar and the seat of his pants, carried him out – I following fast – and held his head over the railing at the stair well, six floors deep saying, 'The next time you put your hands on anybody when I'm around, that's where you go in a hurry, OK?' Once again the man's latihan changed fast.

When I related this to Bapak he responded with laughter and commented, 'Direct action is sometimes necessary.' But I am sure Bapak wasn't recommending such shock treatment as model behaviour for Subud helpers.

Excessive 'spiritualness' is a great temptation it seems. Some of us became holy soon after we were opened. We became so spiritual that we could not bear to go to the supermarket or read a newspaper or a novel and we would sigh like a furnace at the very thought of it. The world was so heavy and materialistic that our hypersensitive souls could not take it. Some of us even wanted Bapak to ban Subud members from reading anything except 'approved Subud literature' which meant Bapak's talks only. Bapak, of course, let that pass by very skilfully like a cricketer raising his bat deftly to let a ball delivered outside the off-stump pass without offering a stroke – a great lesson which I found invaluable as a diplomat and as chairman of the World Subud Council.

When we became helpers we were most in danger of becoming victims of this hyper-spiritual syndrome. That, I suppose, is why when I asked Bapak when a Subud member was ready to be a helper, he said, 'When he or she does not want to.' Becoming a helper *without* being able to sincerely understand that it is not a special status in a hierarchy, but a function that most of us could perform, if we had to, puts us in a dangerous situation because the ego can take hold of it and turn it into a power-trip. In the same way some people elected to serve others in political office soon turn it into a means of self-aggrandisement.

One of the most dire results of this tendency in Subud was that when a term of service as helper or committee person ran out, the holder of that office felt a sense of unbearable emptiness when what the Indonesians call *djumuneng* – the subtle gift with which the holder of a function in Subud is empowered – is taken away, the void is filled not by the spirit of service but by the ego. It was hard for us to realize that the gift is a temporary loan needed for a particular task and not a permanent grant of special powers. A feeling of worthlessness, sometimes amounting to resentful paranoia about imagined slights, fills the empty houses of the heart and mind. So those who experienced the loss often stopped doing the latihan and left Subud. This is what I call the chairman's syndrome. A count of the number of our brothers and sisters who once held prominent office but are no longer in Subud is quite staggering and saddening.

Bapak took pains to explain that in Subud there was no vertical hierarchy, that a group helper – who dealt with the needs of the 'grass-roots' where members did their latihan and lived their daily lives – was by no means a lesser mortal than those who served at the regional, national or international levels, a horizontal series of temporary functions. But though we understood the wisdom of that explanation it was difficult to keep it in the forefront of our consciousness and to practise it in a world organised in vertical structural hierarchies of grades, ranks and special powers reinforced by systems of privileges, rewards and punishments. Priestcraft, alas, was all too often only a short ego-trip away from Subud office.

This caused many difficulties for Subud members, some even staying away for short or long periods from groups. Occasionally the spiritual pretensions of office holders were taken to such extremes and became so obviously nonsensical that they produced great hilarity. A memorable instance of this was offered by an international helper who proposed that no meeting of the International Subud Committee should be held without a full complement of international helpers. It was a great idea, I suggested, but was it practical in view of the shortage of money for international travel? Undaunted, the helper asked whether I did not understand that money should not prevent the decisions of the committee from receiving the special benefit of the presence of international helpers. 'Don't you know, Varindra, that a group helper has one angel on his shoulder, a regional helper two, a national helper three and an international helper four angels on their shoulders?' the helper insisted. He said that material considerations should not be the decisive factor and generously offered to pay for his own fare and that of another. I have a better idea, I said, 'You pay the airfare of all the helpers and I'll pay the fares of the angels.' The Subud brother concerned found my counter proposal as hilarious as the others did and joined in the laughter.

When I told this story to Bapak he referred to it in a talk in New York and asked us to test. 'What is the size of an angel?' and concluded that it might be a bit difficult for a mortal shoulder to carry even a single angel. Some were as big as a Himalayan mountain. I fervently hope that my repeating this story will not offend my brother, the former international helper, for I am aware of his sincerity and indefatigable services to Subud even after he ceased to hold office. I tell the story only because it illustrates the importance of taking Subud functions seriously but not ourselves.

I recall, with some sensation of goose-bumps, the look in Bapak's face when he asked me whether a certain helper from Indonesia had appointed 'special helpers' during a visit to Sri Lanka. Detecting the displeasure in Bapak's tone I promptly became counsel for the defence. Those were the days when I was naive enough to imagine that Bapak could not see through into my mind. I said, 'Not exactly, Bapak. He gave special functions to certain helpers.' Bapak asked, 'Like what?' I said that one was told that his and his wife's speciality was to give explanations, another couple were to do latihan with people who complained they were not feeling it, and another couple was to do latihan with the sick, and so on. Very sternly Bapak said (Anwar Zakir translating), 'You go home and tell the group: no special helpers. No special duties. They are all the same.' I said, 'Please, Bapak, they will not believe me because it was an Indonesian helper and he acted as if he had Bapak's authority. It is better that Bapak should write to the group.' Bapak said he would do so immediately and I could carry the letter home. I replied that I wanted no part of this affair and that it was best for Bapak himself to mail the letter. Bapak relaxed the sternness on his face and smiled understandingly as if to say 'People will be people.' And so it was done.

A few days after I returned home the letter arrived and the helpers concerned came to my home to ask if I knew anything about this or could offer any explanation of this turn of events as they knew I had met Bapak in Singapore a few days before. I pleaded ignorance and I was believed because I too had been 'appointed' to one of those special assignments which I had just lost. I said that the lesson for all of us seemed to be that no helper should be given any 'special' hierarchical status.

It was not easy for some of these brothers and sisters to understand why we had been 'demoted' as one of them expressed it, because that was

the time when we all thought that Indonesian helpers were adepts, especially those who seemed to be 'close to Bapak'. It took us a long while
more to realize that it was not possible for anyone to be 'close' to the
inner Bapak – though his family and the older Indonesians who had been
around with him at Semarang where he received the Subud contact, at
Jogjakarta during the early days of Subud and in Jakarta at his old bungalow in Jalan Java – were certainly 'close' to the physical Bapak. He
himself always said he was an 'ordinary man' whose hand would burn like
yours and mine if he put it in the fire.

That was also the time when there was a great deal of talk in Coombe
Springs, which was then the centre of Subud activity outside Java, about
'real helpers'. A mystique had already spread across the small Subud
world about these real helpers. It was evidently a special category to
which all of us could aspire but only a few could attain. That was why
Bapak took extraordinary pains, it seemed to me, to remind us over and
over again that people appointed as helpers were but 'assistant helpers'
charged with a few necessary functions such as opening those who wished
to receive the Subud contact, giving explanations to those who needed
them, not from theology and theory but from our own experience.

Here is what Bapak said about this at the first international congress
held at Coombe Springs: '. . . You should in no way feel yourself to be the
leader of a group of people exercising, but . . . you should simply do your
own exercise (latihan) together with them. You have the duty of watching to see that there are no collisions and that no one goes out of the
room while still doing the exercise, and that is all. The reason why the
assistant helpers should not feel themselves to be leaders when they carry
out their duties is that if they do, both they themselves and the people
with whom they are exercising will lose the benefits of the exercise.'

In spite of all such injunctions and explanations the myth of special
powers for special people persisted. This wish to assume spiritual distinction decreased in intensity as the years passed because those who held on
to the myth of specialness became less and less credible through their
own excessive claims to be distinctive and often through the evidence of
their own failure to follow in their own lives the advice they gave to others.

But one still comes across the jaunty halo being sported by some who
do not realize the simple truth that if I wear a sombrero – or halo – too
big for my head it will tip over my head and prevent me seeing at all.
This, I suppose, is why Ibu Rahayu – Bapak's older daughter – recently

told the international helpers, 'If you feel God's power, you are nothing . . . you just feel very small . . . The difficulty is how you have to be a helper. Do not pretend that you have helped them. Always pray for guidance so you will not feel proud.'

In a world in which obtaining a status, reaching a higher rung on the ladder of success, being special, outstanding and 'goal oriented' are prime values, the temptation to reach out even to the point of excess is common; it is not easy to 'feel very small'. We cannot learn to feel small when our entire education and upbringing has been geared to competition, ambition and 'upward mobility'. We can pretend to feel small like the famous Rishi who was known far and wide for his humility. People came over hill and dale to offer *darshan* – to gaze upon this humble man. One day a visitor took a look at him and was departing, when the Rishi called out to him, 'Leaving already?' Yes the visitor said, I have gazed at you and now I am leaving. 'But,' asked the Rishi, 'you are leaving without saying a word about my humility?' The Rishi, evidently, was very proud of his humility.

But over the years I came gradually to realize that there is no way to feel humble except by being humble. As Ibu Rahayu suggests, it is only by feeling the greatness of God that we can be small, and that without this power we can do nothing.

The most difficult thing for a helper, I found, is to say 'I don't know'. All of us, as parents, have encountered this problem in our homes. Children expect us to have the answers because we behave as though we do when telling them what to do and what not to do. It took me a long time to realize that it is much better for my children as well as myself to admit ignorance when asked a question about something I do not know or know very little. It was good to be able to say, 'I don't know. Let us find out,' and try to find the answer in a book of reference or by calling someone who might know. This is the way to learn together with those who seek our help.

Another way to deal with a question which baffled one or could not be resolved in testing was to make a joke of it so that it put the mind at rest. Once the group then exercising in Oxford, wrote telling me about a curious problem they were having. At the end of the latihan they found that the shoes they had placed under their chairs around the hall had been switched around by some mysterious process. It was happening often and they had got themselves in a tizzy about it. I told them to congratulate themselves on finding proof of the ancient theory of the transmigration of soles. Evidently this reply satisfied them all – including the man who had played the prank – for I heard no more about it.

4

Of teachers and teaching

THE one 'sin' in Subud is teaching. When Bapak first went to England in 1957 to stay at Coombe Springs, where John Bennett had established an institute for teaching the harmonious development of man, he was hailed and described as a teacher. Mr B, as he was affectionately and respectfully called by everyone, was himself a teacher of the Fourth Way, the system of self-knowledge taught by Georges Gurdjieff and his pupil Peter Damien Ouspensky. Gurdjieff's knowledge, as he said, had been gathered from esoteric groups in 'the East'. He gave out this knowledge garnered from the masters of wisdom in fragments and strictly forbade any of his pupils to synthesise it or formulate it into a coherent doctrine, evidently because he intended to complete his teaching in writing which would be published posthumously when, presumably, his students had matured enough to assimilate it. Indeed the injunction was so severe that when one of his star pupils, Rodney Collis, flouted it by publishing a synthesis, he was, in effect, excommunicated.

But Mr B was not fazed by any of this because he was by nature a teacher in the old pedagogical mode of a learned man who baked the wisdom he had received from his predecessors into fresh food for the minds of those who sat at his feet. He used to say that the 'daily bread' referred to in the Lord's Prayer was not the stuff that the corner grocer sold but 'transubstantial bread' for spiritual sustenance. His work was to teach his pupils to 'see' and understand his esoteric knowledge and to prepare their minds and bodies to be able to digest it. He was a polymath. He was an expert in mineralogy, a mathematician, historian, and a theologian with a profound knowledge of the teachings of all the great religions. He was a linguist who taught himself not only the standard European languages but also Arabic, Turkish, Sanskrit and Russian, of which he told me he learned enough in two weeks to be able to talk to Gurdjieff in his native tongue.

When Bapak arrived in England, Mr B taught himself enough Bahasa Indonesian, again in two weeks, to interpret intelligibly – of course with some inevitable bloopers which sent Bapak's Indonesian entourage into

fits of giggles and despair. One of those early mistranslations has become
an apparently ineradicable part of our Subud jargon – the word 'testing'
with its connotations of examination, experiment, trial or assessment by
someone else, for Bapak's Indonesian word *terima* (as in *terima kasi* or
receive thanks). This mistranslation was inevitable, I suggest, because
that is how a pedagogue would see his role as helper: I test you, and I am
your elder brother assigned to enable you to seek an explanation of the
question you have brought. Mr B found it very difficult to accept Bapak's
insistence that Bapak was not a teacher for it would mean that he himself
would have to forego his own life-time role as teacher. In 1963, soon after
my little book of Subud tales A *Reporter in Subud* was published, Mr B
invited me to have lunch at a small French restaurant he liked in South
Kensington, London. I had told a story in *Reporter* about Bapak saying
that if Bapak was a teacher who knew 10 things he would teach you only
nine, because if he taught you all 10, Bapak would lose his job.

This had touched Mr B at the centre of his attitude to Subud. 'Why
does Bapak say he is not a teacher?' he asked. 'Bapak's book *Susila Budhi
Dharma* is a teaching. It teaches us how to behave, how the food we eat
influences us, how to find a suitable spouse, how to find our true voca-
tions and about a hundred other matters.' I said that I myself had come
from a long line of teachers – my paternal grandfather was a teacher, so
were my parents and I too had started life as a teacher and was deeply
grateful for what he, Mr B, had taught me through many years in the
Gurdjieff work. But since I had been opened, I said respectfully, I had felt
free of the need to subject myself to teaching about spiritual matters by
anyone at all including Mr B himself. I know it was not an adequate
response to his question, but that is all I could say at the time because I
sensed that he had a need to continue his role as a spiritual teacher, and
regarding Bapak as a superior guru would validate that wish.

Soon after – and I do not imply any sort of consequentiality – Mr B
adopted another superior guru, the Sufi master Idries Shah, to whom he
gave Coombe Springs. But his innate nature of being a teacher in his own
right once again proved much too strong for the new relationship with
his new master to last long. He moved himself, his family and his work
to Sherborne House in Gloucestershire where he began teaching
Systematics. He was now called Principal of the International Academy
for Continuous Education. Meanwhile, he had written to Bapak expressing his lasting affection but resigned from being a Subud helper in accordance, he said, with Bapak's advice that helpers should not 'mix' what

was received from within in the latihan with 'other teachings'. Mr B told Bapak in this letter that he had felt for several years that he should return to his Gurdjieff work because the Subud latihan was 'not enough'. He said that he had tested this decision and received affirmation of its rightness. Hence the letter.

I was in Cilandak when the letter arrived and Bapak asked me to read it. Bapak said (Prio Hartono translating), 'You have been a friend of Mr B for a long time. You admire his mind very much do you not?' I said it was one of the greatest minds of our century. Bapak continued 'Yes, indeed it is a great mind. But see what happens even to a great mind when it is used to think about spiritual matters. Mr B says that the Subud latihan is not enough. So what does he do? He uses this inadequate Subud latihan to test and decide on the most important decision of his present life. What is the wisdom of that'?' Bapak looked very sad as he said this and seeing the sadness also on my face he said, 'Oh well. Mr B practised the latihan sincerely for many years. The contact with the Great Life Force remains with him. His mind rules his life on earth but the latihan will direct him to the real human world when he is no longer here.'

He then told me that I should continue to regard Mr B as a friend because I had reason to be grateful to him for being the instrument which brought me to Subud. And although I was not a very good friend in Mr B's last years, my gratitude and affection has never died. In my feelings the 'sin' of teaching was mitigated in Mr B by the fact that he could not be other than a teacher. That was what he was.

I have only one regret. In the first edition of his fascinating autobiography, *Witness*, he took his life story all the way to his encounter with Subud and described it as a culmination of his long spiritual search. It seemed to me that he was affirming his trust in the prediction which, he told me, his master, Georges Gurdjieff, had made to him on his dying bed. The words made such a profound impression on me that I remember them verbatim: 'I am not long for this world. But do not grieve. Someone much greater than I is preparing himself against his coming to the West to continue the work. Look for him in India. Not in your British India but in the India of the Dutch.'

But, in later editions of *Witness* when Mr B had separated himself from Subud and gone his own way, he changed the original record and eventually expunged references to Subud as though that phase of his life had not existed. He may have felt that it would be an act of disloyalty to Bapak personally to be adversely critical of Subud or he may have genuinely believed that his time in Subud was misspent time and was best forgotten. But my regret is that it detracted from the most forthright biography I have ever read. So it is after all a literary regret that I have expressed here.

This digression may not have any meaning for most Subud brothers and sisters who did not know Mr Bennett, and did not come to Subud through association with the Gurdjieff work – as I did – but through other circumstances. My reason for taking space to tell a part of the Mr B story is that it records a bit of my own history – telling stories is essentially a biographical business – and it illustrates the central point of this chapter which is that we need to be constantly aware of Bapak's advice against teaching. I have found, as Mr B did, that it is not easy to distinguish between Bapak's explanations, advice and what we consider to be teaching. When people have asked me about this, I have often said that Subud is not a teaching but that it is a great learning. Most of what I have learned about life-ways and life-values, and my view of the world in my journalism and in my United Nations work have come from Bapak's talks, his conversations and from the stories he has told. I am certain, however, that the meaning of what Bapak has said would have not touched me as it did or changed my perceptions of reality but for the change that the latihan brought about within me, making it possible to understand and accept the explanations Bapak has given us in his words.

And as time passed, I began to see that the 'sin' of teaching was in imposing one's own ideas and interpretations on what another's inner self was receiving in the latihan. One cannot teach the latihan. It is possible and sometimes necessary to talk about one's own experience because it might be helpful to someone else to make sense of his own experience. But theorising about another's experience is teaching. Ibu Rahayu put it very simply recently in talking to the international helpers: 'You had better say (to members who request help) that it is their own life and it is their own decision. All you can do is to work together with the members, by asking for God's help.' It is God's help, not ours. In that, I believe, lies true humility.

I had a memorable indication of this in the latihan once when I was witnessing the opening of a candidate who was a close friend of mine. When the latihan began, I saw that he was not relaxing, but stiff with anxiety to receive the contact. After about 20 minutes of this I became anxious that we would 'lose' this prospective member unless he experienced the opening palpably, since he was a very busy man in his worldly life and would probably not return to the latihan if the opening did not 'prove' itself to him. I silently asked God to make him feel the latihan. The next second I felt I had been given a sharp blow on my head (by my familiar guardian angel?) and I realized instantaneously that it was none of my business. I laughed out loud when this understanding came – it was a huge relief to let go of my anxiety and the *wish* to help. Then it was possible to return to my own latihan which was the only way I could possibly be helpful.

Bapak often used symbols and stories to guide us in applying ourselves to the latihan but he was severe with any helper who told people what to do in the latihan or how the latihan worked. An Indonesian once produced an anatomical chart describing how the Great Life Force coursed through the mind and body, to enable members to see how it worked. Another began to develop a latihan manual – similar to Jane Fonda's slimming instruction book. An instruction was once given to a member in a group to sense the body, part by part – a procedure reminiscent of Gurdjieff's set exercises in self-remembering. All these imaginative spiritual flights were shot down in flames.

A part of the problem it seemed to me, was semantic – the early use of the word 'exercise' as a synonym for receiving the latihan. To defuse the attempt to recreate the self-remembering exercise, Bapak asked Mariamah Wichman to tell the story of an experience she had had when Bapak was visiting Vienna in the early days of Subud's spread in Europe. Mariamah (then Margaret) had been walking across the park towards the apartment where Bapak was staying when she realized she had not practised the self-remembering exercise. She promptly began to be 'aware' of herself. As she was crossing the street, she heard a piercing whistle and 'awoke' from her state to see a traffic policeman on the side walk, arms akimbo, wagging his head at her. 'Madam' he said reprovingly, 'I had switched on the light to let you cross. And *you* were switched off!' The latihan, Bapak said, happens 'by itself'. No teaching aids are necessary. We 'cannot use the mind and the will in the latihan'. We can only be willing, as sincerely as we can, to receive the latihan.

In London Bapak came to a mass latihan held at the great Bloomsbury Hall. Pak Usman and I were attending on him. As we entered, 600 men arranged themselves to face Bapak. When Bapak said 'begin' some members, who had placed themselves right in front, at once began to do their number, lifting their arms and shouting the name of God. Bapak immediately said 'finish' but could not make himself heard in the din; Usman and I went through the crowd relaying the word. When quiet was restored Bapak told us all to arrange ourselves in orderly rows and sit down on the floor. He said 'Bapak does not want to see yesterday's latihan. The latihan is not a practice. It is a receiving which comes when you are relaxed, in a state of *iklas* (sincerity, or willingness to let go)'.

Then Bapak told us of the wayang shadow puppet drama. The puppet master first throws on the screen the triangular shadow representing a great volcano. It is held up to view, still, for a minute or two. And the gamelan orchestra then begins beating a vibrato on the percussion instruments. The shadow starts vibrating, slowly, then faster, and moves to the left and to the right. Bapak began saying *la ilaha ilallah* to the rhythm of the movement of the shadow. 'Now,' Bapak said, 'the drama begins.' We saw the importance of being patient. Patience, I realized, was an essential attribute of sincerity. We had to wait patiently until the vibrations generated by the latihan within us *moved* us. Doing 'yesterday's latihan' was to make movements generated by our minds. It is our will at work, not God's. There was no teaching in what Bapak did and said. But, *mashallah*, there was a great lesson there.

Bapak illustrated the need for sincerity and surrender in the latihan with a parable that I have related often but which never seems to lose its force in the retelling: A man feels he is being attacked by many kinds of fierce animals. So he runs away from them, more and more desperately. But they keep running after him. Tigers and wild dogs snap at his heels. Snakes, spiders and other creepy things crawl towards him. Poisonous plants reach out to grab him. He keeps on running. But they are gaining on him. And when he can run no more, he finds himself on the brink of a deep abyss. But it is only 10 feet wide. Beyond the abyss is beautiful open country with no wild animals, no thorny plants. Even a young boy can leap across the narrow chasm. But he is frightened that he might fall into it. He looks over his shoulder and sees the animals coming. He is at his wits' end. But God is merciful. A rope is dropped from above, suspended above his head. All he has to do now is to clutch it and swing himself across the free and open land. He reaches for it, but it is just six inches beyond his ordinary reach. He must jump up only six inches to grab the rope. But he dares not. He looks at it again but doesn't dare to let go of his fear. So he turns about and begins running again. . .

Often in the quiet time before the latihan, I remember this story, and tell myself I must be willing to let go a little more than I have been doing. Just six inches.

5

Adam and Eve

IN *Assignment Subud*, I reported about my asking Bapak the true meaning of the story of Adam and Eve. He asked, 'You mean about Adam and Eve and the apple?' He paused for a while and said in an exaggerated stage whisper, 'Top secret'. That was 25 years ago. Over the years, he added bits and pieces of information which I squirrelled away avidly and pieced together to explain to myself the meaning of this highly classified mystery. When Bapak was in Paris in the summer of 1964 he stayed in a penthouse apartment in Rue Eugene Manuel. He seemed to me to be in an extraordinary light state during that entire visit which began in Marseilles and, after Paris, continued through many European countries. He slept very little but was constantly looking out for familiar faces to be with. He actually needed to speak to us not only for our sake but for his own. That was what made the occasion extraordinary.

Very late one evening he told us about Adam and Eve (Muhammad Usman translating): Adam was living happily in Paradise when God called him into his office one day and showed him a map of the Universe: 'You see that little planet down there?' Adam nodded. 'I want you to go down there and populate it.' Adam demurred, but God insisted. To make the sentence lighter, God said that it wasn't for ever. He could return to Paradise, in 63 years . . . Adam woke up on the Earth as a *manusia* – Man. It was very different from Paradise and as Adam walked about the gardens and the forests he felt very lonely. God took pity on Adam and split him into two equal parts – Male and Female – so that he could have a companion. Adam and Eve began to populate the Earth with their children. Adam no longer felt lonely and exiled from Paradise. And, indeed, he came to like the Earth and the children and grandchildren that he and Eve had generated. Adam's sixty-third birthday arrived but he showed no sign of wanting to return to Paradise. God asked, 'Adam, how about it?' Adam said 'God, I like it here. Besides, there is a lot more that needs doing here, to look after these people.' So God gave in. Adam lived on much longer. He stayed on for 800 years. And then God said, in a peremptory tone, 'Adam. Time's up. Come on back.' Adam was now an older and wiser man. He bade good-bye to the people on Earth and lay down and died. When he woke up in Paradise he remembered the Earth but realized that Paradise was very different, and much nicer.

He became re-acclimatised and, after a while, wondered why he had been foolish enough to stay on down there. He was enjoying himself. Then one day God sent for him again. 'Adam,' God said, 'I have a job for you.' Adam immediately became alarmed. 'Not that place again, God. Please not there again.' But God said 'Yes, I am afraid it is so. Those people you bred there have gone off the right track in spite of the messages I sent through you. It is necessary that you go back and guide them towards the right path again.' Adam saw that God was in no mood for argument. So he bowed his head submissively and consented to leave his life in Paradise once more and to return to Earth.

I nearly fell off my chair when the story ended. The enormity of what it meant and why Bapak had told it struck me forcibly. Bapak was 63! And he was saying that it was time for him to return but he would stay on for a while yet. I hugged the story close to my feelings for a minute or two as Bapak smoked his cigarette. And then my head began to nag with a question. 'What about the apple?' I asked, the perennial journalist trying to get all the 'facts' in, never mind the wholeness of the Truth in his feelings. Bapak gave me that look and murmured, 'Some other time. *Nanti*; later.' I felt a bit squashed but consoled myself with the thought of the riches we had just been endowed with.

There was plenty of meat in the story for my mind to chew on for years . . . Adam, when he was born, was not a male but Man. The word derives from the Sanskrit *Manu*, the Hand of God. It is not sexually differentiated. Man contained both principles, male and female. Man was halved to make *Purusha* (Male) and *Wanita* (Female). Eve was not a second class citizen, a by-product of a male rib but an equal half of Man. That 'spare' rib myth was invented by male theologians who, at that time – as now – could not accept the notion that Eve, who was made out of Adam, could be an equal partner. Indeed in the Greek Bible, the second oldest extant Bible, the word used is not 'rib' but *corto* or side, the word from which English words like coast (sea-side) derive. On another occasion during that same journey, Bapak elucidated this point very clearly: 'Eve came from God through Adam. She was born second but was not second to him. *Sama-sama*. Same. Equal.'

I recall being in a 'delegation' of Buddhist Subud members in Sri Lanka who were feeling a little resentful that Bapak never seemed to include the Buddha in the line of the great prophets and teachers on whose messages the great religions were founded. Bapak spoke often about Abraham, Moses, Jesus and Muhammad but never, in that context, about the Buddha. As spokesman, I asked Bapak why he did not mention 'our man' as it were. Bapak, in a pained tone, said, 'Bapak often speaks of the Buddha.' I said I'd heard many talks of Bapak but did not remember any mention of the Buddha. Bapak said, 'Oh you mean the Gautama Buddha? Don't you know as Buddhists that Gautama was the twenty-fourth in a long line of Buddhas? The first was Adam. Bapak often refers to the Prophet Adam. "Buddha" means perfected Man. A man in whom both principles, male and female, are perfectly balanced. That is why in depictions of Gautama there is no sexual differentiation. One of the distinguishing marks of a Buddha, according to the scriptural tradition, is that the genitals are retracted into his body. Is that not so? Adam was both male and female – not a hermaphrodite, but Man without sexual differentiation, to symbolize perfection.

'From Adam came two great lines of human beings with the Great Life Force, carrying a message from the Origin. One was the long line of Buddhas who attained perfection by dint of devotion and effort. The other was a shorter line, namely five – Abraham, Moses, Jesus and Muhammad who received the Great Life Force as a gift, without special effort on their part.' I interrupted, 'Who is the fifth?' Bapak waved away my loaded question with a terse answer, 'Adam was the first.'

And he continued to give us a symbolic explanation of the line of prophets: 'The symbol of Abraham is white water representing the seminal fluid which flows through the channel of the law giver, Moses. The child Jesus is born. The child grows up to be a man – the name Muhammad means Man. And now it is time for Man's *jiwa* to grow.' Adam as Man, I realized, was the clue to the mysterious story of Paradise Lost. From occasional fragments of conversational references to the Adam and Eve myth it was possible to compose an account of its meaning which has inspired my own mind.

I offer it here with the forenote that it is my own synthesis, not something Bapak ever spelled out as a whole explanation. So, please be free to reject it as an errant piece of imagination. The meaning of the apple was a crucial clue. Bapak said the apple was half-ripe, half green, representing Right and Wrong, Good and Evil. Since everything in the universe was created by God, so was the apple. The Old Masters who painted scenes of Adam and Eve in the Garden of Eden knew this and painted the apple half red, half green. Even the apples decorating Christmas trees were red and green in earlier centuries. And the tradition is still to be found even in the plastic or glass 'apples' now sold at Woolworths, the difference often being that individual red apples and green apples are sold in the same package, probably because it is easier for the manufacturer not to have to do two-coloured single apples. Of course, this half-ripe, half green idea was exactly appropriate to the myth. The apple tree was the 'tree of the fruit of knowledge of good and evil' that God had planted in Eden.

God had given Adam and Eve the tree but warned them that if they ate of it there would be consequences. The snake, which represents the mind in many oriental myths, the bearer of the diamond of mental illumination, persuaded them, again appropriately, to have a go – to experiment – despite the warning. Adam and Eve, the first human beings on Earth who, according to the Darwinian idea, were the first to evolve from beast to Man, were still being inner-directed by their animal instincts. At first they had no problems with choosing between good and evil since they did only what their instincts suggested. But, the moment they ate of the fruit of knowledge of good and evil, they were liberated from the irresistible power of instinct, and incurred the responsibility for themselves and all their progeny for ever and a day, of having to assume the moral responsibility of choosing between right and wrong, good and evil.

That, for me, was the Fall or separation – not from God's Grace but from total dependency on animal instinct for the decisions we must make and the actions we perform. It was an exile from total control to total freedom modulated by the responsibility to make moral choices. And, as all of us, especially those like me, who have committed many errors in our lifetime – errors of commission as well as omission against ourselves, against our families, against our own societies and against strangers and enemies – know only too well, making moral choices is the most awesome thing about being human.

Where does this story of Adam and Eve take us? Back to the beginning of this book, to the freedom to make responsible choices. On worldly matters – making business decisions, choosing which school our children should attend, which physician to consult, which house to buy, where to go for a vacation, which job to take and the array of 'problems' which beset our workaday lives, we are constrained by practical limits and other material considerations. We cannot avoid using our God-given brains to study the implications of one choice or another, to consult expertise if we do not have it in our own experience, to use that increasingly rare commodity – common sense – when we make a decision. Through many years of practising the latihan, the faculties with which we come to adopt viewpoints, make value-judgements and perform the necessary chores, may be influenced so that, without having to wait for 800 years as Adam did, we might become older and wiser.

So, as we all did at the beginning in Subud we cannot take off our heads with our hats and hang them up, just because we receive God's grace. The latihan does not give us a philosopher's stone which we can use with casual panache to get us easily and safely through this material world. I often tell my younger brothers and sisters who talk to me about their life problems that all I can do as a helper is to assist them from my experience to sort out what is involved and let them make their own decisions and choices.

On one memorable occasion the directors of a successful business corporation in Subud asked me my opinion about a proposal by one of the partners that a set of helpers should be assigned to attend their board meetings. Since my opinion had been sought, I could give it straight. 'If any helper tried to make business decisions for me by testing I would throw him out of the window.' Most of them took it on the bounce but the man who had proposed the idea smiled a bit abashed and spluttered something defensively. My advice did not prevail. His did. This may sound like 'I told you so', but to complete the story it must be said that the business did not last much longer.

Another set of putative entrepreneurs in England went so far as to appoint a spiritual director, a helper with a salary, an office, a telephone and the usual paraphernalia of an executive, to guide them in their day-to-day business decisions. Evidently, the telephone was a hot line to the Almighty and the spiritual director was to give them the inside track in the commercial rat race. I learned of the extraordinary arrangement when, on the advice of the helper, they called me in to ask if I would agree to be the arbitrator should any dispute arise among them about the division of the profits they were going to amass. I remembered the ancient fable about the dairymaid carrying a pot of milk on her head as she walked home dreaming of becoming richer and richer until she became a queen. When her courtiers asked her for favours she would nod regally in agreement and she suited her action to the word and spilt all her milk. I declined the honour.

It has been very difficult for many Subud brothers and sisters not to use testing in making everyday life decisions. Some of them often have asked me why they should not do so since Bapak made business decisions and he was always in a state of latihan, was he not? My usual answer has been, 'Bapak is Bapak'. But even as I have said it, I have known it was too flip an answer. They deserved a clearer and less oracular explanation but I did not have one to offer. I too have had questions in my mind about Subud enterprises and it has taken many years of observing many of them collapsing in ruins before I have been able to make any sense of it at all. But more of that later.

6

Down to earth

THOUGH Bapak often spoke about our life hereafter, he never allowed us to forget our lives here and now. 'Before you become a general,' he said, 'you must first be a good foot soldier and learn to live in the barracks.' And with a sardonic smile, he added, 'And you will have to get used to toilets without doors. This is the satanic world of pain and suffering and injustice where Satan's laws prevail.' I was with him when the news of Martin Luther King's assassination was brought to him. Men like King who had devoted the best part of their lives to assuage human cruelty and injustice towards their fellow-men, fell victim to a single bullet from a madman, he reflected. Gandhi, John Kennedy and Robert Kennedy all died because they worked to mitigate injustice. Assassins often try to kill dictators and tyrants – sometimes ten attempts on their lives are made, but they survive. Sukarno, Bapak said, had been shot at many times but he was unscathed. People believe that he had a magic charm he carried in his mouth whenever he went out of the presidential palace, to protect himself from bullets. He did not need that, Bapak said. The lower forces took care of it.

It was hard for me to accept the notion that this earth was the hell that traditional religions had warned us against in spite of plentiful evidence around us of the truth of Bapak's words. For many millennia the lives of human beings had been grievously distorted by war, internecine conflict, cruel relationships – between wives and husbands, parents and children, grinding poverty for the many co-existing with obscene overabundance for the few, epidemic diseases, constant fear and insatiable greed. This has been the stuff of our great dramatic epics, our music, poetry and novels.

But there always seemed to be the hope of redemption around the corner, in the beguiling wonders of the earth – in its plentitude, the awesome beauty of the land and the sea and the 'goodness' that evidently was present in most human beings, such as qualities of valour and kindness and love, though they were often overlaid with ugliness. We were the products of hundreds of generations of subhuman behaviour, self-willed 'sins' against ourselves, our fellow creatures and against what we called

God's Will, modulated by the environment in which each of us had been raised. How were we to overcome this powerful inheritance? How were we to prevent its baleful influences from being passed on to our children and their children?

At the Coombe Springs congress a member asked Bapak for advice: 'Children are now being born to Subud members. Since they are born with the grace of God in them, how can we protect them from the influence of the lower forces?' Solemnly, but with a trace of amusement in his lips, Bapak replied, 'Truly this question arises from the foolish mind of man. If children have God's power in them, then the real question is how they can be protected from us, not how we can protect them!'

Bapak's talks and responses to members' questions contain a great deal of advice on how we might live our lives and raise our children in this material world through the power of the latihan if we could only let it, by deepening submission, patience and sincerity. The explanations and stories were adventitious aids to put our minds at rest so that we would be willing to surrender and let understanding come to us. Some of this advice was strictly specific and particular, some for general application. The specifics in the replies to letters were often so particular that I was afraid we would take them out of context and use them as patent 'remedies' for general use.

Once I asked Bapak's advice on behalf of a couple, friends of mine, each of whom had come separately to me for help in straightening out their rapidly-collapsing marriage. She had fallen in love with a married man and wanted to leave her husband and their little children and emigrate to live near her lover. He was appalled by her readiness to break up their family and enter into a new relationship which had all the marks of prospective disaster. Bapak heard me out and asked (Prio Hartono interpreting), 'Are you an advocate for either of them?' Laughing, I said 'No, I am more an *amicus curiae*, a friend of the court.'

Bapak, graver now, said, ' In these matters, it is best not to make *ex parte* judgements. It is best to hear both sides of the case. Bapak knows these two friends of yours. It is clear to Bapak that you too feel that she is clearly wrong and he is clearly right. Of course she is wrong to abandon her family and follow her passions. But what you don't know is why such a woman as she is, gentle and kind, should even think of doing this. It is because her life with her husband had been intolerable for a long time. There is a cruel – an almost bestial – streak in him which has distorted their relationship. She is making a mistake by leaving her children and going to this other man. But she cannot continue to live with her hus-band.'

I asked if I should advise them about this. Bapak said whatever I said would not make a difference even if it came from Bapak. So what did I do? Nothing. Except to tell them both about Bapak's concern for their children's well-being.

I tell this story here to make the point that the realities of our individual lives are so complex and specific to each one of us that I have always tried to separate the specific from the general because I am terrified that I would harm rather than help people in trouble by quoting scripture.

The advice and explanations Bapak gave us in his talks was, of course, for general guidance. Sometimes his observations given in private conversations had value in general application. For instance, when Bapak was visiting my home in Colombo, he told me that if I could afford it, I should give each of my children a separate room. They should learn to spend most of their indoor time in their own rooms, doing their studies, amusing themselves, and joining the rest of the family at play time, meal times, and prayer time. (I realized that if we followed this advice in these extraordinary times, one would have to afford not only a room but also a TV set, a VCR and a CD player for each child!) We were partially successful in following Bapak's advice and believe that our children – and we too – benefited. The point, we could see, was not so much the separate rooms, but quietness in the house in which children are raised and the cultivating of their ability to grow as individuals within a family group.

Bapak once asked me whether I struck my children. I said I had, adding quickly in self-defence, but not often. 'But why do you strike them at all? It is like beating your grandfather,' Bapak had said. That lesson sank deep home and though my children often felt the brunt of my irritable tongue and often unfair judgements, since then they rarely had to encounter physical force from me. One such occasion stands out clear in my memory. I was deep in a game of chess which I was losing. Chess is perhaps the most egotistic of all games because it is not a matching of muscle against muscle but mind against mind – the very seat of our self admiration. My son Nuryana, then not more than four, was playing nearby with some friends and they were yelling and screaming away as children will in their excitement. Naturally, I blamed my imminent defeat on him and said curtly 'Stop that.' After losing another piece, I realized the noise had commenced again and repeated my order. When it happened a third time, I picked him up angrily and smacked his little thigh.

He did not cry. He only looked straight at me very calmly and kept on looking. The look was more eloquent than any protest. It said: 'Okay, okay, I am a little boy and I have behaved badly. But why are *you* misbehaving? You are an adult aren't you? You are in a bad way, father.' Subud children are and seem like any other children but, by heaven, they can come through on occasions like my grandfather.

Bapak has told us over and again that the only way to prevent passing on the influences of our hereditary mistakes to our children – at least to the extent that it usually is – is to receive quietly and prayerfully before we start the sexual act which might result in conceiving a child. It was a piece of advice he invariably gave to young people, especially those about to get married. I realized from my own experience and that of my friends that this advice was most often followed only in the breach. One Subud brother caused loud and prolonged laughter when he asked Bapak, 'But Bapak, suppose after we have received and been quiet in bed we no longer want to? Bapak roared with laughter and waggled his head in sheer disbelief that the question had been asked at all.

Such experiences with Bapak were what made me increasingly appreciate Bapak's role as father, apart from his work as messenger. He had pastoral duties as well which he performed night and day until his last days when he became more and more remote from us, withdrawing into his study, into his prayers, and into his family as all of us do as we grow old and frail. So many valuable lessons were given to us in those earlier days. I recall, with goose bumps still coursing through my skin, an evening in Cilandak when all of us who had gathered there for the month of Ramadan were celebrating *idul fitr*, the end of the fast, with Bapak. He spoke to us for a while about the meaning of the fast and concluded with words which glued themselves on my mind (Usman translating): 'Bapak supposes that you have performed your *Id* duties as well as you did your fasting. You have asked and received forgiveness for the offences you have committed against your friends. That is the easiest because if those offences had been really bad they wouldn't still be your friends. Then, you may have asked forgiveness from your enemies. That is more difficult but Bapak hopes you have done so. But Bapak is sure that you have neglected to ask and receive forgiveness from those with whom you are married. The most frequent and hideous offences are committed at home and right there in the bedroom. Husbands and wives try to take these offences for granted and so do not think of cleansing their relationship by asking each other for forgiveness even at *idul fitr*.'

Bapak then said 'Now Bapak would like to see you do so now, right in front of Bapak.' Husbands and wives seated in separate parts of the room rushed toward each other in an urgent gasping scramble to beg for forgiveness. I, seeing my wife near the farther door, charged out through the one nearest me to reach her via the verandah. When I got there, she wasn't there, having joined the *melée* to get to where she had last seen me. I felt as if I was in some Kafkaesque nightmare and scrabbled with heavy limbs through the throng until I reached her looking equally helplessly for me. The tears shed in those few moments had a marvellously detergent quality, not of self-pity but of real penitence.

7
Fasting our habits

WHEN Bapak first suggested that I should follow the Ramadan fast which he had recently urged the residents of Cilandak to undertake, I protested that I did not believe in religious ritual. I was very sassy in those early days. I would talk back (as distinct from speak up) even at Bapak, and take a seat alongside him and cross my legs casually without a thought that I was being impertinent and uncouth. Gradually my behaviour in Bapak's presence changed as intimations of what Bapak might be touched my understanding. 'It is not a ritual,' Bapak said (Prio Hartono interpreting), 'And it's important to experience fasting.' I still demurred, arguing 'If it is not a ritual why should everybody fast at the same time?' Bapak replied, 'Because it is easier to fast when everyone else is fasting.' Complicated question, simple self-evident answer, as usual.

That evening Bapak spoke to us about the 'true meaning' of fasting. He began with an explanation, a parable of fate and destiny (Usman interpreting): 'God sends us his postmen to deliver what we need to live in this world – a suitable wife or husband, children, a house, a job appropriate to our talents, transport for ourselves and our children. The postman's bag contains all our needs and he is willing to deliver them on time. But, influenced by our hearts and minds, we are impatient and ask for this and that ceaselessly and are dissatisfied all the time. So we thrash about, creating a dense fog of passion around us so that the postman cannot find his way to us. What God wills for us is our destiny. Destiny is what should happen to us. Fate is what does happen to us because our hearts and minds, which are influenced by the lower forces, make it difficult for human beings to surrender to God's will for them to reach their destiny. So their lives are ruled by fate rather than destiny . . . Bapak advises Subud members to fast because when you are not ruled by your appetites, the fog around you becomes less dense and the postman may be able to find his way to you.'

The difference between fate and destiny was an important lesson for me. Fate is what *happens* to us because we are under the dominance of material forces. Destiny is what *should* and *could* happen to us if we have been able to put the lower forces in place so that the human force uses them rather than be used by them. As a development reporter and a UN official concerned with human development it was an invaluable working principle. Our task, I urged my younger colleagues, was to help people to move their children away from the line of fate to the line of destiny, the most succinct definition of development that I know. And invariably they understood what I was talking about because people in or out of Subud have a primal sense that responds to such an idea. As more and more of us began to undertake the Ramadan fast Bapak gave us deeper explanations of its meaning.

Everything, Bapak said, has an inner and outer. Even a word has an outer meaning and an inner meaning. Even *zakat* – the obligation of philanthropy – has an outer and inner meaning. A beggar stretches out his hand and you give him a rupiah to get rid of him. You have *done* charity with that rupiah. But you have not *been* charitable. *Doing* charity is very different from *being* charitable. All Muslims go to Mecca and they are proud to wear the white cap to which they are entitled when they have become *hadjis*. The white cap indicates that they have become purified of their sins. Bapak smilingly named an Indonesian who was wearing the white cap in the audience and remarked, 'We all know, and he knows even better, how purified our brother is from his sins. He has been to Mecca by Garuda Indonesian Airways. But has he been to Mecca within? There is a Mecca inside all of us which we should visit in our lifetime.'

Also on the subject of *zakat*, Bapak once said, 'Varindra, you like to help people but when you want to help you don't help enough. If a man is drowning thirty feet away you should not throw him an eighteen-foot rope and claim that you have met him more than half way.'

Ramadan is usually practised as an outer ritual – a form of religious behaviour for a set period during which time food and drink are avoided during the daylight hours. There is nothing wrong with this, Bapak said, because it benefits people to change their habitual pattern of life even for one month in a year. They become more aware of the life of the spirit during their working hours. But the benefits of the fast – not just in its dietary aspect but also in its spiritual aspect – are undone by the widespread tendency to eat even more than usual when night falls. The inner meaning of the fast, Bapak explained, was much more valuable and also more interesting.

Remember, he said, that in ordinary life we all fast for about 13 hours. We eat dinner at about seven o'clock at night and do not eat or drink until possibly eight o'clock in the morning. But most of that time we are sleeping and are therefore unconscious of the change in our bodily and mental states caused by the absence of an intake of food and drink. It is not conscious fasting. The purpose of the Ramadan fast is to become aware of the extent of our habitual dependency on material, vegetable and animal forces.

What do we 'sacrifice' in the fast? What we are stuck on. 'A king,' said Bapak, 'has great lands under his control. It does not mean much to him to give up a bit of it. He needs to give up something he values more, something he thinks he cannot surrender easily such as a little of his power or, better still, his habitual distrust of his ministers!' Then, pointing to me, Bapak said, 'Varindra finds it easy to give up food and water during the fast. But tobacco is not so easy. Even more difficult is reading. Varindra should give up reading books during the fast to know how the habit of reading has got him by his neck.' I protested amidst laughter, 'Bapak I am the kind of fellow who, if he has no book or newspaper to read, will read jam jar labels!' Bapak, joining in the amusement, said 'Yah. Then you'll have to give up jam jar labels.'

There are many inner levels of fasting, Bapak said. The upper, outer layer is fasting from habitual eating and drinking. 'And nowadays, smoking cigarettes!' And looking at the Wilhelm II he was smoking, added, 'Maybe also Dutch cigars!' The second layer of habits from which we should fast are habitual sleep – not sleep which we all need but habitual sleep! And habitual sex. Most people, Bapak said, have sex because it is a habit, or it is the habitual time for it or merely because it is available, not because the inner indicates it. Even deeper than this is the social habits we indulge in so thoughtlessly, for instance, the habit of gossip – useless and harmful tittle tattle that demeans the one who gossips as well as his or her victim.

Bapak said that we, as helpers particularly, should see this tendency in ourselves so that when we meet as a *dewan* we should not use it to pollute the air with 'bad talk'. I suppose the appropriate English word is scuttlebutt. We should be able to see how we have a tendency to enjoy gossip, the juicier the better. I remarked that the taste of gossip was bitter-sweet. Bapak said yes, it is enjoyable but it leaves a bad taste behind on the tongue.

For instance, Bapak went on, the habit of criticism. Being critical is being intelligent, but being habitually critical is being destructive to both the critic and the criticized. It's a form of violence, Bapak said and,

like violence, it does harm to its user and to his victim. As a chronic suf-
ferer from this disease, a critic by nature, by habit and as a professional
critic in my trade, every word Bapak was saying sank into the core of my
heart. I knew the habit well. I knew its colour – bile green. After a week
of Ramadan I knew how clever the material force behind habitual criticism was, how persuasive it was that one was being 'constructive' and
'objective', not malicious and tawdry. Alas, I also learned after repeated
experiences of Ramadan, that whatever cleansing had taken place lasted
no longer than a few weeks, if that, after the lessons of the fast had faded.

Another social habit, Bapak said, was the tendency to be dismissive of
other people, to score easy triumphs off others, to make clever debating
points, to put down other people by being smart and glib. Phew. That
was even closer to where I lived. Allied to this, Bapak continued, was the
habit of wanting to be right, which could be satisfied only if the other
was shown to have been wrong. If you are right, Bapak pointed out, there
is no need to prove that the other man is wrong because rightness comes
from God and does not need any justification by negative proof. Also
allied was the habit of being holier than thou. 'You don't need the stripes
of a corporal or the star of a general for others to know you are holy. If you
need outer symbols of holiness you may get them,' Bapak said, 'but that
is all you will get!'

Many years after we began observing Ramadan regularly Bapak told us
about the *lailat ul quadir*, the gift of God which those who have fasted
sincerely may receive at the end of the month. When in 1972 I went to
Cilandak for the fast, Bapak asked me whether I controlled the newspaper
I was editing. I said that I had complete control of editorial policy and
direction but not the finances. They belonged to the people who owned
the stock. Bapak said that it was a pity and that it was time for me to
move on. Aghast, I replied that it was not easy to find a job in the upper
reaches of journalism. He said, 'You have been a good journalist. Now it
is time, maybe, for something else. You should continue to write but
your work now is not in editing a newspaper. It should now be wider.'

I went into the fast with a heavy heart. I was enjoying my work and
the thought of changing trades was appalling. Also, there were many
financial obligations to carry. What was I to do? I was frightened but I
knew I was going to do what Bapak had suggested though I did not
know how. At the end of Ramadan, I went to ask Bapak permission and
blessing to leave. He asked me whether I had received the *lailat ul quadir*,
my gift from God. I replied that there was nothing noticeable I had

received. Bapak smiled and said, 'People think that the gift of God is like a gift-wrapped parcel that drops from the sky. Surely God is more subtle than that. Very often it is not something that is added to what you have, but something that is taken from you, something you do not need.' I looked a bit bewildered and said I did not understand what had been taken from me. 'How do you feel now about leaving your newspaper? Do you still have fear in you that you will be unable to find the money your children need?'

That was my gift – the freedom from the anxiety I had allowed to enter my heart. I returned to my office feeling confident and clear. In the huge pile of a month's mail there were three offers of jobs. All of them had their attractions and none of them felt right. I cabled refusing them. A day or two later a senior UN officer called to offer me what he called 'a challenge' – to use my journalistic experience, particularly in the developing world, to make people aware of the world's population situation. I had been a severe critic of the population policies being enunciated in Washington, London, Bonn and Stockholm. And the challenge seemed right. I accepted the work and went back to Cilandak to ask Bapak for a spiritual briefing on population problems. It has served me well but that is another story. All I need to say here is that the advice Bapak gave me enabled me to help many powerful people in the field understand that the population 'problem' would not be solved in the uterus but in the human mind, that people would not willingly reduce the size of their families unless they could be certain that the children they already had, had a chance of surviving, and that people would not readily regulate their lives unless their lives were worth living.

The lessons of Subud, praise God, are not airy 'spiritual' fantasies but commonsensical, practical and humane.

8

Matters of life and death

BAPAK hardly ever read a newspaper. I once saw him reading a newspaper as I entered the room, and remarked that it was the first time I'd seen him do so. He grinned, a bit embarrassed, it seemed, as though he had been caught doing something unbecoming and said (in English), 'Bapak was reading the advertisements. They are all lies. But not so much lies as the news.' As a newspaperman, I understood very well. The advertisements were blatant lies, so blatant that the reader was aware of it. But the lies in the news column were subtle, much more subtle, because the reporter was an expert at selecting his 'facts' to fit his particular truth and was often skilled at braiding these preferred facts and opinions so that the reader could not easily tell them apart and took it all in as 'truth'. How often had I opened the eyes of my children as they grew up to detect this professional legerdemain. When she was very young, my daughter Anuradha observed that whenever a reporter starts a sentence with 'In fact,' he is about to give you an opinion. (Journalism schools please note.)

Bapak's inner was profoundly aware of the weight and direction of political trends but he would not clutter his mind with the breathless ephemera of the daily press. He once told me of his awareness of the movements of the nuclear submarines of the US and the USSR playing their deadly war games in the Indian ocean. He said their material vibrations often woke him in the early hours of the morning. He was deeply concerned at the build-up of lethal weapons and asked me about what was going on in the international scene at the United Nations.

I was his Man of the World. He would often greet me with the question 'So what is happening out there?' I told him of the highlights of the political and economic events making the current headlines and Bapak would listen and make comments about what it all meant. One evening when I had arrived in Cilandak from New York, I told him about the first heart transplant carried out by Dr Christian Barnard in South Africa. Bapak was silent for a long time and then remarked (Usman translating) that the world-wide interest in transplant surgery came from a misunderstanding about the meaning of living and dying. Human beings were being increasingly regarded as mechanical things composed of a multitude of parts which could be repaired or replaced by 'spares' taken from dead bodies of other humans or animals or even wood and metal. The human body and brain were made up of material things but what made a human being different from a mechanical object was the *jiwa*, the human soul which must return to its origin when the body dies. Scientists are very clever people and their surgery is a highly skilled art but they know nothing about death. Death is necessary to life but unnecessary death is unnecessary. So these clever surgeons serve a useful function but they should know about necessary death.

My mind was racing along trying to understand. Bapak seemed to have had his say on this subject, so I told him about the controversy raging between the legal profession and the medical profession about when death occurred. The legal people were sticking to the old theory that death occurs when the heart stops and the medical people were insisting that death occurs when the mind stops.

Bapak began again, 'Usman says that Varindra is alive. Bapak asks why do you say Varindra is alive? Usman says it is because Varindra can hear and see and touch and taste and smell and move and feel the breeze and the heat on his skin. Bapak asks how does Varindra do these things? Because he has ears and eyes, a tongue, nose and limbs and a nervous system. Suppose that Varindra dies at this very moment. He is dead. But his ears, eyes, nose, tongue, limbs and nervous system are still there. You can recognize his features as Varindra's. But he is dead. What is the difference? The power that gave life to these organs is no longer there. The common process of death is that as a human being grows old, this power is gradually withdrawn. The eyes cannot see so well, the ears cannot hear so well, the body does not move so well and so on. And there comes a time when there is no more power to animate the senses and the brain. It has been separated. Sudden death is shocking because it happens without notice!'

After another long pause Bapak said, 'In the case of people who have been touched by the power of God, the ears die but the hearing does not, the eyes die but the seeing does not, the nose dies but the smelling does not, the tongue dies but the tasting does not, the limbs die but the moving does not. It is not the eyes, ears, nose and limbs that go to the True Human World. They belong to this earth and return to it. What is the use of these clumpy legs and heavy body in heaven? It is the purified seeing, hearing, smelling and moving that leave this earth and return to the origin.'

I recalled a hymn – a 16th century Christian hymn, which a wonderful Subud voice had sung at my daughter's wedding:

God be in my head
And in my understanding
God be in my eyes
And in my looking
God be in my mouth
And in my speaking
God be in my heart
And in my thinking
God be at my end
And at my departing

Bapak nodded as if to say yes, that is it.

Another time, in Calcutta, when Bapak was staying at the marvellous marble apartment on Alipur Road in which Ian and Muftiah Arnold lived for many years, an Indian member asked Bapak, 'What's the meaning of Christ's resurrection?' When the question was interpreted to him Bapak acted as though he had not heard it. He went on puffing his cigar (these were the days when people were not as sensitive as they now seem to be to tobacco smoke) and looked out of the window as if there was a new species of bird sitting on the neem tree outside. I thought that he was going to let that one go by unaddressed, or that he was splaying his inner fingers about to judge if he should answer the question, in that particular audience. Then, smiling, Bapak said (Usman interpreting), 'There is this old Mercedes Benz. Its body is dented badly. It is covered with thick coats of grime. Its tyres are flat and the wheels need aligning. It has no brakes. And above all, there is no spirit. The owner wants to upgrade it.

'He aligns the wheels and puts new tyres on them. He fills the tank with benzene. Then he knocks out the dents. If the Mercedes Benz could feel, it would be a very painful process. Now begins the task of cleaning off the grime. The owner washes the body with soap and water. There is more grime underneath. He takes a wire brush to it and scours deep. It is quite painful. But after a while something marvellous begins to happen. On each separate part of the Mercedes Benz, from under the grime, appears the name of its maker: MB, MB, MB, MB, Allah, Allah Allah ...' Then Bapak pointed at the person who had asked the question and said,

'Meaning of resurrection.'

Once during Bapak's visit to Marseilles, I asked him one of my off-the-wall questions: 'What happens to a man when he dies?' I remember being ready to be slapped down but not in quite the way it happened. 'Varindra, you as a reporter should learn to ask sharper questions,' Bapak said (again, Usman interpreting). 'What's the point of asking what happens to a man when he dies? Which man? What happens to one man when he dies will be very different from what happens to another man when he dies.' It was now obvious to me that my question was inane and I felt very abashed and hung my head. After a while, Bapak relented and said, 'You are not ready to receive and understand the full answer. But Bapak will tell you something you can understand. A temporary explanation. Bapak will speak in very broad terms and if you speak or write about it you should always point out that it is a broad explanation. An explanation for now, not the whole explanation.

'There are three broad categories of possibilities for human beings after death. The first and the largest category is people who are so completely influenced by the material forces of the earth that when they die, their *jiwas* are so heavily encrusted with material forces that they revert to the material earth along with their bodies.' I must have looked horrified at this prospect not only for them but for myself too – just in case – for Bapak immediately added, 'But there is always God's mercy. One of their progeny, within seven generations, may receive the grace of God and that person's worship would influence the soul of the earth-bound ancestor and enable it to begin progress to the origin.

'The second category is the people who have worshipped God as sincerely as they can. They attend the mosque and church, regularly perform their *shariat* and are referred to as "God fearing" men and women. Their *jiwas* may not be as heavily encrusted by the material forces and when they die, their *jiwas* do not revert to earth but hover about on its surface. These are what people often see as "ghosts". They have two possibilities of redeeming themselves. One of their progeny within seven generations may come in contact with the Grace of God and this will touch them and set them off on their way to the true human world. The second possibility is rebirth. If a man and woman in a state of being similar to that of the dead person while he was on earth, are entering into a procreative act, the "hoverer" could enter the crucible of that union and become the soul of the child who may be born from it. That child might come into contact with the grace of God in its lifetime and, at death, will begin the journey to the true human world.

'The third category is the smallest and includes Subud members who have received the contact with the power of God. Depending on the sincerity of this person's surrender and the degree of purification reached in his or her lifetime, their soul, when separated from the body, will soon be on its ascendance to the true human world. It will not remain in earth's atmosphere but will go beyond this solar system, making its way eventually to the origin.' Bapak stopped, and feeling the solemnness his explanation had caused in Usman and me, he cracked a joke: 'No guarantees!' And then, he repeated his warning that he was 'speaking broadly' and that this was only a partial explanation. I share this with others in Subud because I must, and I must repeat the proviso that Bapak was 'speaking broadly' and giving only a partial provisional explanation.

Bapak made very few references to dying and death in his public talks. In smaller groups and in private conversations, he spoke about death not as an event but as part of a process, a passage between one life and another. A progression to the true human world or 'paradise'. I once asked him, point blank, whether what he spoke of as the true human world was a spiritual state of being or an actual place in the universe. Bapak replied, 'Ya, it's a place beyond this solar system.' I never raised the subject with him again. His tone sounded so final.

But from the occasional testing Bapak did with us and from hints in his talks and conversations I came to understand that the prevalent notion that life exists only on this planet is one of those absurd enormities of human geocentricity, an arrant piece of anthropoid hubris. We look for life in outer space, in other planets and beyond, but we want to 'recognize' it, to see and hear people like us out there, with a head and facial features, torso and limbs, speaking the languages we are familiar with — even if its sound was electronic like the voices of the Daleks and the Jeddis of science fiction. Is it not possible that there are other unrecognizable kinds of life? I suppose it is beyond the capacity of our minds to visualize anything beyond its familiar experience just as a person born blind cannot 'recognize' the colour red or blue except in terms of analogy or metaphor. But in spite of that limitation could we not make a leap of imagination and guess that the beings on, say, Jupiter might be composed of light, so clear that they are invisible to our earthly eyes?

It may be the same for 'intelligent' beings on other planets in our own or other galaxies who might be trying to find intelligent life on earth. They must have realized by now that there isn't any. I can imagine a report already filed somewhere out there concluding that the planet Earth is inhabited by small metal bugs on wheels, scampering about feverishly. When the bugs stop for a while, smaller two legged parasites emerge from them and rush about, carrying briefcases or plastic bags and return to their host-bugs which then tear away again. Ergo, there is no intelligent life on that small planet in that small solar system down there. And if they only heard the conversation which took place between two astronauts who landed on the moon and spoke these deathless lines which went very like this, they would have no doubt about that conclusion:

> 'Gee. Ain't this sump'n?'
> 'Yeah, ain't it?'
> 'Ain't this sump'n else?'
> 'Yeah, sump'n else'
> 'Ain't it?'

But I babble. All I need to suggest is that unless our inners become clear and sensitive enough to receive the reality beyond, as Bapak's could, we shall never 'know'. We may have to wait for that 'other life' before we can understand.

Bapak explained many times that the other life was a 'continuation of this, not in the same body or form but in quality.' The quality with which we end our lives in this world would determine the quality of the beginning of our lives in the other world. He often even joked about it. Once he did a mime of a well known *wali* or holy man who, when the angel of death whispered in his ear that he was summoned upstairs, he hurriedly clutched at his money wallet to check if it was safe. Another mullah, famous for his submissiveness to Allah, when told of his impending death, began counting his gold to be sure he would have enough to carry with him to paradise. 'Holiness,' it seems, 'is not the way upstairs.'

One evening in Cilandak Bapak told a few brothers about my asking him about what happened to a man when he died. An Indian member had written asking about 'reincarnation' and Bapak recalled what he had told me about rebirth in this world. 'Reincarnation,' Bapak said (Prio Hartono interpreting) 'is for a very few. If a man's *jiwa* has reached complete purification in this world, he would, at death, return directly to paradise. There, he may come under orders to perform many duties in the universe. He may even be "ordered" to carry out an assignment on planet earth. Then he could incarnate himself in the form needed for the task. He could be born on earth as a Palestinian or as a Javanese or in another form he chose. He would live and die on earth as long as he needed to, and return to paradise.'

We were all weeping silently as Bapak spoke. I remembered Adam. There was no sadness in our tears. Only a quiet joy and gratitude that we were fortunate to hear what he said from his own lips. There was a long silence in which I dozed off (it was nearly midnight). I woke up with a pleasant aroma in my nose. Bapak was fast asleep. So that, I thought, that is the smell of a reincarnated soul.

9

Meanings and origins

THERE must have been something in each one of us, some peculiar bit of genetic character inheritance or learned trait that brought us to Subud. In my case I suppose it was the need to find meaning in my daily life and the myriad events occurring around me and in the alternating feelings of hope, despair, fear, like and dislike, acquisitiveness and detachment which coursed through my mind. The religious 'knowledge' and practices in which I had been raised were never rigorous and demanding. My father was the principal of a small Buddhist school in a village not far from Colombo, the capital of our country. He was a lay leader of the local monastic Buddhist temple but though he performed his public religious duties, he was very relaxed about domestic religious observances.

My mother had been a Protestant Christian till she married my father but she never tried to impose Christian or Buddhist theology on her rapidly-growing brood. She bore and nurtured 13 of us through epidemics of malaria and childhood disorders and did it so well that all of us, my parents included – are alive at this time of writing. In my teens, I used to label myself a Free Thinker. There was more freedom than thinking skulking under that label. And by the time I reached university, I was accustomed to scoff at the mention of God, Brahma, Heaven and Hell and all the attendant beliefs of devout aunts and family elders.

It was predictable, I suppose, that I would gravitate towards Marxism and associate myself politically with faculty members and colleagues who called themselves Trotskyites – not because Trotsky had any relevance to the plight of the people in our country but because he was an enemy of Joseph Stalin. We knew nothing at the time of Stalin's gulags and their brutalities, but we saw his abortive pact with Hitler and the subsequent alliance with imperial France, Britain, and with nationalist China and the United States. This was all the evidence we needed to justify our loathing of him as an opportunist who was betraying Lenin and the promise held out by the great revolution of October 1917 by joining forces with the oppressors of colonial people. I wrote party pamphlets and had a whale of a time playing at cops and robbers. The Trotskyite party was banned during the war and its leaders jailed, and we claimed to be operating 'underground', the romantic milieu of all youthful rebels against authority.

A small group of us young undergraduates belonged to a training cell headed by a senior English teacher. He had a wide reputation as the party theoretician and as a brilliant literary critic. At the first training class he held at his house, he shattered and impressed us with a startling opening. 'Comrades', he said (how pleasing it was to be addressed thus by such a formidable character), 'Comrades, this country feeds and excretes through Colombo Harbour. We must get control of this aperture.' I did not fancy being a sphincter muscle, but I admired the succinctness of his description of our single channel of economic metabolism. The country had been completely colonised and reduced to total dependency on imports and exports, largely from imperial Britain. Control of movement of goods in and out through organising the big harbour workers' unions would put a clamp on the effort to win the war (this was in the early 40s), a way which we considered to be the last violent gasp of the imperial age – which is what it turned out to be.

My participation in all this underground work was to write the occasional polemical pamphlet and distribute it on my bicycle to whoever would stop to collect it, and I enjoyed the sense of belonging to a party which, in the words of the title of one of Trotsky's policies, was 'against the stream'. It had meaning for me because the pompous panoply of British imperialism present in all its glory in my country had no meaning at all except the intention to make us feel second-class citizens, inferior to the mangiest sales clerk at Millers, Cargills and Whiteways – the great British owned department stores through which post-season garments and other shoddy goods which were unsaleable in London were passed on to the 'native' elites.

But as we got deeper into the fray and into our training, a few incidents occurred that reduced my sense of dangerous elation. Our cell leader once said that we needed a copy of one of Trotsky's works which had been banned by the British government. The only copy, he said, was in the private library of the professor of English who was a friend of ours but not a member of the party. I was ordered 'to get hold of the copy' for translation into Sinhalese and Tamil. Dutifully, I went to the professor's house and asked to borrow the book. He denied my request saying that his books were his life and he never lent them out. I could read it in his house and work on it if I wished but the book should not be taken out. I thought this was very inconvenient but reasonable and so reported to our

leader at the next meeting of the cell. He went into a rage. 'You bloody
fool,' he screamed, 'I told you to get a hold of the book, not to borrow it.
We need it badly. We must get it by hook or by crook.'

I realized that what he was saying was that I should have simply stolen
the book from our friend. The end, evidently, justified the means. The
idea that one should use whatever means that would 'work' to attain a
desirable end had always troubled me theoretically as a harsh proposition
that the imperial powers had consistently used to vindicate their actions.
But its full meaning and venomous motive had not struck me forcibly
until I came face to face with it as I now did. As time passed, such con-
tradictions in action that claimed to be exclusively virtuous and progres-
sive became increasingly harder to swallow. Though my own lifestyle
could in no sense be described as virtuous, I gradually began to recognize
the relationship between personal values and public action. This was not
being sanctimonious but, rather, a recognition of the truth I came to realize much later, that means *were* indeed ends because they determined the
quality of the result attained. A war is won by violence but it only breeds
further violence and war. My association with party politics withered
away before long because it no longer had meaning for me.

I searched for meaning in my life in religion and in my reading.
Religion claimed to have the answers to the question 'why' – the key to
the quest for meaning. Why was I born? Why do so many tyrants and
crooks thrive in the world while honest and gentle people who care about
others suffer intolerably? Why do people fall ill and age and die, many
prematurely? But, the religious answers were often given in the form of
assertions wrapped in mystery which, we were told, could not and should
not be questioned or unravelled. Any attempt to make sense of them –
that is, to satisfy the mind – or ask for proof – was seen as an absence of
faith.

This attitude repelled me because I wondered how one could have
faith in anything one had not experienced and thereby got to know to be
true. I asked tacitly and sometimes out aloud – getting myself into all
kinds of trouble – how the priests and gurus, who preached about these
assertions of heaven and hell and the mysteries in which dogma and doctrine were wrapped, themselves knew about all this without direct experience of what they were saying. My questions, I was told, were illegiti-
mate because they arose from some dark place in my mind, some black
hole of unbelief. Faith, trust and belief in the assertions of the great masters – or rather, as they were reported – was essential if one wished to

find an answer to the great question 'why?'

The scientists I knew and had read never addressed that question. They were exclusively concerned with other questions: 'how?' and 'what?' They rejected questions relating to purpose and meaning – the 'why?' questions – as being 'unscientific' since they did not lend themselves to testing by the scientific method of establishing proof through replicable experiment and conclusive 'proof'. And yet, the great scientists such as Albert Einstein seemed to share an attribute of the great religious teachers – the ability to reach beyond immediately provable conclusions, to make a leap of faith. The lesser scientists and those whose scientific knowledge was obtained mostly from paperbacks, newspapers and the goggle box – a category in which most of us belong – seemed to be labouring under the pathetic logical fallacy that absence of proof was proof of absence.

Loren Eisely, American hobo poet and philosopher, whose work is widely unknown, grappled with the same questions in his unfinished book *How Man Came*, and offered some clues which gave some grist to my mind's mill:

'His living organs, his eyes, backbone, his hands and feet – even his remarkable brain – have originated in far places and in different eras of time. He is a mosaic of odd parts drawn together as one might rifle a cosmic junkyard to make a more than usually complicated tin woodman or a scarecrow. Some of the parts have been bent to other than their original purposes, some are obsolescent.

'None of these facts make man unique. All living creatures, because of the changing nature of life, are constructed of similar wandering bits of material strung together by a peculiar little alphabet or set of instructions, a kind of "do-it-yourself kit" which all plants and animals carry in their bodies and pass from one generation to another.

'Man can give names to these processes, lengthy scientific names like DNA, but their wonder remains. In short, we are stardust that somehow assembled itself first into life and finally into consciousness. This implies strange forces in the universe that no amount of naming by man can make ordinary. Man can use terms like evolution and try to position himself in time, but when, behind all these processes, he asks why they are, or come to be, he has reached the borders of science and has entered a realm of thought which can never be tested in a laboratory. This is the realm of what used to be called final questions, the questions asked by the philosopher. We can reason about such questions in a division of thought called metaphysics. Or we may explain them in terms of religious faith. But unlike the domain of science, with its palpable causes and effects which we have come to take as given and to be studied either in the experimental world of the laboratory or the wider, more confusing world of nature, we can only think what we are informed of by our senses. By the nature of things we are denied a scientific answer to the question Why? We can only accept the universe as given and proceed to examine how it seems to operate . . .'

And when Eisley began to scrape the barrel of his descriptive resources he told a story – the familiar resort of all word people like me: 'The Plains Indians had a favourite story motif and an opening line that began, "Once there was a poor orphan." This was once a true statement of man's condition, and although man has since attained to material riches he is a poor orphan still – an orphan armed with dangerous weapons he has picked up by the wayside that threaten to destroy not the fearsome creatures that once threatened him, but himself. He needs, in other words, another little kit that is studied by genetic instructions not carried in his body. This strange little kit instructs his body how to shape itself. What the orphan now needs for the freedom given him by nature is a new kit of instructions about how to live.

'Man himself must write this book. He has been trying for many ages all over the earth, but he has found the task difficult, and even more difficult the task of observing the rules he has devised for himself. This is part of the problem of being human and an orphan in a world where other creatures go about with another little set of instructions known as instinct, which tell them to be what they are, as for example an otter, a beaver or a serpent. By contrast man has gotten lost in a desert of terrible freedoms. He does not know clearly what he is and he frequently falls into violent argument as to how to behave. At such time the wise among his kind know that he is still an orphan and that he needs a new instruction . . .'

The latihan, for me, was a renewal of that 'instruction', the guiding force which was different from 'instinct' and flimsy as it was, seemed to be more whole and more persuasive than the prissy rigors of scientific and logical enquiry which could not give us a hand to help us choose between what Eisley called those 'terrible freedoms'.

There was something in me which was repelled by the aridity of Aristotelian or Cartesian logic. Post-Newtonian physicists and chemists, who reduced the human being to a mechanical contraption of atoms, irredeemably subject to the whims of pervasive material forces operating without purpose, were meaningless to me. I detested their assumption that man was similar to a Model T Ford made up of parts which, when over-used or corrupted, were repairable by skilled mechanics, and replaceable, part by part, with spares. There had to be some other explanation of human existence than was suggested by this atomistic view.

What was there in us that was attracted to painting and music and poetry? What was there within us which recognized truth when we heard it? What was there in us – whatever nation or ethnic group or age-group we belonged to – that was revulsed by wanton cruelty towards vulnerable beings, whether they were humans or animals or insects or plants? What outraged us when we saw unjust discrimination (and I don't mean unlawful), being done in the name of politics, nationality, ethnicity, skin-pigmentation, class, caste and gender? Even those who violated the canons of ordinary decency seemed to have spasms of remorse. Where did this originate?

I recall a story about Alfred Russell Wallace, a young British natural scientist, who set out for the Dutch East Indies in the middle of the 19th century and tramped around the islands looking for explanations of all things great and small. One of his discoveries was that there was a dividing line between the fauna of Australasia and those of Asia. This line snaked between the islands of the Archipelago, even separating Bali and Lombok which were only 15km apart. The fauna of Bali were never seen in Lombok and vice versa. When we were in primary school, our atlases called it Wallace's Line, but it is no longer noted in modern maps. Wallace made a brilliant guess – that it had something to do with a division in the sea bed. That was long before we knew anything about tectonic plates. He wrote about it in his The Geographical Distribution of Animals (1876).

But what he was even more noted for was his 'receiving', during a strong malarial delirium, of the principle of natural selection. He wrote it down on 30 pages of foolscap, tottered to the nearest port of the Moluccas, found a British ship leaving for London, and sent his paper to Charles Darwin Esq., care of the Linnaean Society. Darwin had returned from the Galapagos Islands with a similar theory of evolution but was waiting for corroboration, and here it was, in spadefuls. He read Wallace's letter out to the Society with his own annotations. Later Darwin and Wallace worked together on the theory of human evolution which we loosely call Darwinism.

The point here of my story, and this part of it may well be apocryphal, is that Wallace said to Darwin one day after 12 years of collaborations, 'Charles, we have taken this theory as far as we can. We have developed a defensible theory of the evolution of the physical body of man. But I believe that man is more than his physical body.' To which Darwin's reply was, 'About that, only God knows.' And they parted company. What was that missing element?

When I asked Bapak whether Darwin was right or wrong, Bapak replied (Anwar Zakir interpreting), 'Darwin was right. But his followers were not so right. Darwin was a humble man who believed in the existence and power of God. But his followers did not see that there was a vast gulf between the most advanced ape and the least advanced human being. So they interpolated a "missing link" to bridge the gap,' And Bapak bent towards me in a stage whisper and said, 'This link will always be missing.' He explained that when man's physical body had been 'prepared' the human soul arrived from the true human world beyond our solar system and lodged in that body. That was how Adam was born.

I told this story to Arthur C. Clarke, the science fiction writer, who was a friend and neighbour in Colombo. He had asked me to tell him what Pak Subuh has said about creation and the origin of the species. Arthur heard me out and, as I expected, his only response was a scientific snort. Years later, I saw his *2001: A Space Odyssey* in which the apes touched a monolith that had come from beyond Jupiter and received the impulse which transformed them into human beings. His snort had evidently not expunged Bapak's explanation from his mind. It had lurked somewhere in its crevices, forgotten by his consciousness as some powerful impressions do, and reappeared much later in the form of his own creative imagining. When I challenged him, jokingly, about plagiarism, Arthur was honest enough to remember the story I had told him.

My interest in meanings and origins that had brought me to Subud and motivated my persistent curiosity about Adam and Eve and evolution, tickled Bapak and he indulged me when he was in the mood. He once told me of a Mexican Subud member who had told Bapak about the 'sighting' of a UFO at a place near Guadalajara. She described how these space-men had landed in their space craft and walked out of it in the full sight of many people. Had Bapak any comments on this? Bapak asked, 'And I suppose these space-men spoke English? Or was it Spanish?' That quip did not quell her curiosity (good for her, I thought) and she looked

on at Bapak expectantly. Bapak said, 'If you only knew what this means .
. . you will not sleep of nights.' And did not say any more to her or to me.
It seemed to me that although Bapak did not wish to keep anything from
us, he was judicious about the time and place at which he let himself go.
And he was wary about stirring our imaginative faculties and giving us
cause for *akalfikiran*, needless thinking.

But one evening when Bapak was visiting France he was in the mood
to talk. It was July 14, Bastille Day, and there Bapak was with about half
a dozen of us on the penthouse terrace of a building in Rue Eugene
Manuel where he was staying, watching the fireworks bursting in the
clear sky. I marvelled at his child-like enjoyment of the star bursts of red,
white and blue and the brilliance of the display celebrating a historic liberation from tyranny. My enjoyment of such things is more inward, rather
colonial-British, which makes me more British than the British. I
expressed myself in a sort of half smile canopied by raised eyebrows. But
Bapak was uninhibitedly having a ball. At midnight the fireworks sput-
tered out and all was still. We sat silently with Bapak in one of those
extraordinary spells of quietness – which no one felt obliged to break by
chatter, unlike most moments of silence when people feel embarrassed
and awkwardly responsible for their inarticulateness.

The silence stretched for five, six, seven, eight minutes and then Bapak
said 'Varindra, look out and tell Bapak what you see.' I scanned the skies
and said 'Space, Bapak.' 'Yes, space,' said Bapak, 'But it may be not space
as you know it. As Bapak is right now, Bapak can see the whole universe.
It is not broken up. It is one, single, intricate machine. Not like the
machines you use. Not like your typewriter, Varindra. Or your car. It is
more like (and he bent over to Muhammed Usman for a phrase and continued) more like electronic grid or like (he spoke to Usman again) a
field of force. This force starts from the origin and moves outward in a
circular direction eventually returning to the origin.'

Anxious to seize the moment for a key answer to my constant questioning, I asked, 'What is the point of origin?' Bapak looked a bit exas-
perated and dismissed the question with a question, 'What is the origin
of a circle?' Feeling foolish, I shut up. 'As it moves out, this force con-
denses into lumps. We call them stars and planets. Each of one of these
lumps becomes refined in time and de-lumps itself to be able to rejoin
the flow of force and return to the origin. And you Varindra, are a two-
legged lump walking about on one of the smallest of these planetary
lumps. And you say "This piece of this lump is my country. And within

this small lump is a smaller lump called my property." But surely the refining process we call purification is to enable you to de-lump yourself so that, at the end of your life on this lump we call earth, you can rejoin the flow of force on your way back to the origin.'

We were enthralled by the completeness of this parable on our existence, given so clearly, briefly and lightly. It was all there. 'Are you sitting on that chair, or is the chair sitting on you? Are you drinking that whisky, or is the whisky drinking you? Do you own your property, or does your property own you?' There was no call for 'renunciation' there. But there was a call for the appropriate relationship between what I am and what I have. This parable has constantly been with me ever since, as the only explanation of the why and wherefore of life that calmed my turbulent mind. Bapak did not say more that night though I am certain that it was only what he had chosen to say. It was plenty for the time being.

But a few months later, during the month of Ramadan in Cilandak, Bapak talked to us again about creation and the latihan (Usman interpreting), 'Before the universe was created, there was emptiness and God. You will ask how there can be emptiness and something else. But Bapak cannot explain that to you now. If you would, take it from Bapak that there was only emptiness and God. There was no light because there was no darkness. Only emptiness. God created the light. The light was not God but God's creation. Light is a vibration. That was the original vibration. The vibration of creation. This vibration produced material things. The stars and planets are made up of this materiality which has its own vibrations. Material forces have their own vibrations.

What you experienced when you received the Subud contact, the contact with the great life force, was a contact with the original vibration. When you do your latihan, after long purification, you will be able to distinguish between that original vibration of light and the material vibrations of the earth.'

I felt elated that another piece of the 'explanation' had fallen into place. But, *bismillah*, there was so much more to learn from Pak Subuh, the non-teacher, and I will regret for the rest of my days that I had not taken the trouble to learn enough of Bahasa Indonesian to draw him out when he was in the mood to reveal his experience and understanding. I realize I should not be ungrateful for the opportunities I had to be with Bapak more often than most Subud members, and I know that Bapak told me many things because he knew that I was by nature a communica-

tor and would share them with others. But I might have been better
equipped for it if I had taken more trouble.

10

The business of Subud

MANY Subud members, including me, had great difficulty in coming to terms with Bapak's continuous emphasis in our engaging our time, skills and energies on enterprises. Part of my problem was the socialist cast of my mind, which was conditioned to abhor capitalism and its profit nexus as the devil's invention to set up greed as the prime motive force behind our use of the earth's resources and human skills. Despite my early atheism and vociferous anti-religiousness, Gautama Buddha's mordant observation that greed, envy, fear and ignorance were the predominant determinants of human behaviour was – and continued to be – a constant thought underlying my world view. My reading of history seemed to confirm and validate this attitude. It was clear to me that the hideous human toll of war throughout recorded history had been caused by the greed of despots and, later, by private greed organised into businesses which were not accountable to their trading partners but to their stockholders who demanded annual assuagement of their greed for more and more dividends.

As a very young man writing polemical party pamphlets and occasionally writing for magazines and newspapers, I had been given the opportunity to meet Mahatma Gandhi. That was in the winter of 1946 and the meeting was to be in New Delhi at the home of the Ceylon Representative who was my father-in-law at the time. I prepared myself sartorially for the great occasion. I got myself a spanking new suit of Royal Air Force blue from Phelps and Co, the British military tailors and a sober Tootal tie and a breast pocket handkerchief to go with it. On that Sunday morning under the brilliant Delhi winter sky, Mahatma Gandhi was seated on a rattan settee wearing his familiar *dhoti* around his loins with a handwoven shawl covering his torso and shoulders, his stick beside him on the carpet spread on the lawn.

There were about 20 guests standing well away from him offering *darshan* – the respect of their eyes, no one daring to go near, as is usual in Asia where distance is a measure of reverence. As I was taken to be introduced to him, he looked up, saw this vision of tailored splendour before him,

smiled broadly and said in a sardonic tone, 'Oho, one of our smart south-
ern neighbours!' Mahatma Gandhi who had shed his snappy colonial suit
and tie many decades before, found tropical colonials clad in British
clothes absurd and made no bones about it.

The gawking guests burst into laughter as people do when a great man
makes a joke. My face must have gone white with embarrassment.
Mahatma Gandhi heard the laughter, saw my discomfiture and immediately took compassion on me. He patted the space on the settee beside
him and said, 'Sit down, sit right here,' to make it up to me. I sat in gin-
gerly awkwardness at the edge of the chair, desperately thinking how on
earth I was ever going to lift my head again. But, as the smart schoolboy
gets out of a jam by asking an intelligent question, I produced one to get
out of my predicament. 'Gandhiji,' I said, 'All of us in Asia are soon
going to be free because of your work. If you had one piece of advice for
all of us, what would it be?' His face purpled in a sort of sad seriousness
and he looked down at the carpet for a few seconds, then he looked up at
me, smiling that beautiful toothless grin of his, and said, 'Reduce your
wants and supply your needs.' And then he added, perhaps unnecessarily,
'Our needs make us vulnerable enough. Why increase our vulnerability?'

Those extraordinary words have lodged in my head ever since as a permanent part of its furniture, although like many Asians, I cannot say that
the brunt of the advice has been followed in my life. I have indulged my
'wants' far beyond my needs as my income has increased over the years.
But the power of Mahatma Gandhi's words has never dimmed in my consciousness. It was very much in tune with the sub-continental ethos of
renunciation of material attachments which bind us to the earth.
Mahatma Gandhi had made it an essential feature of his own lifeways. It
also proved to be a tremendous political strategy. He had proved the
truth that real power comes not from what you *have*, but from what you
are, that the less and less you have, the less vulnerable you are to the
power and blandishments of the forces set against you. The British government could get no leverage at all on him to bend him to their will. He
had no estate they could confiscate, no house, no automobile – nothing at
all except his loin cloth and chappals, and he would have readily parted
with those if they had demanded them. He did not even set great store by
his personal liberty which he was so often willing to surrender in prison
for the sake of the freedom of his country.

The only 'greed' he had was for independence from colonial rule. He
destroyed the mightiest empire in history without the use of a single gun

and started the astonishing domino process of decolonisation which changed the world in a quarter of a century. And when he had accomplished that, he refused to accept political appointments in free India, and even the honours they offered him as the father of independent India.

Another great Indian, Jawaharlal Nehru, was very different from Mahatma Gandhi. He rejected many 'Gandhian' values – even non-violence, the most precious gift from the Mahatma. But he too shared the loathing of material values as the measure of human worth. I once asked him one of those blunt questions I often asked as a journalist to get an interview going. 'Prime Minister, why do you hate the Americans?' He reflected on this for a while, refusing to make a kneejerk response and said, very quietly, 'I do not hate the Americans. Not at all. I have neither time nor inclination for hate. But I have some difficulty in coming to terms with the crassness of some of them.'

He then told me of his being given a great banquet by a group of American businessmen during his first visit to the United States. The president of US Steel at the time was the chief host and said in the course of his toast, 'Mr Prime Minister, the measure of our great admiration and regard for you is that round this table are the heads of corporations representing more than fifty billion dollars.' He may have been free of hatred but Nehru was by no means free of moral finickiness and, though he was a modern Indian raised in the values and attitudes he learnt at Harrow and Cambridge, the contempt for money and being measured by quantitative criteria rather than by quality, seared his mind. I asked, 'Do you think that the president of US Steel represented the values of all, or most, Americans?' He said 'Not at all. American people obviously have more civilized values. Their literature and art prove that.'

Such attitudes to business – particularly big business and its antihuman relationship towards people, such as the hiring and firing of workers without a qualm in the interests of profits and 'efficiency', which was a way of making more profit – were very much in accordance with my own long-set ideas. The result was that when Bapak spoke about enterprises, an automatic cut-out in my mind began operating, not only because it was unpalatable to the conditioning of my mind, but also because I was loath to let myself harbour any negative thoughts about Bapak.

I realized that he had been advocating enterprises from as long ago as 1959, at the first world congress held at Coombe Springs. In response to questions from a group, its chairman, Sir Victor Goddard, a Subud stalwart of the time, asked Bapak for guidance about the conduct of Subud enterprises. Bapak said; 'Although money-making may be included in the field of our activities and although to all outward appearances this may be just the same as any other similar concerns, in reality it is quite different. In the ordinary way it is the nature of those who are engaged in making money to be dominated and influenced by it, whereas we, when we work with money are not overpowered by it, but are its masters, and it is we who have power over it.' (*Subud and the Active Life.*)

I could understand easily that it was necessary for business people in Subud to set up enterprises to produce funds for Subud education, health and other human welfare purposes. I told myself, 'fair enough, but not for me'. I was no businessman, I was a writer and I would stick to my pen, and a percentage of whatever I made from my work I would give to Subud. But when in later years the emphasis on Subud enterprises became more vocal and frequent, I watched with growing alarm how everyone felt impelled to become entrepreneurs. So poets began businesses, which collapsed after a few stumbling steps and businessmen began to write bad poetry.

Bapak had told a story at the congress about a farm in Indonesia which was failing until it was taken over by a Subud member called Karjo, who made it work because the material, vegetable and human forces in him were able to get the farm working properly. His reward was the hand of the owner's daughter. This was promptly – and perhaps inevitably – taken to mean that because we are in Subud, whatever we put our hands to would go well. Some of us plunged into real estate with no knowledge at all about land values and land laws; some, who couldn't tell the front of a cow from its behind, became livestock farmers; some set up factories with little capital and no knowledge of the rigours of cash-flow. It was all going to be like Karjo and the owner's daughter's hand was a cinch.

But what we had not heard was the rest of Bapak's explanation: 'We cannot obtain money from God because money is a human factor and is made by man, not by God. Therefore, if we look to God to provide us with money, we may not get any, for God has never created it. It is clear that when man needs money, it is through other men, through human agency, that he must obtain it. However, the most important thing in our lives here is that we should be able to allow the various powers in us to work properly and to make proper use of them; that we should know how these forces work and operate in us.' (*Subud and the Active Life.*)

Bapak once gave us a quick explanation of the power that material things have over us. He said (Prio Hartono interpreting), 'Here is a piece

of blank paper. It has no value. The four of you here agree to give it some
value. You say, let us decide that this piece of paper is worth one hundred
dollars. You have created value with your minds. But the following week,
you are fighting over this paper. The thing you yourself created now has
power over you, enough to make good friends fall out.'

My scepticism about enterprises was mitigated by Bapak's explanation
that the working principle of business should be that both the seller and
the buyer should be equally satisfied. This meant honesty and clarity in
all our transactions and, above all, no hype, and no 'spiritual' fancies
about any special providence for Subud members doing business. I began
to hope that Subud enterprises would set new standards of integrity in
business, that there would be examples of capitalism with a human face,
where success in commerce would go hand in hand with social justice for
everyone concerned, because the ultimate purpose was to free Subud
members from dependency on the iron whims of some faceless gnome in
Zurich, Wall Street, or the City of London, and produce sufficient
resources for Subud education, Subud health facilities and other human
welfare programmes.

It did not take long to realize that I was counting my chickens long
before they were hatched. There was much more for all of us to learn.
And it has been a very painful and expensive learning process. I learned,
for instance, that the material forces of this earth are not waiting passively to serve Subud enterprises. They are not queuing up with buckets of
cement and sand to pour into a Subud building site.

Bankers are not twiddling their thumbs impatiently waiting for a
Subud entrepreneur to come along asking for a loan to finance a business.
Politicians and central bankers do not take into account Subud enterprise
needs with their calculations when they decide to change exchange regulations or devalue currencies. On the contrary, the material forces are
actively opposed to allowing Subud enterprises to thrive. They liked the
way business was done in the familiar market place with its 'I'm all right,
Jack' values and its penchant for increasing consumerism by constant,
strident appeals to man's greed. 'You have a 1988 Ford? Get rid of it and
buy the new, bigger and shinier 1989 model,' and so on – the hype that
assails our eyes and ears every moment of the day and night. Subud enterprises, run as Bapak described them and for the social purposes for which
they were intended, were highly undesirable to these forces and they did
their damnedest to plague them. We, for our part, made openings for
these inimical elements to do their work by quarrelling among ourselves

and by using spiritual imagination rather than our minds to make business decisions.

We wondered why the businesses suggested by Bapak himself were not assisted by the good angels. Why did they not provide the money, the steel and the sand to prevent us over-shooting estimates by delays in financing? Why did they not warn us that the Indonesian government was going to devalue the rupiah so that we could have timed that foreign bank loan to our advantage rather than cause us to suffer a 40 percent loss overnight? It took a long while for us to begin to understand that business was not the angels' business, nor was it Bapak's. Bapak was our spiritual guide, not our business manager. Bapak was concerned with the well-being of Subud members and could 'see' a project ahead of us, a bank, a hotel, a conference centre, a development programme in the thick rainforests of Kalimantan, and he would tell us about it, urging us to take advantage of the opportunity he had foreseen for our benefit. It was up to us to find our way towards it, to make it real. It was up to us to put together the brains, the skills and the means to give his vision form and substance.

Apart from the intrinsic value of increasing the resources of the brotherhood for members and their families in terms of Subud 'development' – schools, hospitals, homes for the ageing and disabled who needed care – it became increasingly clear to me that Bapak had another purpose in pressing us to go into enterprises. This was to get us to use our minds for that sort of productive work instead of thinking about spiritual matters and into 'organizing' Subud. Over the years many of the disputes within the brotherhood had been caused by a few members who had good brains and no work to use them on. 'Working for Subud' became their full-time occupation. They felt very virtuous about their indefatigable dedication but had not the slightest suspicion that they were doing any damage to themselves as well as to the brotherhood. Engaging these energies in enterprises was one way of preventing this while deploying them for a purpose beneficial to everyone.

After the second London congress in 1983, I called on Bapak to receive my marching orders. I asked him about the purpose of Anugraha, which had not been completed as a conference centre then as it had originally been intended. I pointed out that even if it had been completed, we would still have had to resort to the giant tent we had used to accommodate 3,000 members. Bapak said (Sjarif Horthy interpreting) that we needed a conference hall not only to raise funds for Subud and for a centre where Subud members could use for their meetings but also as an attractive place where Subud and the world outside would 'interface' in a way that was useful to both, where non-Subud people would realize that Subud was not one of those other-worldly cults devoted to mystic concerns.

Subud members, Bapak explained, should be interested in *this* world as long as we are in this world because the quality of our lives in the world hereafter would be determined by our lives here and now. Bapak said the latihan was all we needed to do for our inner life. Our hearts and minds should be deployed for the improvement of our outer life. That is why, Bapak added, in old times people's minds and energies were used to build churches and temples and mosques. I asked, 'Anugraha, then, is our mosque?' Bapak replied smiling, 'Yes, only more useful.'

11
A star at the window

PEOPLE have come to Subud for all sorts of reasons and nonreasons. If you took a microphone around to each member in a group – as I have done – and asked, 'How did you come to join Subud?' nearly everyone will begin, 'It was very strange . . .' or 'It was a funny coincidence . . .' In the beginning many of the people who came to Subud were 'seekers' looking for a way to live their lives with less gormlessness than they had been able to find in books and in their workaday experience. Some were refugees from religious dogma and trumpery ritualism. Others – like me – had been members of ways and systems which they had followed as far as they could, and had turned to Subud when they found themselves up against an impenetrable blank wall.

Still others came for 'faith healing'. Eva Bartok's 'miracle cure', sensationalised in the London press and in *Paris Match*, induced hundreds to seek the help of the Miracle Man from Java. One of them was Soraya, the Empress of Iran, who wanted a meeting with Bapak to ask him to intercede with the Almighty so that she could produce a male heir to the Peacock Throne. (Bapak said it was 'up to God' and she lost interest and eventually her throne.) Another, a frequent customer of health spas, joined Subud to lose weight. (He still frequents fat farms.)

Some others had been persuaded, prevailed upon by a friend or teacher they respected, to receive the contact in Subud. Many had read John Bennett and later, Ronimund von Bissing and Edward van Hien, the first of several Subud authors. The chapter on Subud in Jacob Needleman's *The New Religions*, published during the Maharishi explosion of the 60s, brought many Americans to the latihan. I suspect that George Lucas, the writer-producer-director of *Star Wars*, had derived the idea of surrendering to The Force from the Subud members he worked with. It was done tongue-in-cheek but it was respectful and knowledgeable in the same way as Needleman was, though neither Lucas nor Needleman ever joined Subud.

Most people attributed the reason for their joining Subud to coincidence – or as the Americans felicitously call it – happenstance. I never believed it. Coincidence is not necessarily meaninglessly random. I have always thought that we were all brought to Subud by one means or another – coincidences, brief encounters or seemingly casual happenstance. Peter (Lester) Barrett, who was on an ocean liner sailing from London to Rio de Janeiro to meet Yma Sumac's voice tutor, found a copy of John Bennett's *Concerning Subud* in the ship's library. He realized that he needed things other than his voice repaired and took the very next ship back to London to receive the latihan. The coincidence of that book being in his ship's library and that he should decide to choose it when his own preoccupation – even obsession – was on something very physical, seemed to me to be no accident.

Even the 'reason' given by the man who came to reduce his adipose tissue was not absurd. There was something already within him that moved him in the direction of Subud. Even those who soon dropped out of doing the latihan had been brought to Subud for a purpose. John Bennett gave Subud a footing in the West and went his own way. But many of us who had come to Subud through his instrumentality have now been practising the latihan for more than 30 years. There was a disabled New Yorker who came to the Subud house in a wheelchair to get his legs 'fixed'. He walked out after his opening, leaving his chair behind. He never returned. When Francis von Kahler telephoned him some months later to ask him about his health and to seek a contribution for a new Subud house the man said, 'Ah yes. That place on East 21st. Yes. It did me good. I'll put a cheque in the mail today. Oh, by the way, could you arrange to have that wheelchair returned to me? . . . I have an appointment, must run.' He must be running for some reason, I suppose.

What amazes me is not the mystery of why and how people came to Subud but why we stay in Subud in spite of all the tribulations we have encountered in our lives. All the early propaganda (which Bapak constantly warned us against) about miraculous cures and the spiritual 'protection' from all sorts of pain and suffering have proved to be disappointing. Subud members have been subject, like everyone else, to fatal motoring accidents, they have been victims of cancer and other ravaging diseases, and some of them play petty power games over other members as 'normal' people do in their offices and social associations

All we have is the latihan. We have no grand architecture – great cathedrals and mosques and stupas decorated by the Old Masters of painting and sculpture; we have no great 'theatre' – ornate basilicas, brocade costumes, intricate liturgical ceremonies, sonorous organ music and chorales . . . We go twice a week to a cramped leased space in some ordinary building (I've just done two latihans among the word processors and calculating machines in a secretarial school where the Subud group in Austin, Texas, meets) and, dressed down rather than up in our Sunday best, we close our eyes, make funny movements and utter extremely unmusical sounds for half an hour and go back home. And we have gone on doing this for years and years. Now even Bapak does not visit us to give us that lift we enjoyed occasionally over the years. And we still go on. Why?

The answer I have given to myself is based on something Bapak told us at the very beginning of Subud's coming out of Indonesia into the world. He said that ancient people who worshipped God relied on their capacity for faith. They were less complicated and less caught up in material existence. Modern men and women need to worship in a way that gives them 'proof'. The proof lies in the palpable experience of the latihan: the vibrations felt in the body and on the skin and the movements we make that arise from within, when the mind ceases 'by itself' to direct us.

Bapak once told me that when someone interested in knowing about Subud kept on asking questions ad nauseam, I should say clearly to him, 'Enough talking; now experience. Then we can talk more if you like.' But that after experience, his questions would be different. More real. Bapak said, 'It is like the experience of eating a mango. If you tell someone who has never eaten a mango that the arumanis mango is the best mango in the world he would ask you what makes it so special, why is it better than Indian or Sri Lankan mangoes and on and on interminably. But if you give him an arumanis mango and he likes its taste and texture, his questions will change or, maybe, he will have no more questions.'

Someone present asked 'But, if someone said that he had experienced the same sort of vibration as in the latihan from a different source than Subud, maybe in Africa or India, what then?' Bapak replied, 'Then what? *Sama sama*. If the experience is the same what's the problem? Subud does not claim a monopoly of the power of God.'

That, then, is it. It is the ability to experience the latihan and to put ourselves in a state of willingness to experience it time after time that gives us proof of its reality. That is why I have continued in Subud. After a while it becomes a part of us, as much a part of us as our skin and bone. It is *there* – beating its flimsy butterfly wings inside us whenever we let go of our minds even for a moment. That is why it is unthinkable for me that anyone could 'leave' Subud. It would be like leaving oneself.

But our minds look for more proof – apart from proof of the reality of the latihan. We look for proof in its effects on our work, and in our relationships with our families and with others in society. I have been lucky to find that evidence outside myself, since I have spent my life writing and I can detect significant changes in it over the years, which I cannot honestly attribute to biological maturescence or increasing worldly 'knowledge'. I make a simple balance sheet: what has improved in my work, I credit to the latihan. What hasn't, I charge to myself. Often Bapak has asked us to 'let it' work in our daily lives so that the latihan is reflected in the way we act and behave, and show up in our 'culture'. The key words for me are to 'let it'. And then there is outward proof of the effects of an inner process. And one day, I fervently hope, we shall be able to give the world the proof it demands in the form of Subud hospitals, schools and businesses, and good and able people running them.

As for me, questions never ceased even when I was given scintillating explanations. As a professional disbeliever and a chronic doubter it seemed I needed more frequent 'proof' than almost anyone else. I was fortunate enough to have ready access to Bapak and to ask him all my questions. I had wonderful children, I had work which suited my talents, I could earn what money I needed and I had the latihan. What more could I want? I wanted renewed reassurance from time to time that Subud was what Bapak said it was – a fresh gift of the power of God sent to help human beings to avoid being overwhelmed by the material forces which were omnipresent in this world. In my peregrinations as an international journalist and as an international civil servant, I saw the ubiquitous power of weapons and money and the internecine power-plays among cultured people such as academics, politicians, business leaders, social workers. No one seemed to be interested in human values in action but only in the 'do-able' and cost-efficient, whatever the human price.

Seeing how pervasive this material power was, I often wondered how the latihan I felt tingling across my pate and on my skin and in my blood, this 'force' which seemed to have the tensile strength of gossamer, this grace from God which joined Subud members together in a web of brotherhood and sisterhood – the smallest spiritual movement in the world, no more than six or seven thousand active members, at best, scattered in fifty different countries – would make any difference. I went to Bapak as often as I could, every month, even oftener in the early years, to recharge my spiritual batteries and my confidence. I often went into the Big House with a craven dispirited heart and came out feeling on top of the world – a Subud member armed with the latihan in his inner, ready to confront the world again. But I wanted more proof of who Bapak was and of the cosmic place of Subud.

The proof was given on two blessed occasions. In 1969, I lived in Singapore while my wife Lestari lived with our son, Imran, in a tiny two-roomed apartment in the back of the Wisma Subud compound in Cilandak – a 'temporary' line of tenements appropriately called Skid Row. Bapak had advised Lestari not to live in Manila where my headquarters were or in Singapore – where we had rented a beautiful home – because he felt that she was too sensitive to live in 'heavy' places. I was evidently coarse enough to handle it. I asked what we should do with the house we had furnished. With a grin and a chortle, Bapak said, 'You furnished it for Bapak to stay in whenever he passes by Singapore.' Once a month I was able to visit my family and, occasionally, I would ask Bapak's permission to borrow my wife for a shopping trip to Singapore. But it became intolerably lonely especially on the week-ends. One Friday afternoon, returning from the *Straits Times* to my empty house, I could not face it; I told my driver to take me to the airport and set off for Jakarta.

I arrived unexpected in Cilandak at about eight o'clock and saw Lestari and our little boy running up to greet me while I paid off the taxi. She told me that Bapak had popped into our place not five minutes before to ask if I was due that evening. She had said I was not coming back for another week. Bapak had said, 'But that is very odd. Surely Varindra knows it is Bapak's birthday tomorrow?* And he's not going to attend the party Bapak is giving at his house?' All this had been said in a joking tone but we had learned that Bapak's jokes had a serious purpose which we were able, if at all, to decode only later. Lestari said that Bapak was due to talk to the men later that evening and I had arrived just in time.

Bapak seemed pleased to see me, invited us all to the birthday party and spoke for three hours about death. That was the evening when he said we should 'learn to die to things before they die on us,' a lesson I have found profoundly valuable, especially in dealing with the reality of the death of my wife, and the cosmic event of Bapak's own death on earth. That was also the evening when Bapak made a curious statement, again using me as the butt for it. 'Varindra travels all over the globe and knows the world well,' he said. 'It is necessary to know this world. That is why you are here. But when Varindra dies and his *jiwa* is separated from his

*Honestly, I am not a birthday person and had forgotten all about it.

body, it will experience its new freedom and then say to itself, "Ah ha, but I have not yet been to Alaska. I must get to know Alaska. Only after seeing Alaska can I leave this earth".'

None of us understood it fully but none of us took it literally, and, reader, I hope you will not either. Alaska was only a remote place, the name of which had popped into Bapak's mind as he spoke. But 'getting to know Alaska' became a private joke for Lestari and me as we traipsed around the world through Latin America, Russia, China, Africa, Canada, India, Australia and scores of other places.

Back in our little hidey hole, I reported Bapak's talk to my wife. Then we made love and turned over, back to back as we usually did, to sleep. It was about three in the morning. Hardly had we closed our eyes when the room was flooded with a bright light through the small open window that Abdullah Pope had made for Lestari only a few weeks before. I heard Lestari say, 'Varindra, Varindra, look, look!' I turned over and saw something extraordinary happening. There were trees just outside with a 20 foot-diameter circle left open by the foliage, and into this circle a bright light was streaking in from far away. As it reached the circle it stopped, apparently adjusting itself to occupy the very centre, and began to flash its light at us. It could have been 20 feet away, or two miles away or 200 million miles away; it had no relationship to perspective, it seemed. It was a many-sided star, looking about 18 inches deep and wide. It was so translucent and the light, bright as it was, was so soft that it did not dazzle us, so that we could see clearly its farther points. I glanced at my watch by habit, as a reporter will. It was three twenty. We watched it, hardly daring to breathe.

After a while Lestari whispered, 'What is it? Is it what they call a UFO? or is it a message?' I whispered back 'It must be a message for Bapak. A birthday greeting.' After half an hour Lestari said, 'It is Erling Week's turn at being watch-man tonight. Why not call him so that he too can see it? Clad only in my sarong, barebodied, I ran out to find Erling somewhere in the compound. I was sure I would, since Erling does everything thoroughly and he would still be up and about. But he was nowhere to be found. I saw a light burning in one of the guest rooms and rushed to the open window to see a young Italian, who never had seemed to need any sleep, lying on his bed with one leg trailing on the floor, fast asleep with Erling's flashlight in his hand. He had volunteered to take over Erling's watch and fallen asleep. Try as I did, I could not wake him.

I did not want to miss any more of the star and was running back when I met an Indonesian, also a tenant of Skid Row. I said 'Mas, look at that,' pointing to the star, which I could see over the low roof. 'Where? What?' he said wagging his head. I realized he could not see what was plain to me and bid him *selamat pagi* and rejoined my wife. The star was still there flashing its message.

Of course there was no sleep for us that night. In the morning we waited anxiously for the Big House to open so that I could tell Bapak about our experience. At about eight o'clock we saw Pak Usman walking towards Bapak's house for his daily orders, and I joined him. Bapak and members of his family were supervising the rearrangement of the living room for the evening's party. Usman and I offered Bapak our *sunkum* and wished him well on his birthday. Bapak offered me a seat and, after a while, in a rather stern tone asked '*Apa?*' I sobbed out my story, Usman hardly able to follow my tripping words to translate them. He had another difficulty. He was weeping as deeply as I was. So were the family. Tears without a twinge of sadness. Tears of awe and wonderment. Cleansing, inspiring tears. Bapak alone remained stern.

A moment or two after I finished, Bapak said, still in that stern manner, 'Yes. It was a message for Bapak.' Then he added, 'Don't you go and write about this.' I felt suddenly terrible, as though inveterate reporter that I was, I had snooped into something that I had no business in, that I had invaded Bapak's privacy. I mumbled '*Minta maaf*, Bapak,' apologetically and slunk away thinking that Bapak had warned me not to send cables all over the Subud world saying, 'Star of Bethlehem sighted again,' or some such sensational inanity. I was hobbling down the back steps in a sort of shame when I heard Bapak's steps. He had walked to the top of the flight and now he smiled. 'You may tell your friends about it,' he said, making it all right for me again.

The message was for Bapak but it had appeared at my window I figured, because I was Bapak's messenger boy. When I told my friends Sudarto, Brodjo and Prio my story, Pak Darto laughed uproariously and said, 'So? You are the great disbeliever in miracles. So you are given extraordinary proof. And in case you disbelieved that too, your wife was there to corroborate it!'

On another occasion in Cilandak, I had a dream in the early hours of the morning. I saw points of light, like little stars on the ceiling which I knew was the sky. I counted them. There were 40. The dream seemed to last a long time but did not move and change. The 40 lights twinkled away without revealing their meaning. All I experienced was a sense of calm happiness and a suggestion that it was somehow important. That morning I told Bapak about my dream. He closed his eyes and received for a long time so strongly that I could hardly bear it so that I broke again into a spasm of tears. Bapak said (Prio Hartono interpreting), 'This is an experience of what will happen when Bapak dies. There will be 40 Subud members around the world who will attract people to Subud and will have earned the trust of Subud members because they understand the importance of surrendering to the will of Almighty God and the meaning and purpose of Subud. Seven of them will be from Indonesia. The rest will be from many other countries. They will be able to recognize one another. It will be like a *dewan* when Bapak is in the other world'.

Lestari and I resolved we would not tell this story at that time except to our closest friends. We were afraid that if it was widely known many would begin tagging people with stars, and some helpers who had spiritual ambitions would make a play to become one-star generals. Besides, we felt certain at the time that Bapak would outlive all of us and that the 'stars' would be not any of us then alive but possibly our grandchildren and their children. I tell this story publicly now not because I think the danger of it being misused and misinterpreted has passed, but only because now that Bapak is no longer with us, I feel I have no right to keep it from my brothers and sisters to do with it as they will.

Both these experiences with stars associated with Bapak and with the brotherhood of Subud have already given me what I needed most – the conviction of Bapak's greatness and the reassurance that, despite the scattered evidence pointing to the contrary, all will be well for Subud, *insh' Allah*, since it is God's will that will prevail, not ours.

12

A world without Bapak

AS the 31 years since I received the Subud contact from Bapak at Coombe Springs in Kingston-on-Thames passed by, there was a constant sense of joy in my being that we, the first generation of Subud members, were especially blessed by living on this earth at the same time as Muhammad Subuh. Whenever we spoke to one another of this feeling, we wondered what it must have been like to be living in Bharat (India) at the time of Gautama Buddha or in West Asia at the time of Jesus and Muhammad. Apart from being able to see and hear and touch Bapak from time to time we were conscious of belonging to the generation of practitioners of the latihan who did not have to rely on the scriptures written and published later, to try and understand the sense and weight of his explanations directly.

We were in his physical presence as he spoke so that we had the advantage of seeing the expression on his face changing from gravitas to joviality and hearing the modulation of his voice from directness to irony or lightness, and to appreciate the meaning in the pauses, which no grammatical punctuation can convey. And we could understand the intention in his gestures which, of course, were never recorded on film because it would have been profanely uncouth to have flashed electric bulbs and photographed him in the state of receiving he was in when he gave us his talks.

And, most of all, the vibration of his voice would touch our inner ears when we were able and willing to 'let go' of the effort to seize meaning with our brains, so that even those of us who knew no Bahasa Indonesia would sense the benefit of what he was saying without it being mediated through the mind.

Yes, we were enormously lucky to inhabit this planet and raise our children at the time of Muhammad Subuh's earthly existence. But we were also full of rubbish. Aware of the extent, depth and variety of that rubbish in my own life, the Doubting Thomas in me questioned why, if this coincidence of lifetimes was indeed a blessing, it should have been vouchsafed (what a marvellous old word, that!) to me, a man with a barrow full of garbage to get rid of before I could possibly deserve any spiritual blessing at all, let alone such a special good fortune. My mind often jeered at my sense of wonderment that I was able to see Bapak and talk with him, pointing out that Bapak himself had often said that he was 'an ordinary man,' that he was not a Teacher, nor a prophet, that he was 'only' the bearer of a message, that we should never forget that it was to God, not to Muhammad Subuh, that we should be grateful for the blessings of the latihan.

As a journalist and as a Sri Lankan, I could detect what was distinctly Javanese in Pak Subuh as a physical presence and in his modes of thinking, his relationships with his extended family, his idiom and metaphor which came from a feudal agrarian society, his cultural allusions to the Mahabaratha and the Ramayana which had been assimilated into ancient indigenous archipelagic lore, quite distinctive from the way they had been internalised by the Thais, the Burmese, the Indians and the Sri Lankans who also had been influenced by those classics. What was essentially discernible as Indonesian in Pak Subuh often stood in the way of my wish to regard him as a man living above and beyond the limitations of national and cultural boundaries. He evidently 'knew' the essence of other cultures and could distinguish between their effect on the behaviour patterns (how does an Englishman walk, how does a a woman from Solo greet her husband?) and the mores of people all over the globe. I marvelled to observe how Bapak's own movements changed in a subtle way as he travelled – a slight loose-limbed swagger in California, a subtle stiffening of his gait in London, a clear formality in a tea-house in Japan, a relaxed homeyness in Colombo when he was nearer Jakarta.

But when the Paris group took Bapak to the ballet, some of them were a little put out that he did not seem to enjoy himself as all of us had. When they asked me why he had not applauded, my riposte was to ask why the ballet company had not applauded Bapak for taking time to see them dance. But even as I said this, I felt it was just a glib mot from a loyal courtier and not a helpful answer from an older brother. I should have said I don't know, let us ask Bapak, and I did not because I too had noticed the Javanese gentleman being uncomfortable with the unfamiliar. In the early days when Bapak used to speak about the way Subud went abroad from Java – how a 'French Countess' had offered the money for Bapak to go to Malaya and from there to the West – I smiled affectionately at how Pak Subuh, the 'assistant book keeper from Jakarta,' as he referred to himself; was displaying the testimonials he had received from the rich and the mighty.

All this baffled me, not much but enough to prevent me from sus-
pending my disbelief altogether. It took many years of being with Bapak
and doing the latihan for me to understand that Bapak too had – and was
entitled to – an inner and an outer like all human beings. He had been
incarnated as a Javanese and his *jiwa* was lodged in the body of a Javanese
who was an Indonesian in the same way that I was a Sri Lankan. There
was Pak Subuh, the Indonesian (who insisted on making the first national
contribution as an Indonesian from his own pocket to an international
undertaking), and there was Bapak the messenger with a *jiwa* wide
enough to contain all of us and the multifarious ambiences in which we
Buddhists, Jews, Christians, Muslims and even the agnostics and atheists
among us had come from.

At the time when President Sukarno was trying to make Indonesia the
capital of the world – his cartographers were instructed to move zero
meridian from Greenwich to Jakarta, and he had taken Indonesia out of
the United Nations, determined to establish a United Nations of the
New Emerging Forces (UNNEFO) in Jakarta or Bandung – Bapak
remarked that this sort of chauvinism was retrogressive politics influenced by Sukarno's unbounded *nafsu*. He explained to a small group of us
at Cilandak (Prio Hartono interpreting) that when a baby is born it is
only concerned with its own needs and comforts, and cries constantly for
attention. The baby is hungry or cold or too hot or wet and demands
immediate attention. As it grows up the baby 'recognizes' its mother and
father and its siblings, the whole family. Later the child recognizes himself or herself as a member of a community, a village or a small area of a
town. Later still, as a member of a cultural-linguistic group, or a state as
in India, and then as a citizen of a nation.

There most of us are stuck. Nationhood, Bapak said, is not an end, it is
a stage of political and spiritual evolution. We all belong to one human
race, whatever our outer distinctions. That is why God has sent the latihan to human beings, this time with the possibility of the contact with
the Great Life Force being transmitted from person to person across
national, cultural or economic barriers so that one day all human beings
will realize that in their inner being they are all relations of one another.
Bapak then pointed to me and said, 'Varindra gets into trouble with his
government because he does not believe in the theory of MY country,
right or wrong. He criticizes the government because he loves his country, but he does not think that the Sinhalese people are better than the

Tamil people or that the Buddhists there are better than the Christians in the world. He is lucky. He can go anywhere and feel at home among fellow human beings.' And then, with a grin of irony he added, 'In fact, at this time he can go anywhere in the world except his own country.' He was referring to the time when I was impelled by government threats to flee with my family to many years of involuntary self-exile.

There was no doubt about my being lucky. I had extraordinarily civilised parents who had raised us in such a way that we were free from any form of unfair discrimination against other people on grounds of caste, creed, class, colour or language, the common tribal barriers erected against other human beings, although the Buddha, like all great leaders, had taught his followers to respect 'all living things,' not just ourselves and what we found to be 'like' us. My father, the wisest school teacher I ever knew, once advised me not to try to memorise anything at all. He said I should first understand the principles which underlay any problem rather than try to remember and bind myself to mechanical formulae. 'Always go back to first principles and work your way up from there. Then you don't have to remember,' he told me. It has been one of the most valuable guidelines to living I ever learned. In later years, to deal with whatever problem I encountered as a journalist, international civil servant or as a man, I went back to first principles. They were valid, I found, whether one was confronted with the 'problem' of poverty, population growth, epidemics, famine, war and violence as a way of resolving disputes, conflicting ideologies and ethnic or gender differences, whether they arose in Asia, Africa or any other continent.

When my parents were opened in Subud and accepted Pak Subuh as Bapak – though my mother was the same age as Bapak and my father was older than he, I felt that what I learned from the latihan and from Bapak's explanations were a natural deepening and broadening of my parents' guidance. There was no discontinuity whatever and no conflict in values. Indeed, I was lucky, as lucky as many of the Subud members I know who had the natural benefit of being raised by considerate parents who had time for them and the natural 'luck' of receiving the Subud contact which Bapak brought to us.

Bapak advised us to realize that one religion was in no way 'better' or 'higher' than any other. 'Only earlier or later, not lower or higher,' he said (Usman interpreting). 'A wall to paradise may be built with bricks. But one brick is not better than another brick. You place one on top of another but they are all essential and equally important parts of the whole wall.'

These are some of the miraculously simple lessons of the message Bapak brought to us. And now he is no longer with us. What are we left with? How shall we manage to live the rest of our lives without Bapak and how shall the new generation grow without the benefit of his physical presence here on this planet? Those questions were in my mind for 25 years before the event. Bapak himself had advised us to experience 'the inevitable' in our inner feelings before it happened so that we were prepared for it. Bapak's death was one of those inevitabilities – for us in Subud the most traumatic – and I felt we should be courageous enough to think unthinkable thoughts and contemplate their implications.

At my first meetings with members of international Subud committees appointed at world congresses, I suggested that each of us separately and all of us together should confront the possibility of Bapak dying during our term of office so that we would respond to that awesome cosmic circumstance with mature understanding. At the back of our minds was the ironic thought that Bapak would outlive all of us and make nonsense of our preparedness. And when he once indicated that he might live beyond his 100th birthday, this sense of irony seemed apt. But Bapak was never dependent on even his own wishes and predictions. As we saw on so many occasions, he was totally subservient to God's will and would surrender to it at any given moment.

Shortly before the Toronto world congress we learned that Bapak's heart had been playing up again and my wife Lestari and I made a special trip to Indonesia to dissuade him from making the long journey to Canada. When we were ushered into the great living room upstairs at the Big House, we noticed a wheel chair partially hidden behind a sofa. There was a slipper lying beside it and we gave ourselves a knowing smile. Bapak, who liked to keep his illness from bothering Subud members, had evidently risen from his wheel chair and hurried away to change and prepare himself to receive us.

After a few minutes he walked in unaided, straight and self assured as he usually was, trying to give us the impression that he was in fine fettle, never felt better. The next few moments were spent in the marvellous minuet of 'When did you arrive?' 'How long are you staying?' 'How is your son?' 'And how is the UN?' and so on.

And then I spoke our piece. I said we had heard about Bapak's illness and had come to suggest that he should not undertake the journey to Toronto until he was well again. Bapak looked at me as though I was being a bit dotty and said, 'But members will be disappointed if Bapak does not attend.' I replied that we had no intention of holding a congress without Bapak and that though I had canvassed only a few brothers and sisters I was certain that the entire brotherhood would not wish to risk Bapak's health for a congress. We could put it off or move it to Jakarta or somewhere near for Bapak's convenience.

Bapak became quiet for a minute or two and said, very gravely (Sjarif Horthy interpreting), 'Bapak thanks Almighty God that people who have received the latihan are able to feel in this way. But, because in these matters Bapak does only what God wishes, Bapak will go to Toronto. If anything should happen, even if it is Bapak's death, it will be not because of Bapak's wish but because of God's will. Bapak learns how you both love Bapak and is grateful for your concern. But please arrange for Bapak's journey to the congress.'

As a part of my 'preparation' for the eventuality of Bapak's death, I studied the history of what had taken place in other parts of the world when the great messengers had died. Lessons from the past were clear: soon after the obsequies were over there was a temptation for some of the followers to regard the absence of their guide or teacher as a power vacuum which, as does Nature, they abhorred and felt had to be filled. In each case they had not respected the truth constantly enunciated by their teacher that the Power was God's alone and that no human being should try to usurp it. But some people were crass enough to make the attempt, either by making a play for power directly for themselves or indirectly by 'promoting' someone – such as a member of the family of the beloved teacher – as the true inheritor of the messenger's mantle. This, of course, led inevitably to the schisms, theological conflicts and wars for power over the faithful.

Would the same history repeat itself in Subud after Bapak? Whenever I asked myself this question, I was reassured by an inner nudge which offered promise that since the Subud contact could be transmitted from person to person, the latihan would be constantly renewed and experienced afresh by succeeding generations so that the brotherhood and sisterhood of people who practised it would not allow it to crystallise into a hierarchical bureaucracy which deadens inner growth through power games, regulations, 'systems' and new forms of priestcraft. Bapak, I realized, saw the possibility of even Subud being subject to these pathological pressures despite the evergreen impulse of the latihan and, long before his death, he made very clear public statements that there could be no successor to Bapak – that the latihan for which he was a channel was the only and true successor.

Despite all my preparation for Bapak's passing, news of his death opened a void in front of me. I felt no sense of calamity for the future of Subud but the sense of personal loss was profound. I became intensely conscious of how my life and that of my family had been changed from the time I had stood before him in that small bare room in the west wing of John Bennett's house in Coombe Springs, how Bapak had saved me from certain assassination for my political writings, how kind he had been to Lestari when she needed to be directly in his care at Cilandak for three years, how he had carried my son Imran, then three, out of his bedroom that the little boy had infiltrated with childish insouciance at siesta time and how Bapak had handed him over to me saying, without a trace of annoyance that his rest had been disturbed, 'Your son is more clever than you. He knows where the good things are!'

I wept quietly in the aeroplane as I travelled through Turkey, Switzerland, Britain and back to New York, mourning for myself. As I met Subud members here and there, I saw that they too felt this personal sense of loss. But, as an older member, I was immensely heartened by the natural grace with which they seemed to have accepted the inevitable and adjusted to it. It was as though children who had held on to their father's hand, tottering along the path, found themselves suddenly free from dependency and were now walking on their own, more confidently because they now had, perforce, to be self-reliant.

But we should not be so naive as to imagine that everything will be nice and tidy in the brotherhood of Subud. There will be some among us for whom Bapak's absence may seem as an opportunity to indulge in some power-tripping. There will be those among us who want to control other people's lives, using Bapak's guidance not as the gentle touch it was but as sharp goads to prod us in the direction they want other people to go. Some of us will take the trees for the wood and others the wood for the trees. But, as long as most of us remember that the organisation is for the latihan and not the other way round, no permanent damage will be done and Subud will go on in this world for 10,000 years as Bapak hoped. I pray that the inner feelings in us will prevail over the emotions of the *nafsu* because Subud, as Bapak once said, is our last chance.

During his lifetime Bapak guided us in our fumbling efforts to produce the living institutional framework for existing and growing as a community spread around the world, albeit very thinly. His advice about the functions of helpers and committees and their relationships with each other as well as with the members in general is to be found stated over and over again in his recorded talks. In that too we have been lucky. Unlike former epochs when the guidance given to communities of the spirit were carried from memory by word of mouth or scratched on bits of leather or on papyrus or on hard stone a long while after the event, we have had recourse to technology which records immediately and replicates the message almost infinitely. We were not very diligent about that at the start of Bapak's mission and a great deal of precious words went unrecorded, so that once again we have to rely on the retentive capacity of the memory cells of those who happened to hear him. I have often pleaded with his interpreters and those who attended on him closely to keep journals of the days in the life of Bapak. But for one reason or another that did not materialise.

Never mind. Let us be thankful for the treasures we have in the archives rather than regret what we may have missed. I, for one, intend to spend a considerable part of whatever time is left to me in helping to preserve, protect and propagate Bapak's word as the living relic of Muhammad Subuh, the most extraordinary ordinary man of our time.

Subud

SUBUD is an international spiritual movement of men and women who have received a renewed contact with the Great Life Force and practise the *latihan kejiwaan* or inner training which arises from experiencing the contact.

This contact was first received in the modern era by Muhammad Subuh Sumohadiwidjojo, an Indonesian, when he was a young man living at Kampong Sari, a small hamlet in the town of Semarang, East Java. A supernatural energy entered him, leading to an unfamiliar vibration within his being, followed by physical movements and many new and extraordinary experiences. At first, Muhammad Subuh – 'Bapak' – spoke about this only to a few close friends in the neighbourhood but, later, he received inner intimation that he could and should transmit the contact he had received to any other who wished to share his experience.

Before long it became clear that this contact could also be transmitted by those who had already received it to others who asked for it, in a chain reaction, each individual's reaction being different from that of any others. The continued experiencing of this vibration in the latihan, or inner training, causes inner change in people. They feel different, think differently and are, in many ways, different in the eyes of their families and friends. Over a period of time it is possible for each one to know whether this change has been beneficial to his or her relationships at home or at the workplace and for the person's own inner and outer development.

Subud is not a religion. The membership of the Subud brotherhood and sisterhood consists mostly of Muslims, Christians, Jews, Buddhists, Hindus, Parsis, Shintoists and others born into and 'belonging' to other formal religious groups. Many people also join who are disaffected by formal religion. Subud members are people who have had an experience which they come to believe is a contact with the power of God.

When they join Subud they are not 'converted' to a new religion but may choose to follow their own religion or any other they might prefer, aided by the inner guidance they receive.

Subud does not stand for nor connote the organisation of Subuh, its founder. The similarity of the two names is coincidental. Subud is a contraction of three Javanese words of Sanskrit origin – Susila Budhi Dharma – which means worship of God in a sincere and genuine way according to one's capacity.

Subud is not a monastic cult nor another of the *kebatinaan* or spiritist groups which abound in Indonesia and other parts of the world. It is a movement of people who have, through experience, recognized the importance of a human being not being 'used' by the material forces of this Earth but, rather, using these forces for personal, familial and social development.

Subud is not a teaching. Muhammad Subuh, its originator, in his explanations of the latihan, frequently said that all the teaching humankind needs has already been given by the founders of the great religions. What is needed is to understand and follow better their messages. To do this, human beings need inner strength and guidance. This is what is given by the *latihan kejiwaan* of Subud.

(Muhammad Subuh was born in 1901 and died in June 1987.)